WordPress® FOR DUMMIES®
5TH EDITION

by Lisa Sabin-Wilson

Foreword by Matt Mullenweg
Cofounder of WordPress

WILEY

John Wiley & Sons, Inc.

WordPress® For Dummies®, 5th Edition

Published by
John Wiley & Sons, Inc.
111 River Street
Hoboken, NJ 07030-5774
www.wiley.com

WILEY

About the Author

Lisa Sabin-Wilson has worked with the WordPress software since its inception in 2003 and has built her business around providing technical support, hosting, and design solutions for bloggers who use WordPress. She reaches thousands of people worldwide with her WordPress services, skills, and knowledge regarding the product. Lisa is also the author of *WordPress All-In-One For Dummies* and *WordPress Web Design For Dummies*.

Lisa operates a few blogs online, all of which are powered by WordPress. Her personal blog (`http://lisasabin-wilson.com`) has been online since February of 2002; her design business at E.Webscapes (`http://ewebscapes.com`) has been online since 1999. Lisa is also the co-founder and Lead Creative Designer at Allure Themes (`http://ithemes.com/find/allure`) — a commercial theme company providing ready-to-use WordPress themes designed for women.

When Lisa can be persuaded away from her computer — where she is usually hard at work providing design solutions for her WordPress clients — she sometimes emerges for public speaking appearances on the topics of design, blogging, and WordPress. She has appeared at national conferences such as the annual South By Southwest Interactive Conference, BlogWorld & New Media Expo, BookExpo America, American Association of Journalists and Authors, and various WordCamps nationwide.

Lisa consults with bloggers both large and small. Bloggers come in thousands of different flavors, from business to personal, from creative to technical, and all points in between. Lisa is connected to thousands of them worldwide and appreciates the opportunity to share her knowledge through *WordPress For Dummies*. She hopes you find great value in it, as well.

When she's not designing or consulting with her clients, you can usually find her at her favorite coffee shop sipping espresso, on a mountaintop somewhere hitting the slopes with her husband and kids, or 100 feet beneath the ocean waters, scuba diving with her husband and swimming with the fishes.

Dedication

For my father, Donald Sabin — for him, his love, and his undying support and encouragement of my crazy choices in life. I miss you, Dad . . . rest in peace.

Author's Acknowledgments

Many, many thanks and kudos to Matt Mullenweg, the WordPress core development team, and every single person involved in making WordPress the best blogging platform available on the Internet today. To the volunteers and testers who destroy all those pesky pre-release bugs for every new version release, the WordPress community thanks you! And to each and every WordPress plugin developer and theme designer who donates his or her time, skills, and knowledge to provide the entire WordPress community of users with invaluable tools that help us create dynamic blogs, thank you a thousand times! Every person mentioned here is an invaluable asset to the overall WordPress experience; I wish I could name you all, individually, except that there are literally thousands of you out there!

Extra special thanks to my friends and colleagues within the WordPress community who inspire and teach me every day.

Huge thanks to Amy Fandrei and Leah Michael from Wiley for their support, assistance, and guidance during the course of this project. Just the mere fact they had to read every page of this book means that they deserve the Medal of Honor! Also, many thanks to technical editor, Mitch Canter, and other editors of the project who also worked hard to make sure that I look somewhat literate here.

To my family and close friends whom I have neglected during the process of writing this book, thank you for not abandoning me — your support sustains me!

Publisher's Acknowledgments

We're proud of this book; please send us your comments at http://dummies.custhelp.com. For other comments, please contact our Customer Care Department within the U.S. at 877-762-2974, outside the U.S. at 317-572-3993, or fax 317-572-4002.

Some of the people who helped bring this book to market include the following:

Acquisitions and Editorial, and Vertical Websites

Senior Editorial Manager: Leah P. Michael
  (Previous Edition Project Editor: Susan Christophersen)

Executive Editor: Bob Woerner

Copy Editor: Amanda Graham

Technical Editor: Mitch Canter

Supervising Producer: Rich Graves

Editorial Assistant: Leslie Saxman

Sr. Editorial Assistant: Cherie Case

Cover Photo: © Richard Newstead / Getty Images

Cartoons: Rich Tennant (www.the5thwave.com)

Composition Services

Project Coordinator: Sheree Montgomery

Layout and Graphics: Corrie Niehaus, Laura Westhuis

Proofreader: Shannon Ramsey

Indexer: Ty Koontz

Special Help: Teresa Artman and Barry Childs-Helton

Publishing and Editorial for Technology Dummies

  Richard Swadley, Vice President and Executive Group Publisher

  Andy Cummings, Vice President and Publisher

  Mary Bednarek, Executive Acquisitions Director

  Mary C. Corder, Editorial Director

Publishing for Consumer Dummies

  Kathleen Nebenhaus, Vice President and Executive Publisher

Composition Services

  Debbie Stailey, Director of Composition Services

Table of Contents

Bonus Chapter 2: Hosting Multiple Sites with WordPress............BC47

Bonus Chapter 3: Ten Great Sites That Use WordPress as a CMS BC75

Foreword

. . . .

*T*here used to be a program from Microsoft called FrontPage that was the first visual interface for creating Web sites that I saw. It worked like Word or Publisher, so with very little knowledge, I was able to hack together the world's worst Web site in just a few hours without worrying about what was going on under the hood.

Years later when I look back at that Web site, I cringe, but at the time it was incredibly empowering. The software, though crude, helped me publish something anybody in the entire world could see. It opened up a world I had never imagined before.

Now, using software like WordPress, you can have a blog or Web site light-years beyond my first one in both functionality and aesthetics. However, just as my first Web experience whetted my appetite for more, I hope that your experience entices you to explore the thousands of free plugins, themes, and customizations possible with WordPress, many of which are explained in this book.

WordPress is more than just software; it is a community, a rapidly evolving ecosystem, and a set of philosophies and opinions about how to create the best Web experience. When you embrace it, you'll be in good company. WordPress users include old media organizations such as CNN, *The New York Times,* and *The Wall Street Journal,* along with millions of personal bloggers like myself for whom a WordPress blog is a means of expression.

Matt Mullenweg
Cofounder of WordPress

Introduction

*I*t was 2003 when I discovered the WordPress blogging software. Way back then (and in Internet years, that's actually quite a lot of time) I used Movable Type as my blogging platform. My friend Chelle introduced me to the WordPress software. "Try it," she said. "You'll really like it."

As a creature of habit, I felt reluctant to make the change. But I haven't looked back. I've been with WordPress ever since.

Blogs are here to stay. Authors, students, parents, business owners, academics, journalists, hobbyists — you name it — use blogs as a matter of course.

WordPress has been a huge part of the blogging boom. Today, it's the most popular blogging platform for personal, business, and corporate bloggers alike.

To a brand-new user, some aspects of WordPress can seem a little bit intimidating. After you take a look under the hood, however, you begin to realize how intuitive, friendly, and extensible the software is.

This book presents an insightful look at two popular versions of WordPress:

- ✔ The hosted version available at WordPress.com
- ✔ The self-hosted version available at WordPress.org

The book also covers managing and maintaining your WordPress blog through the use of WordPress plugins and themes.

If you're interested in taking a detailed look at the blogging and website services provided by WordPress, you happen to have just the right book in your hands.

About This Book

This book covers all the important aspects of WordPress that new users need to know to begin using the software for their own blog (or blogs). I cover the two most popular versions of WordPress, highlighting all the important topics, such as these:

✔ Setting up and using a hosted blog at WordPress.com

✔ Locating good hosting services for the self-hosted version of the software (available at WordPress.org)

✔ Installing and setting up the WordPress.org software

✔ Navigating the Dashboards of both the hosted and self-hosted versions of WordPress

✔ Adding media files to your blog

✔ Finding and installing free themes to use in your WordPress blog

✔ Using basic coding to design your own WordPress theme or modify the one you're using

✔ Using templates and tags in WordPress

✔ Installing, activating, and managing WordPress plugins

✔ Choosing to use the multiple-site WordPress Network option to host a network of multiple blogs on your domain

✔ Discovering the potential pitfalls associated with each version

✔ Understanding the challenges you face when running a WordPress-powered site, such as dodging comment and trackback spam

✔ Exploring RSS feed syndication

✔ Migrating your existing blog to WordPress (if you are using a different blogging platform, such as Blogspot, Movable Type, or Typepad)

✔ Discovering the power of WordPress as a Content Management System (CMS) to create a full website, not just a blog

✔ Upgrading your WordPress blog and staying up to date and informed about ongoing WordPress software development

✔ Finding support, tips, and resources for using the WordPress software

With WordPress, you can truly tailor a blog to your own tastes and needs. All the tools are out there. Some of them are packaged with the WordPress software; others are third-party plugins and add-ons created by members of the WordPress user community. It takes a little research, knowledge, and time on your part to put together a blog that suits your needs and gives your readers an exciting experience that keeps them coming back for more.

Conventions Used in This Book

Throughout the book, I apply the following typography conventions to guide you through some of the information I present:

- ✔ When I ask you to type something, the text that you're supposed to type is in **bold.**

- ✔ When I suggest a keyword that you may want to enter in a search engine, that term appears in *italics.*

- ✔ Text that appears in this `special font` is certain to be a URL (web address), e-mail address, filename, folder name, or code.

- ✔ When I use a term that I think you may not be familiar with, I apply *italics* to that term to let you know that I'm defining it.

- ✔ In some instances, I give you a basic idea of what a web address or block of code looks like. When the text that you see may be different, depending on your settings and preferences, I apply *italics* to that text.

What You Are Not to Read

Read what you need and leave the rest — or pass it on to a friend.

This book covers the details of how to set up, use, and maintain the blogging tools available at WordPress.com and WordPress.org. I don't intend for you to read this book from cover to cover (unless you're my mother — then I won't forgive you if you don't). Rather, hit the Table of Contents and the Index of this book to find the information you need.

If you never intend to run a hosted WordPress blog on your own web server, you can skip Chapters 6–8.

If you have no interest in setting up a hosted blog at WordPress.com, skip Chapters 3–5.

If you aren't interested in digging into the code of a WordPress template, and don't want to find out how to apply CSS or HTML to enhance your design, you can skip Part V of this book (Chapters 12 and 13).

Long story short: Take what you need and leave the rest.

Foolish Assumptions

I'll never know what assumptions you've made about me at this point, but I can tell you a few things that I already assume about you:

- ✔ You know what a computer is. You can turn it on, and you understand that if you spill coffee on your keyboard, you'll have to run out and get a replacement.

- ✔ You understand how to hook yourself into the Internet and know the basics of using a web browser to surf websites and blogs.

- ✔ You have a basic understanding of what blogs are, and you're interested in using WordPress to start your own blog. Or you already have a blog, are already using WordPress, and want to understand the program better so that you can do more cool stuff and stop bugging your geeky best friend whenever you have a question about something. Or, even better, you already have a blog on another blogging platform and want to move your blog to WordPress.

- ✔ You know what e-mail is. You know what an e-mail address is. You actually have an e-mail address, and you send and receive e-mail on a semi-regular basis.

How This Book Is Organized

This book is made up of six parts that introduce you to the WordPress platform, including detailed information on two very popular versions of WordPress: the hosted version of WordPress.com and the self-hosted version of WordPress.org. Also included is detailed information on WordPress themes and templates.

Part 1: Introducing WordPress

The first part gives you an overview of WordPress and the advantages of making it your blogging platform. You may think of WordPress as coming in two "flavors": vanilla (WordPress.com hosted solution) and chocolate (WordPress.org self-hosted solution). In this part, you also discover some of the fun aspects of blogging, such as RSS feed syndication and reader interaction through comments.

Part II: Using the WordPress Hosted Service

Part II takes you through signing up with the hosted service for a blog. You tour the WordPress.com Dashboard, explore writing and managing your blog, find out how to change the various themes available in this version, and discover how to enhance your blog with widgets.

Part III: Self-Hosting with WordPress.org

Part III explores the single-user version of the WordPress software available at WordPress.org. You install this software on your own hosted web server, so I give you valuable information about domain registration, web-hosting providers, and a few of the basic tools (such as FTP) that you need to have in place before you set up a WordPress blog. I also familiarize you with the WordPress.org Dashboard, where you personalize your blog and explore many of the settings that you need to manage and maintain your WordPress-powered blog.

Part IV: Flexing and Extending WordPress

This part shows you how to add images to your pages, including how to create a photo gallery on your site. In addition, you discover how to find, install, and use various WordPress plugins to extend the functionality of your blog. This part also steps into the world of WordPress themes, showing you where to find free themes (including some that I designed at `www.dummies.com/go/wordpressfd5e`), as well as how to install and activate them.

Part V: Customizing WordPress

Part V takes an in-depth look at the structure of a WordPress theme by taking you through the templates and explaining the template tags each step of the way. You find information on basic CSS and HTML that helps you tweak the free theme that you're using or even create your own theme.

If the topics covered in this part aren't ones you're interested in, make sure that you look to the bonus chapters at `www.dummies.com/go/wordpressfd5e`. There you find information on using WordPress as a Content Management System (CMS) to power a full-blown website as well as a blog. Additionally, these chapters show you how to configure the WordPress Multisite feature to allow multiple sites, which gives you the option of running a network of sites with one single installation of the WordPress software.

Part VI: The Part of Tens

The Part of Tens is in every traditional _For Dummies_ book that you will ever pick up. This part shows you ten popular free WordPress themes that you can use to create a nice, clean look for your blog. Further, in this part you discover ten great WordPress plugins that you can use to provide your visitors (and yourself) with some great functionality.

Icons Used in This Book

Icons emphasize a point to remember, a danger to be aware of, or information that I think you may find helpful. Those points are illustrated as such:

Tips are little bits of information that you may find useful.

I use this icon to point out dangerous situations.

All geeky stuff goes here. I don't use this icon very often, but when I do, you know you're about to encounter technical mumbo-jumbo.

When you see this icon, read the text next to it two or three times to brand it into your brain so that you remember whatever it was that I think you need to remember.

Where to Go from Here

As I mention in the "What You Are Not to Read" section of this introduction, take what you need, and leave the rest. This book is a veritable smorgasbord of WordPress information, ideas, concepts, tools, resources, and instruction. Some of it will apply directly to what you want to do with your WordPress blog. Other parts deal with topics that you're only mildly curious about, so you may want to skim those pages.

Also remember that this book has a couple of companion websites that I encourage you to check out:

- ✔ www.dummies.com/cheatsheet/wordpress: Visit this site and find the Cheat Sheet for *WordPress For Dummies,* 5th Edition.

- ✔ www.dummies.com/go/wordpressfd5e: The three bonus chapters that you find on this page tell you all about using WordPress as a content management system (CMS). You also find a chapter listing ten great sites that use WordPress for just that purpose. Finally, you get a chapter on how to host multiple websites, and whether and when to bring in the professionals. But that's not all! You also find five free themes designed by me that you can use for your own site. (You'll need the instructions from Chapter 11 to access them.)

Part I
Introducing WordPress

The 5th Wave   By Rich Tennant

In this part . . .

Ready to get started? I know I am! This part of the book provides a brief introduction to WordPress and blogging. WordPress is unique in offering two versions of its software, and I tell you about each version so that you can choose the one that's right for you.

Chapter 1

What WordPress Can Do for You

In This Chapter

▶ Seeing how WordPress can benefit you

▶ Participating in the WordPress community

▶ Understanding the different versions of WordPress

*I*n a world in which technology advances in the blink of an eye, WordPress is blogging made easy — and free! How else can you get your message out to a potential audience of millions worldwide and spend exactly nothing? There may be no such thing as a free lunch in this world, but you can bet your bottom dollar that there are free blogs. WordPress serves them all up in one nifty package.

The software's free price tag, its ease of use, and the speed at which you can get your blog up and running are great reasons to use WordPress to power your personal or business blog. An even greater reason is the incredibly supportive and passionate WordPress community. In this chapter, I introduce you to the WordPress software so that you can begin to discover how effective it is as a tool for creating your blog or website.

Discovering the Benefits of WordPress

I work with first-time bloggers all the time — folks who are new to the idea of publishing on the Internet. One of the questions I'm most frequently asked is "How can I run a blog? I don't even know how to code or create websites."

Enter WordPress. You no longer need to worry about knowing the code because the WordPress blogging software does the code part for you. When you log in to your blog, you have to do only two simple things to publish your thoughts and ideas:

1. Write your post.

2. Click a button to publish your post.

That's it!

WordPress offers the following competitive advantages as the most popular blogging tool on the market:

- ✔ **Diverse options:** Two versions of WordPress are available to suit nearly every type of blogger:

    - *WordPress.com:* A hosted turnkey solution

    - *WordPress.org:* A self-hosted version to install on the web server of your choice

    I go into detail about each of these versions later in this chapter, in the "Choosing a WordPress Platform" section.

- ✔ **Ease of use:** WordPress setup is quick, and the software is easy to use.

- ✔ **Extensibility:** WordPress is extremely extensible, meaning that you can easily obtain plugins and tools that let you customize it to suit your purposes.

- ✔ **Strong community of users:** WordPress has a large and loyal members-helping-members community via public support forums, mailing lists, and blogs geared to the use of WordPress.

The following sections fill in a few details about these features and point you to places in the book where you can find out more about them.

Getting set up the fast and easy way

WordPress is one of the only blog platforms that can brag about a five-minute installation — and stand behind it! Both versions of WordPress take you approximately the same amount of time to sign up.

Mind you, five minutes is an *approximate* installation time. It doesn't include the time required to obtain domain registration and web hosting services or to set up the options on the Dashboard (find information on web hosting services in Chapter 6).

When you complete the installation, however, the world of WordPress awaits you. The Dashboard is well organized and easy on the eyes. Everything is clear and logical, making it easy for even a first-time user to see where to go to manage settings and options.

The WordPress software surely has enough meat on it to keep the most experienced developer busy and happy. At the same time, however, it's friendly enough to make a novice user giddy about how easy getting started is. Each time you use WordPress, you can find out something exciting and new.

Extending WordPress's capabilities

I've found that the most exciting and fun part of running a WordPress blog is exploring the flexibility of the software. Hundreds of plugins and *themes* (designs) are available to let you create a blog that functions the way *you* need it to.

If you think of your blog as a vacuum cleaner, plugins are the attachments. The attachments don't function alone. When you add them to your vacuum cleaner, however, you add to the functionality of your vacuum, possibly improving its performance.

All WordPress blogs are pretty much the same at their core, so by using plugins, you can truly individualize your blog by providing additional features and tools to benefit yourself and your readers. When you come upon a WordPress blog that has some really different and cool functions, 98 percent of the time you can include that function in your own blog by using a WordPress plugin. If you don't know what plugin that blog is using, feel free to drop the blog owner an e-mail or leave a comment. WordPress blog owners usually are eager to share the great tools they discover.

Most plugins are available at no charge. You can find out more about WordPress plugins and where to get them in Chapter 10. Chapter 14 lists my top ten choices for popular WordPress plugins available for download.

In addition to using plugins, you can embellish your WordPress blog with templates and themes. WordPress comes with a real nice default theme to get you started. Figure 1-1 shows the default Twenty Eleven theme, created by the team from WordPress, which is displayed by default after you install and set up your blog for the first time.

The theme's default form is blue and white, with a handy application built in to the preferences that allows you to change the background color and insert an image to use as a header image. (You can find more about tweaking WordPress themes in Chapter 13.)

The Twenty Eleven theme (shown in Figure 1-1) includes all the basic elements that you need when starting a new WordPress blog. You can extend your WordPress blog in a hundred ways with plugins and themes released by members of the WordPress community, but this default theme is a nice place to start.

Figure 1-1:
Start a new
WordPress
blog with a
theme.

Taking part in the community

Allow me to introduce you to the fiercely loyal folks who make up the user base, better known as the vast WordPress community. This band of merry ladies and gentlemen comes from all around the globe, from California to Cairo, Florida to Florence, and all points in between and beyond.

In March 2005, Matt Mullenweg of WordPress proudly proclaimed that the number of WordPress downloads had reached 900,000 — an amazing landmark in the history of the software. But the real excitement occurred in August 2006, when WordPress logged more than 1 million downloads, and in 2007, when the software had more than 3 million downloads. The number of WordPress downloads has broken the ceiling since 2007, and the number of WordPress users has climbed to the tens of millions and is growing daily. WordPress is easily the most popular content management system available on the web today.

Don't let the sheer volume of users fool you: WordPress also has bragging rights to the most helpful blogging community on the web today. You can find users helping other users in the support forums at `http://word press.org/support`. You can also find users contributing to the very helpful WordPress Codex (a collection of how-to documents) at `http://codex.wordpress.org`. Finally, across the blogosphere, you can find multiple blogs about WordPress itself, with users sharing their experiences and war stories in the hope of helping the next person who comes along.

You can subscribe to various mailing lists, too. These lists offer you the opportunity to become involved in various aspects of the WordPress community as well as in the ongoing development of the software.

Joining the WordPress community is easy: Simply start your own blog by using one of the two WordPress software options. If you're already blogging on a different platform, such as Blogger or Movable Type, WordPress enables you to easily migrate your current data from that platform to a new WordPress setup. (See the Appendix for information about moving your existing blog to WordPress.)

Choosing a WordPress Platform

Among the realities of running a blog today is choosing among the veritable feast of software platforms to find the one that performs the way you need. You want to be sure that the platform you choose has all the options you're looking for. WordPress is unique in that it offers two versions of its software, each designed to meet various needs:

- ✔ The hosted version at WordPress.com. (Part II of this book focuses on this version.)
- ✔ The self-installed and self-hosted version available at WordPress.org. (Part III focuses on this version.)

Every WordPress blog setup has certain features available, whether you're using the self-hosted software from WordPress.org or the hosted version at WordPress.com. These features include (but aren't limited to)

- ✔ Quick and easy installation and setup
- ✔ Full-featured blogging capability, letting you publish content to the web through an easy-to-use web-based interface
- ✔ Topical archiving of your posts, using categories
- ✔ Monthly archiving of your posts, with the ability to provide a listing of those archives for easy navigation through your site
- ✔ Comment and trackback tools
- ✔ Automatic spam protection through Akismet

- ✔ Built-in gallery integration for photos and images

- ✔ Media Manager for video and audio files

- ✔ Great community support

- ✔ Unlimited number of static pages, letting you step out of the blog box and into the sphere of running a fully functional website

- ✔ RSS (Really Simple Syndication) capability with RSS 2.0, RSS 1.0, and Atom support (see Chapter 2 for more information on RSS)

- ✔ Tools for importing content from different blogging systems (such as Blogger, Movable Type, and LiveJournal)

Table 1-1 compares the two WordPress versions.

Table 1-1	Exploring the Differences between the Two Versions of WordPress	
Feature	*WordPress.org*	*WordPress.com*
Cost	Free	Free
Software download	Yes	No
Software installation	Yes	No
Web hosting required	Yes	No
Custom CSS* control	Yes	$15/year
Template access	Yes	No
Sidebar widgets	Yes	Yes
RSS syndication	Yes	Yes
Access to core code	Yes	No
Ability to install plugins	Yes	No
Theme installation**	Yes	Yes
Multiauthor support	Yes	Yes
Unlimited number of blog setups with one account	Yes	Yes
Community-based support forums	Yes	Yes

*CSS = Cascading Style Sheets
** Limited selection on WordPress.com

Choosing the hosted version from WordPress.com

WordPress.com is a free service. If downloading, installing, and using software on a web server sound like Greek to you — and like things you'd rather avoid — the WordPress folks provide a solution for you at WordPress.com.

WordPress.com is a *hosted solution,* which means it has no software requirement, no downloads, and no installation or server configurations. Everything's done for you on the back end, behind the scenes. You don't even have to worry about how the process happens; it happens quickly, and before you know it, you're making your first blog post using a WordPress.com blog solution.

WordPress.com has some limitations, though. You cannot install plugins or custom themes, for example, and you cannot customize the base code files, nor are you able to sell advertising or monetize your blog at all on WordPress.com. But even with its limitations, WordPress.com is an excellent starting point if you're brand new to blogging and a little intimidated by the configuration requirements of the self-installed WordPress.org software.

The good news is this: If you ever outgrow your WordPress.com-hosted blog in the future and want to make a move to the self-hosted WordPress.org software, you can. You can even take all the content from your WordPress.com-hosted blog with you and easily import it into your new setup with the WordPress.org software.

So in the grand scheme of things, your options are really not that limited. Look for information about WordPress.com in Part II of this book.

Self-hosting with WordPress.org

The self-installed version from WordPress.org (covered in Part III) requires you to download the software from the WordPress website and install it on a web server. Unless you own your own web server, you need to lease one — or lease space on one.

Using a web server is typically referred to as *web hosting,* and unless you know someone who knows someone, hosting generally isn't free. That being said, web hosting doesn't cost a whole lot, either. You can usually obtain a good web-hosting service for anywhere from $5 to $10 per month. (Chapter 6 gives you the important details you need to know about obtaining a web host.) You need to make sure, however, that any web host you choose to work with has the required software installed on the web server. Currently, the minimum software requirements for WordPress include

- ✔ PHP version 5.2.4 or greater
- ✔ MySQL version 5.0.15 or greater

After you have WordPress installed on your web server (see the installation instructions in Chapter 6), you can start using it to blog to your heart's content. With the WordPress software, you can install several plugins that extend the functionality of the blogging system, as I describe in Chapter 10. You also have full control of the core files and code that WordPress is built on. So if you have a knack for PHP and knowledge of MySQL, you can work within the code to make changes that you think would be good for you and your blog. Find information about PHP and MySQL in Chapter 2.

You don't need design ability to make your blog look great. Members of the WordPress community have created more than 2,000 WordPress themes, and you can download them for free and install them on your WordPress blog. (See Chapter 11.) Additionally, if you're creatively inclined, like to create designs on your own, and know CSS, you'll be glad to know that you have full access to the template system within WordPress and can create your own custom themes. (See Chapters 12 and 13.)

The self-hosted WordPress.org software lets you run an unlimited number of blogs on one installation of its software platform, on one domain. When you configure the Network options within WordPress to enable a multisite interface, you become administrator of a network of blogs. All the options remain the same, but with the Network options configured, you can have additional blogs and domains and allow registered users of your website to host their own blog within your network, as well. You can find out more about the WordPress Multisite feature in Bonus Chapter 2, which resides online at `www.dummies.com/go/wordpressfd5e`.

Some examples of sites that use the Network options within WordPress are

- ✔ Blog networks can have more than 150 blogs. The popular electronics retail store, Best Buy, uses WordPress to power 1,050 local store blogs (example: `http://stores.bestbuy.com/577`).
- ✔ Newspapers and magazines, such as *The New York Times,* and universities such as Harvard Law School use WordPress to manage the blog sections of their websites.
- ✔ Niche-specific blog networks, such as Edublogs.org (`http://edublogs.org`), use WordPress to manage their full networks of free blogs for teachers, educators, lecturers, librarians, and other education professionals.

Chapter 2

WordPress Blogging Basics

In This Chapter

▶ Considering blog types

▶ Finding out what blog technology can do for you

▶ Outlining your initial blog plan

A lot happens behind the scenes to make your WordPress blog or website function. The beauty of it is that you don't have to worry about what's happening on the back end to manage and maintain a WordPress site — unless you really want to. In this chapter, I delve a little bit into the technology behind the WordPress platform, including a brief look at PHP and MySQL, two software components required to run WordPress.

This chapter also covers some of the various blogging technologies that help you on your way to running a successful blog, such as the use of comments and RSS feed technology, as well as information about combating spam.

This Crazy Little Thing Called Blog

Blogging is an evolutionary process, and blogs have evolved beyond personal journals. Undoubtedly, a blog is a fabulous tool for publishing your personal diary of thoughts and ideas; however, blogs also serve as excellent tools for business, editorial journalism, news, and entertainment. Here are some ways that people use blogs:

✔ **Personal:** This type of blogger creates a blog as a personal journal or diary. You're considered a personal blogger if you use your blog mainly to discuss topics that are personal to you or your life — your family, your cats, your children, or your interests (for example, technology, politics, sports, art, or photography). My blog, which you'll find at `http://lisasabin-wilson.com`, is an example of a personal blog.

✔ **Business:** This type of blogger uses the power of blogs to promote a company's business services, products on the Internet, or both. Blogs are very effective tools for promotion and marketing, and business blogs usually offer helpful information to readers and consumers, such as tips and product reviews. Business blogs also let readers provide feedback and ideas, which can help a company improve its services. ServerBeach is a good example of a business that keeps a blog on the hosted WordPress.com service at `http://serverbeach.wordpress.com`.

✔ **Media/journalism:** More and more popular news outlets, such as Fox News, MSNBC, and CNN, have added blogs to their websites to provide information on current events, politics, and news on regional, national, and international levels. These news organizations often have editorial bloggers as well. Editorial cartoonist Daryl Cagle, for example, maintains a blog on MSNBC's website at `http://blog.cagle.com/author/cagle`, where he discusses his cartoons and the feedback he receives from readers.

✔ **Citizen journalism:** The emergence of citizen journalism coincided with the swing from old media to new media. In old media, the journalists and news organizations direct the conversation about news topics.

With the popularity of blogs and the millions of bloggers who exploded onto the Internet, old media felt a change in the wind. Average citizens, using the power of their voices on blogs, changed the direction of the conversation. Citizen journalists often fact-check traditional media news stories and expose inconsistencies, with the intention of keeping the media or local politicians in check. An example of citizen journalism is the Power Line blog at `http://powerlineblog.com`.

✔ **Professional:** This category of blogger is growing every day. Professional bloggers are paid to blog for individual companies or websites. Blog networks, such as B5Media (`http://b5media.com`), hire bloggers to write on certain topics of interest. Also, several services match advertisers with bloggers so that the advertisers pay bloggers to make blog posts about their products. Is it possible to make money as a blogger? Yes, and making money (at blogging) has become common these days. If you're interested in this type of blogging, check out Darren Rowse's ProBlogger blog at `http://problogger.net`. Darren is considered the grandfather of all professional bloggers.

Dipping Into Blog Technologies

The WordPress software is a personal publishing system that uses a PHP and MySQL platform. This platform provides everything you need to create your own blog and publish your own content dynamically, without having to know how to program those pages yourself. In short, all your content is stored in a MySQL database in your hosting account.

PHP (which stands for *PHP: Hypertext Preprocessor* — and PHP itself originally stood for *personal home page,* as named by its creator, Rasmus Lerdorf) is a server-side scripting language for creating dynamic web pages. When a visitor opens a page built in PHP, the server processes the PHP commands and then sends the results to the visitor's browser. MySQL is an open source relational database management system (RDBMS) that uses Structured Query Language (SQL), the most popular language for adding, accessing, and processing data in a database. If all that sounds like Greek to you, just think of MySQL as a big filing cabinet in which all the content on your blog is stored.

Every time a visitor goes to your blog to read your content, he makes a request that's sent to a host server. The PHP programming language receives that request, obtains the requested information from the MySQL database, and then presents the requested information to your visitor through his web browser.

In using the term *content* as it applies to the data that's stored in the MySQL database, I'm referring to your blog posts, comments, and options that you set up on the WordPress Dashboard. The theme (design) you choose to use for your blog — whether it's the default theme, one you create for yourself, or one that you have custom designed — isn't part of the content in this case. Those files are part of the file system and aren't stored in the database. So create and keep a backup of any theme files that you're using. See Part IV for further information on WordPress theme management.

When you look for a hosting service, choose one that provides daily backups of your site so that your content/data won't be lost in case something happens. Web hosting providers that offer daily backups as part of their services can save the day by restoring your site to its original form. More information on choosing a hosting provider is found in Chapter 6.

Archiving your publishing history

Packaged within the WordPress software is the capability to maintain chronological and categorized archives of your publishing history, automatically. WordPress uses PHP and MySQL technology to sort and organize everything you publish in an order that you, and your readers, can access by date and category. This archiving process is done automatically with every post you publish to your blog.

When you create a post on your WordPress blog, you can file that post under a category that you specify. This feature makes for a very nifty archiving system in which you and your readers can find articles or posts that you've placed within a specific category. The Archives page on my personal blog (see it at `http://lisasabin-wilson.com/archives`) contains an Archives by Subject section, where you find a list of categories I've created for my blog posts. Clicking a link below the Archives by Subject heading takes you to a listing of posts that I wrote on that topic. See Figure 2-1.

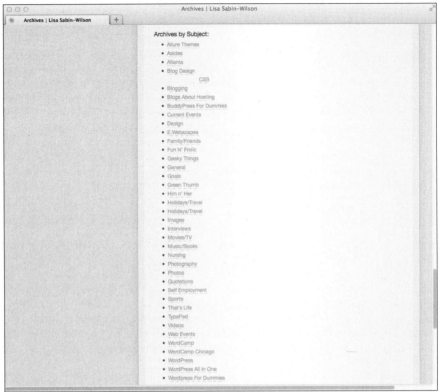

Figure 2-1:
An archive
of my blog
posts by
subject.

WordPress lets you create as many categories as you want for filing your blog posts by topic. I've seen blogs that have just one category and blogs that have up to 1,800 categories — WordPress is all about preferences and options for organizing your content. On the other hand, using WordPress categories is your choice. You don't have to use the category feature.

Interacting with your readers through comments

One of the most exciting and fun aspects of blogging with WordPress is getting feedback from your readers the moment you make a post to your blog. Feedback, referred to as *blog comments,* is akin to having a guestbook on your blog. People can leave notes for you that are published to your site, and you can respond and engage your readers in conversation about the topic at hand. See Figures 2-2 and 2-3 for examples. Having this function in your blog creates the opportunity to expand the thoughts and ideas that you presented in your blog post by giving your readers the opportunity to add their two cents.

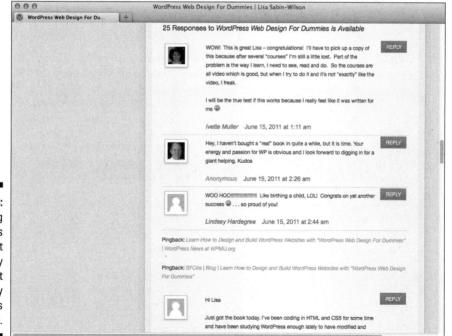

Figure 2-2:
Readers use
the form to
leave their
comments.

Figure 2-3:
Blog
readers
comment
on my
blog about
one of my
WordPress
books.

On the WordPress Dashboard, you have full administrative control over who can and can't leave comments. In addition, if someone leaves a comment with questionable content, you can edit the comment or delete it. You're also free to choose not to allow any comments on your blog. Chapter 7 has the information you need about setting up your preferences for comments on your blog.

Some blog users say that a blog without comments isn't a blog at all. This belief is common in the blogging community because experiencing visitor feedback through the use of comments is part of what has made blogging so popular. It's a personal choice, though. Allowing comments on your blog invites your audience members to actively involve themselves in your blog by creating a discussion and dialog about your content. By and large, readers find commenting to be a satisfying experience when they visit blogs because comments make them part of the discussion.

Feeding your readers

An RSS (Really Simple Syndication) feed is a standard feature that blog readers have come to expect. The Introduction to RSS page on the resource site WebReference.com

```
www.webreference.com/authoring/languages/xml/rss/intro/
```

defines RSS as "a lightweight XML format designed for sharing headlines and other Web content. Think of it as a distributable 'What's New' for your site."

Readers can use feed readers to download your feed — that is, their feed readers automatically discover new content (such as posts and comments) from your blog. Readers can then download that content for their consumption. Table 2-1 lists some of the most popular feed readers on the market today.

For your blog readers to stay updated with the latest and greatest content you post to your site, they need to subscribe to your RSS feed. Most blogging platforms allow the RSS feeds to be *autodiscovered* by the various feed readers: that is, the blog reader needs to enter only your site's URL, and the program will automatically find your RSS feed.

Most browser systems today alert visitors to the RSS feed on your site by displaying the universally recognized orange RSS feed icon, shown in the margin.

Table 2-1	Popular RSS Feed Readers	
Reader	*Source*	*Description*
Bloglines	`http://` `bloglines.com`	Bloglines is a free online service for searching, subscribing to, and sharing RSS feeds. You have no software to download or install; Bloglines is all web based. You need to sign up for an account to use this service.
FeedDemon	`http://` `feeddemon.com`	This free service requires that you download the RSS reader application to your own computer.
Google Reader	`http://google.` `com/reader`	This free online service is provided by Internet search giant Google. With Google Reader, you can keep up with your favorite blogs and websites that have syndicated (RSS) content. You have no software to download or install to use this service, but you need to sign up for an account with Google.

WordPress has built-in RSS feeds in several formats. Because the feeds are built in to the software platform, you don't need to do anything to provide your readers an RSS feed of your content. Check out Chapter 8 to find out more about using RSS feeds within the WordPress program.

Tracking back

The best way to understand trackbacks is to think of them as comments, except for one thing: *Trackbacks* are comments that are left on your blog by other blogs, not by actual people. Sounds perfectly reasonable, doesn't it? Actually, it does.

A trackback happens when you make a post on your blog, and within that post, you provide a link to a post made by another blogger in a different blog. When you publish that post, your blog sends a sort of electronic memo to the blog you've linked to. That blog receives the memo and posts an acknowledgment of receipt in a comment to the post that you linked to. Chapter 13 gives you information on how to use HTML to create links on your blog.

That memo is sent via a *network ping* — a tool used to test, or verify, whether a link is reachable across the Internet — from your site to the site you link to. This process works as long as both blogs support trackback protocol.

Sending a trackback to a blog is a nice way of telling the blogger that you like the information she presented in her blog post. All bloggers appreciate the receipt of trackbacks to their posts from other bloggers.

Dealing with comment and trackback spam

Ugh. The absolute bane of every blogger's existence is comment and trackback spam. When blogging became the "it" thing on the Internet, spammers saw an opportunity. Think of the e-mail spam you've received — comment and trackback spam is similar and just as frustrating.

Before blogs came onto the scene, you often saw spammers filling Internet guestbooks with their links but not leaving any relevant comments. The reason is simple: Websites receive higher rankings in the major search engines if they have multiple links coming in from other sites. Enter blog software, with comment and trackback technologies — prime breeding ground for millions of spammers.

Because comments and trackbacks are published to your site publicly — and usually with a link to the commenters' websites — spammers get their site links posted on millions of blogs by creating programs that automatically seek websites with commenting systems and then hammering those systems with tons of comments that contain links back to their own sites.

No blogger likes spam. As a matter of fact, blogging services such as WordPress have spent untold hours in the name of stopping these spammers in their tracks, and for the most part, they've been successful. Every once in a while, however, spammers sneak through. Many spammers are offensive, and all of them are frustrating because they don't contribute to the ongoing conversations.

All WordPress systems have one very major, very excellent thing in common: Akismet, which kills spam dead. Chapter 10 tells you more about Akismet, which is brought to you by Automattic, the makers of WordPress.com.

Using WordPress as a Content Management System

You hear something like the following a lot if you browse different websites that publish articles about WordPress: "WordPress is more than a blogging platform; it's a full content management system." A *content management system (CMS)* is a platform that gives you the capability to run a full website on your domain. This means that in addition to hosting a blog, you can build pages and have additional features built into your website that have nothing to do with the content on your blog.

Exploring the difference between a website and a blog

A website and a blog are really two different things. Although a website can contain a blog, a blog doesn't and can't contain a full website. I know it sounds confusing, but after you read this section and explore the difference between the two, you'll have a better understanding.

A *blog* is a chronological display of content, most often posts or articles written by the blog author. Those posts (or articles) are published and, usually, categorized into topics and archived by date. Blog posts can have comments activated, which means that readers of a blog post can leave their feedback and the blog post author can respond, thereby creating an ongoing dialog between author and reader about the blog post.

A *website* is a collection of published pages and sections that offer the visitor a variety of experiences or information. Part of the website can be a blog that enhances the overall visitor experience, but it usually includes other sections and features that might include things such as the following:

- ✔ **Photo Galleries:** This specific area of your website houses albums and galleries of uploaded photos, allowing your visitors to browse through and comment on the photos you display.

- ✔ **E-Commerce Store:** This feature is a fully integrated shopping cart through which you can upload products for sale, and your visitors can purchase your products via your online store.

- ✔ **Discussion Forums:** This area of your website allows visitors to join, create discussion threads, and respond back and forth to one another in specific threads of conversation.

✔ **Social Community:** This section of your website allows visitors to become members, create profiles, become friends with other members, create groups, and aggregate community activity.

✔ **Portfolio of Work:** If you're a photographer or web designer, for example, you can display your work in a specific section of your site.

✔ **Feedback Forms:** You can have a page on your website with a contact form that visitors can fill out to contact you via e-mail.

✔ **Static pages (such as a Bio, FAQ, or Services page):** These pages don't change as often as a blog page does. Blog pages change each time you publish a new post. Static pages contain content that doesn't change very often.

The preceding list doesn't exhaust what a full website can contain, but instead lists some of the most often seen sections of a website. In Bonus Chapter 3 on the companion website (`www.dummies.com/go/word pressfd5e`) for this book, I provide you with a showcase listing of ten websites that use WordPress as a CMS effectively.

Viewing examples: Blog versus website

I include a couple of figures in this section to further illustrate the difference between a blog and a website. Figure 2-4 shows the front page of my personal blog located at `http://lisasabin-wilson.com`. Notice that the site displays a chronological listing of the most recent blog posts I've made. On my personal site, I use WordPress primarily as a blogging tool.

In contrast, my business website, located at `http://ewebscapes.com`, uses WordPress as a CMS to publish a full website. This site includes a static front page of information that acts as a portal into the rest of my site, where you find a blog, my portfolio of work, a contact form, an order form, and various static pages used to tell my visitors more about my business. The static pages include services, FAQ (Frequently Asked Questions), Terms of Service, Privacy Policy, and more. Check out Figure 2-5 for a look at the front page of my business site at E.Webscapes and notice how it's quite a bit different from my personal blog site, shown in Figure 2-4.

Using WordPress as a CMS means that you're using it to create not just a blog but an entire website full of sections and features that offer a different experience for your visitors.

Figure 2-4:
My personal
blog uses
WordPress
as a
blogging
tool.

Figure 2-5:
My business
website uses
WordPress
as a CMS.

Moving On to the Business of Blogging

Before getting started with blogging, you need to take a long look at your big plans for your website. A word of advice: Organize your plan of attack before you start. Have a good idea of what types of information you want to publish, how you want to present and organize that information, and what types of services and interaction you want to provide your audience.

Ask this question out loud: "What am I going to blog about?" Go ahead — ask it. Do you have an answer? Maybe you do, and maybe not — either way, it's all right. There's no clear set of ground rules you must follow. Having an idea of what you expect to write about in your blog makes planning your attack a little easier. You may want to write about your personal life. Maybe you plan to share only some of your photography and provide very little commentary to go along with it. Or maybe you're a business owner and want to blog about your services and the current news within your industry.

Having an idea of your subject matter helps you determine how you want to deliver that information. My design blog, for example, is where I write about web design projects, client case studies, and news related to design and blogging. You won't find pictures of my cats there, but you will find those pictures on my personal blog. I keep the two blogs separate, in much the same way as most of us like to keep a distinct line of separation between our personal and professional lives, no matter what industry we work in.

When you have your topic and plan of delivery in mind, you can move forward and adjust your blog settings to work with your plan.

Part II
Using the WordPress Hosted Service

"It all started when I was researching recipes for Baked Alaska and frozen custard for my baking blog."

In this part . . .

*I*f installing software on a web server and hosting your own blog sound like activities you'd like to avoid, WordPress.com may be your answer. In this section, you find out how to get — and use — a free, hosted blog from WordPress.com.

Chapter 3

Getting Started with WordPress

In This Chapter

▶ Signing up for a blog

▶ Familiarizing yourself with the Dashboard

▶ Understanding important options to set before you begin

*I*f you're just starting out and don't want to spend money purchasing a domain name and hosting your site with a third-party web host, WordPress has a great solution for you.

This book takes a complete look at the hosted service offered at WordPress, and in this chapter, you discover how to create a free blog through this service. You also find out how to get your hosted blog up and running.

Don't confuse WordPress with the blogging software available for download at `WordPress.org`! Both were created and developed by the same folks and they do have the same name; however, they are different varieties of WordPress. See Part III for information on installing and using the self-hosted version of WordPress.org.

Creating a WordPress Account

To create your WordPress user account, follow these steps:

1. **In the address bar of your browser, enter the URL** `wordpress.com`.

2. **On the page that appears, click the Get Started button shown in Figure 3-1.**

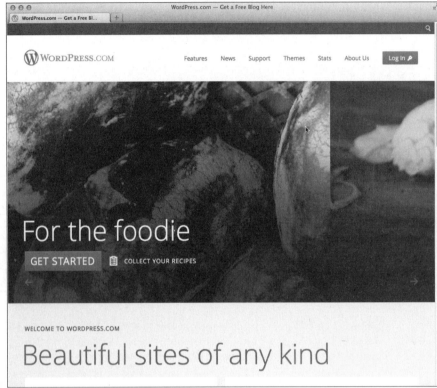

Figure 3-1:
On the
WordPress
main page,
click the
Get Started
button.

You're taken to the WordPress signup page at `wordpress.com/signup`.

3. **In the Blog Address text box, type the word you've chosen as your blog address.**

Whatever you enter here becomes the URL address of your blog. It must be at least four characters (letters and numbers only), and don't worry about choosing the perfect thing; you can change this later. You can use any blog address you want; however, if you choose a blog address that doesn't follow certain rules, WordPress displays a message, as shown in Figure 3-2. If you see this message, you need to pick a new one because WordPress doesn't allow duplicate blog addresses. Keep in mind that search engines catalog your content based on your chosen URL, so use a domain name that relates well to your site's content.

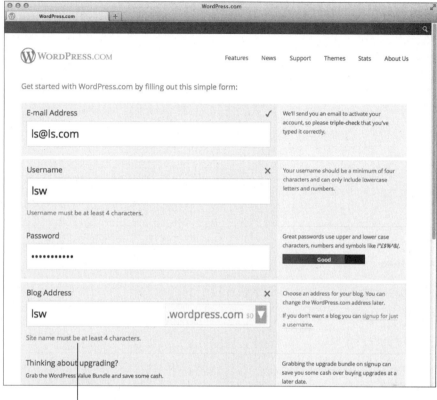

Figure 3-2:
WordPress
has rules
about the
length of a
site name.

Try again!

4. Select the suffix for your blog address.

In the drop-down list to the right of the Blog Address text box, you have several options. One is free and the others cost you $18 to $25/year. In Figure 3-3, I typed `lswtester` as my blog address and chose the `wordpress.com` suffix, which creates the full blog address of `http://lswtester.wordpress.com`. However, WordPress gives me the option to purchase the available domain name `lswtester` if I want to spend an additional $18. WordPress also makes the `.net`, `.me`, and `.org` suffixes available for purchase. See Chapter 6 for more information about domain names and suffixes. For now, select the free `wordpress.com` suffix; you can always upgrade to a paid domain later if you want.

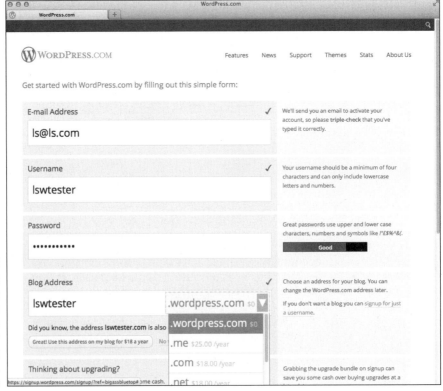

Figure 3-3:
Select
the free
WordPress
suffix for
your blog
address.

5. **In the Username text box, enter the name you want to use to log in to your blog from now until forever.**

   Your username must be at least four characters with letters and numbers only. WordPress automatically fills in the username box with the same username as the blog address you typed in Step 3; however, you don't have to use that one and can choose to type in your own, unique username. For security purposes, choose a username that's different from your blog address because that makes it more difficult for anyone to guess. You can change the username on the blog you're creating right now after you log in and have access to the Dashboard. (See the "Setting your public profile: Tell us a little about yourself" section later in this chapter.)

6. **Type a password of your choice, in the Password text box.**

   You use this password to log in to your new WordPress account. Choose and then type a password that you'll remember, but not one that would be easy for anyone to guess. Your password must be at least four characters. WordPress gives you a visual indicator of the strength of your password choice, with *strength* meaning how easy or difficult it is for someone to guess what your password is.

7. **Type your e-mail address in the E-mail Address text box.**

   This address isn't made public on your blog; rather, it's used for communication between you and WordPress. You can change this address later, in the Options section on your WordPress.com Dashboard.

8. **Review upgrade options.**

   WordPress has several upgrade options such as domain names, space upgrades, and custom design. During the signup process, WordPress offers a Value Bundle that provides you with upgraded features for $99, which you can add to your blog by clicking the Upgrade button in this step. For now, though, click the Create Blog button to obtain a free blog and you can learn more about the upgrades offered by WordPress in Chapter 5.

9. **Click the Create Blog button.**

   This completes the signup process, and a new page opens with a message that WordPress has sent you an e-mail containing a link to activate your account. As you wait for that e-mail to arrive, take a moment to fill out the Update Your Profile! form on this page. Enter your first name, last name, and a few sentences about yourself. Then click the Save Profile button. Later, you can choose to display your profile information on your blog. (See the later section "Setting your public profile: Tell us a little about yourself".)

   By clicking the Create Blog button, you also indicate that you fully agree to, and understand, the WordPress Terms of Service. If you'd like to read the fine print, you can find the Terms of Service at wordpress.com/tos.

10. **Choose a theme and start blogging.**

    The final signup step is to choose one of several themes (or template designs covered in Chapter 5) that WordPress provides for your blog. Don't worry about your choice here because, as you discover later in this book, you can come back and change your theme anytime. For now, find the Twenty Eleven theme (on the screen shown in Figure 3-4) and select it for your blog by clicking its thumbnail.

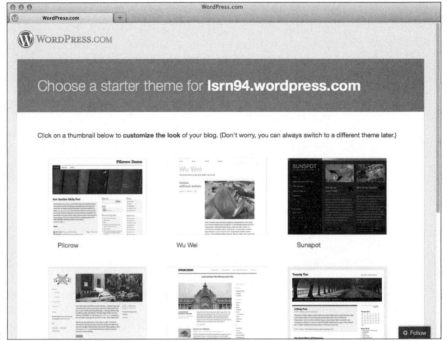

Figure 3-4:
Choose a
theme and
start
blogging.

11. **Check your e-mail and click the Activate Blog link in the e-mail message from WordPress to activate your new WordPress blog.**

    The Dashboard for your WordPress account loads in your browser window with a message welcoming you to WordPress. The Dashboard also displays a few helpful items to help you get started, including

    • A video entitled "Welcome to WordPress.com" that gives you a quick tutorial of the WordPress.com services.

    • A link to the WordPress Zero-to-Hero guide that gives you an introduction to WordPress: learn.wordpress.com

    • A link to the WordPress 24/7 support documentation: support. wordpress.com

    If you don't want to see the Welcome box at the top of your Dashboard page, click the Hide This Screen link in the bottom-right corner of the Welcome to WordPress.com box, as shown in Figure 3-5.

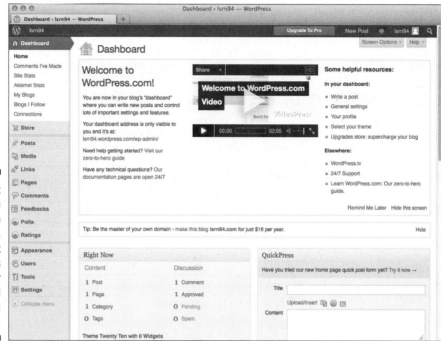

Figure 3-5:
The
Welcome to
WordPress.
com box
appears
on your
Dashboard
when you
first log in.

Your new blog is yours to use for the life of your blogging career on WordPress.com. You can log in to your blog anytime by going to wordpress.com and clicking the Log In button in the top-right corner of the WordPress website (refer to Figure 3-1).

Have you ever signed up for a service on the web only to forget your user-name and/or password for that service mere weeks later? Yep, me, too. File that e-mail from WordPress in a safe place for future reference — just make sure you remember where you put it. Or you can tell WordPress to remember you each time you enter the site. To do so, select the Remember Me check box. WordPress places a cookie in your browser files that tells it to remember your login credentials the next time you visit the site. (You need to have cook-ies enabled in your browser configurations for this feature to work.)

If you delete your cookies in your browser and then visit WordPress again, you won't see the WordPress menu bar and will have to log in again. Likewise, after you delete the cookies in your browser, when you visit your new blog, it appears to you as though you are a visitor (that is, you see no menu bar with quick links for logging on to your Dashboard). In this case, you have to revisit the WordPress main site to log in again.

You can get help and support for your WordPress account in the Support Forums here: `wordpress.com/forums`. Find answers to frequently asked questions here: `learn.wordpress.com`.

Navigating WordPress

When you successfully log in to your new account from the main WordPress home page, WordPress returns you to the main WordPress website — only this time, you see a slightly different display on the home page — a tabbed navigation menu shown in Figure 3-6. The navigation menu contains shortcut links to some important areas of interest:

- ✔ **New Post:** Click this tab to write and publish a post on your WordPress blog. The WordPress Dashboard, covered in the next section of this chapter, has the full post interface; however, this part of the WordPress home page provides you with a quick way to publish a quick post.

- ✔ **Reader:** Click this tab to discover new posts and updates from the WordPress.com blogs that you follow.

- ✔ **Notifications:** Under this tab, you find updates from blogs that you subscribe to in the WordPress.com network, as well as discussions and comments that you subscribe to.

- ✔ **Stats:** Click this tab to view the statistics of your WordPress blog in graphical format. At a glance, discover who is visiting your blog and where they are coming from.

- ✔ **My Blog:** This tab displays quick access links to blogs that you own within the WordPress network.

- ✔ **Freshly Pressed:** Click this tab and discover the latest posts from bloggers within the WordPress.com network.

You find the same links when you hold your mouse pointer over the small WordPress logo displayed at the top left of your browser window. The links appear in a drop-down menu for easy access.

Quick access links to important areas of your WordPress Dashboard appear after you log in to your WordPress account. You see a bar at the very top of your browser window, on the right side. This bar also appears at the top of any WordPress blog you surf to, as long as you are logged in to your WordPress account. This menu bar consists of several helpful quick links for you to access your account, your Dashboard, and various options.

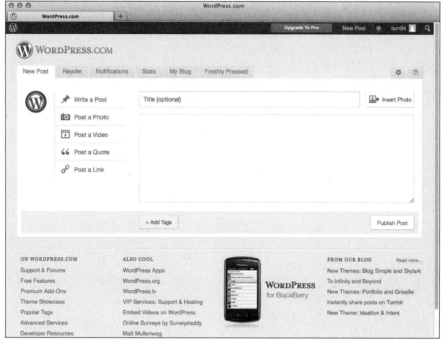

Figure 3-6:
Navigation
tabs are
on the
WordPress
home page.

Hover your mouse over your username at the top right of your browser and you see the following links in a drop-down menu:

- ✔ **Your name:** Click this to visit Account Settings where you can edit your own user profile, password, e-mail address, and applications (or third-party applications such as Twitter or Facebook).

- ✔ **Find Friends:** Click this link to visit the Find Friends page where you can locate your friends in other networks such as Twitter, Facebook, and Google Plus. You can also find friends and/or blogs within the network by using the Recommended Blogs link, or explore the topics to find blogs of interest to you.

- ✔ **Manage My Blogs:** This takes you to the My Blogs page on your WordPress Dashboard where you see a list of all the blogs you own; WordPress allows you to operate more than one blog in its network.

- ✔ **Help:** Click this link to visit the support area of WordPress.com at support.wordpress.com where you can find helpful articles and tutorials on using your WordPress account.

Using the WordPress Dashboard

When you click the Dashboard link under the My Blog navigation tab (covered in the preceding section), you go directly to your WordPress Dashboard page shown in Figure 3-7. Several modules on the Dashboard provide you with information about your blog, as well as actions you can take to navigate to other areas of the Dashboard, such as writing a new post and adding a new link or blogroll.

You can configure the Dashboard modules by moving them around on the page and changing the way they display. Hover your mouse pointer over the title bar of the module you want to move. Click and drag the module to the spot you'd like to move it and release the mouse button. This drag-and-drop capability is available not only on the Dashboard page but also on all the inner pages of the WordPress Dashboard, so you can truly configure the panel to suit your needs. You can also expand (open) and collapse (close) the individual modules by clicking the mouse anywhere within the gray title bar of the module.

This configuration feature is really nice because it allows you to use the Dashboard to see just those modules that you use regularly. The concept is easy: Keep the modules you use all the time open and close the ones that you use only occasionally — you can open those modules only when you really need them. Additionally, you can click the Screen Options tab at the top right of your Dashboard screen to configure other options for your Dashboard display, such as which modules you would like to show or hide.

The navigation menu on the WordPress Dashboard appears on the left side of your browser window. When you need to get back to the WordPress Dashboard, click the Dashboard link that appears at the top of the navigation menu of any page on your WordPress Dashboard. Each navigation item that appears in the menu has a submenu of links associated with it — hold your mouse pointer over a menu item and the submenu flies out on the right side of the menu, so you can click any of the submenu links.

Right Now

The Right Now module of the Dashboard gives you some stats on what's happening in your blog this very second. Figure 3-7 shows what was happening in my WordPress blog when I took a picture of it.

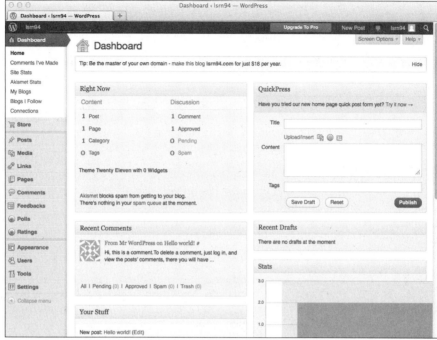

Figure 3-7:
The
Dashboard
page serves
as the
control
center of
your blog.

The Dashboard displays the following information under the Content header in the Right Now module:

- ✔ **The number of posts:** The number here always reflects the total number of posts you currently have in your WordPress blog. Figure 3-7 shows that I have 1 post on my blog. The number is blue; click the number, and you go to the Edit Posts page where you can edit the posts on your blog. I cover editing posts in Chapter 4.

- ✔ **The number of pages:** This is the number of pages on your blog, which will change as you add or delete pages. *Pages,* in this context, refer to the static pages you created in your blog. Figure 3-7 shows that my blog has 1 page.

  Clicking this link takes you to the Edit Pages screen, where you can view, edit, and delete your current pages. Find the difference between WordPress posts and pages in Chapter 4.

- ✔ **The number of categories:** This is the number of categories you have on your blog, which will change as you add and delete categories. Figure 3-7 shows that I have 1 category for my blog.

  Clicking this link takes you to the Categories Page, where you can view, edit, and delete your categories or add brand new ones. For details about the management and creation of categories, see Chapter 4.

✔ **The number of tags:** This is the number of tags you have in your blog, which will change as you add and delete tags in the future. Figure 3-7 shows that I have 0 tags.

Clicking this link takes you to the Tags page where you can add new tags and view, edit, and delete your current tags. You can find more information about tags in Chapter 4.

The Dashboard displays information about comments on your blog under the Discussion header in the Right Now module. Specifically, you find the total number of comments currently on your blog. Figure 3-7 shows that I have 1 Comment, 1 Approved, 0 Pending (waiting to be approved), and 0 Spam. Clicking any of these four links takes you to the Edit Comments page where you can manage the comments on your blog. I cover the management of comments in Chapter 4.

The last section of the Dashboard's Right Now module shows the following information:

✔ **Which WordPress theme you're using:** Figure 3-7 shows that I'm using the Twenty Eleven theme. The theme name is a link that takes you to the Manage Themes page where you can view and activate themes on your blog (see Chapter 5 for more).

✔ **How many widgets you've added to your blog:** This is the number of WordPress widgets you're using in your blog. Figure 3-7 shows that I have 0 widgets. The number is a link that takes you to the Widgets page where you can change your widget options by editing them, moving them, or removing them. I cover widgets in detail in Chapter 5.

✔ **Akismet spam stats:** This is the last statement in the Right Now section and it gives you a quick look into how many spam comments and trackbacks the Akismet application has successfully blocked from your site. Figure 3-7 shows that Akismet hasn't blocked any spam comments on my site; because it's a pretty new blog, spammers haven't found it yet.

Recent Comments

The next module is Recent Comments. Within this module, you find

✔ **Most recent comments published to your blog:** WordPress displays a maximum of five comments in this area.

✔ **The author of each comment:** The name of the person who left the comment appears above the comment. This section also displays the author's picture (or *avatar*) if she has one.

✔ **A link to the post the comment was left on:** The post title appears to the right of the commenter's name. Click the link and you go to that post on the Dashboard.

✔ **An excerpt of the comment:** This is a snippet of the comment left on your blog.

✔ **Comment management links:** Hover your mouse pointer over the comment, and five links appear that give you the opportunity to manage those comments right from your Dashboard. (I discuss comment management in Chapter 4.)

  • *Unapprove:* This link appears only if you have comment moderation turned on.

  • *Reply:* This link displays a text box in which you can quickly reply to the comment right from your Dashboard.

  • *Edit:* This link opens the Edit Comments page (Chapter 4) where you can edit the comment.

  • *Spam:* Clicking this link marks that comment as spam.

  • *Trash:* Clicking this link deletes the comment from your blog.

✔ **All link:** Click this link to see all the comments that have been left on your blog. Clicking the All link takes you to the Comments page (Chapter 4), where you can view and edit, moderate, or delete any comments that have been left for your blog.

Your Stuff

Scroll further down the Dashboard page, and you find a module titled Your Stuff; in it, you see the following sections:

✔ **Today:** Click the links here to go to a page with options that let you manage today's posts. This page contains new or updated posts you've made during the day.

✔ **A While Ago:** Click the links here to go to a page with options that let you manage posts and updates you made in past days.

What's Hot

Last but not least, the What's Hot section provides information about happenings in and around WordPress, including WordPress news, top blogs, top posts, fastest-growing blogs, and the latest posts made to blogs on WordPress. This section helps you stay in touch with the WordPress community as a whole.

The tabs across the top of the What's Hot Module include navigation for

- ✔ **WordPress.com News:** Listing of posts about WordPress from the official WordPress blog
- ✔ **Top Blogs:** Listing of the top blogs within the global WordPress network
- ✔ **Top Posts:** Listing of the most recent top blog posts (or most popular) from within the global WordPress network
- ✔ **Latest:** Listing of the most recent posts from within the global WordPress network

QuickPress

The QuickPress module is a handy form that allows you to write, save, and publish a blog post right from your WordPress Dashboard. The options are very similar to the ones I cover in the section on writing posts in Chapter 4.

Recent Drafts

If you're using a brand new WordPress blog, the Recent Drafts module displays the message `There are no drafts at the moment` because you have not written any drafts. As time goes on, however, and you have written a few posts in your blog, you may save some of those posts as drafts to be edited and published later. These drafts will be shown in the Recent Drafts module. Figure 3-7 shows the `There are no drafts at the moment` message in my Recent Drafts module.

WordPress displays up to five drafts in this module and displays the title of the post, the date it was last saved, and a short excerpt. Click the View All button to go to the Manage Posts page, where you can view, edit, and manage your blog posts. Check out Chapter 4 for more information on that.

Stats

The last module of the Dashboard page is Stats (Figure 3-8). It includes a visual graph of your blog stats for the past several days. These stats represent how many visitors your blog received each day. The bottom of the Stats module shows some specific information:

✔ **Top Posts:** This display lists the most popular posts in your blog, determined by the number of visits each post received. It also shows you exactly how many times each post has been viewed.

✔ **Top Searches:** This area tells you the top keywords and search phrases people used to find your blog in search engines.

✔ **Most Active:** This area tells you which posts in your blog are the most active, determined by the number of comments left on each post. You can click the title of a post, and WordPress loads that post in your browser window.

✔ **View All:** Click this button to view all stats for your blog on the My Stats page.

Figure 3-8:
The Stats
section
of the
WordPress
Dashboard
has an
easy-to-
read graph.

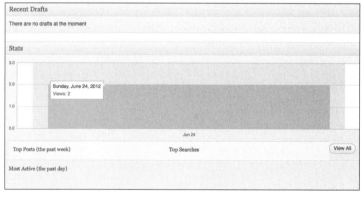

If you find that you don't use a few modules on your Dashboard page, you can get rid of them altogether by following these steps:

1. **Click the Screen Options tab at the top-right of the Dashboard.**

   Clicking this tab drops down the Screen Options menu, displaying the title of each module with check boxes to the left of each title.

2. **Deselect the module you want to hide on your Dashboard by clicking the check mark in the check box.**

   The module you deselected disappears from your Dashboard. If you have hidden one module and find later that you really miss having it on your Dashboard, you can simply enable that module again by selecting it from the Screen Options menu.

Setting Important Options before You Blog

The options in this section help you get started managing your own WordPress blog. In this section, you discover how to set the primary options that personalize your blog including creating your user profile, setting the date and time stamp (based on your own time-zone settings), and uploading a picture of yourself.

Setting your General options

To begin personalizing your WordPress blog by setting the General options, follow these steps:

1. **Hover your mouse pointer over the Settings menu item in the navigation menu.**

2. **Click the General link on the Settings submenu.**

   The General Settings page opens, as shown in Figure 3-9.

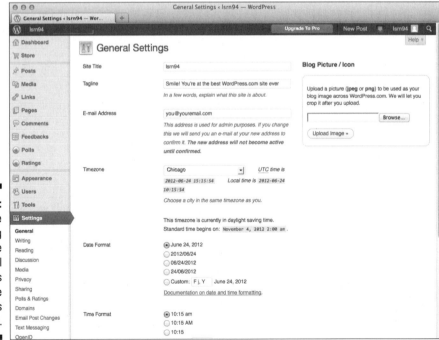

Figure 3-9:
Personalize your blog with the General Settings page on the WordPress Dashboard.

3. **Enter the name of your blog in the Site Title text box.**

   You can revisit this page anytime and change the blog name as often as you like.

4. **In the Tagline text box, enter a slogan or a motto that describes you or your blog.**

   The tagline should be a short (one line) phrase that sums up the tone and premise of your blog. Figure 3-9 shows I used the tagline: `Smile! You're at the best WordPress.com site ever`, which goes along with my chosen Site Title of lsrn94.

5. **Enter your e-mail address in the E-mail Address text box.**

   Enter the e-mail address that you used to sign up with WordPress. You can change this address, but be warned: If you change the e-mail address here, it won't become active until you confirm that you are in fact the owner of said e-mail address. Confirmation is simple: WordPress sends an e-mail to that address, providing a link you click to confirm that you are the owner. This e-mail address is used for administrative purposes only, which consists mainly of communication between you and WordPress.

Adjusting your Date and Time settings

After you configure the name, tagline, and e-mail options that I discuss in the preceding section, the remaining items on the General Settings page include setting your local time zone so that your blog posts are published with a time stamp in your own time zone no matter where in the world you are. Use the following options to establish your settings in this area, as shown in Figure 3-10.

✔ **Timezone:** Choose your UTC time from the drop-down menu. This setting refers to the number of hours that your local time differs from Coordinated Universal Time (UTC). This setting ensures that all your blog posts and comments left on your blog are time-stamped with the correct time. If you're lucky enough, like me, to live on the frozen tundra of Wisconsin, which is in the Central time zone (CST), you would choose –6 from the drop-down menu because that time zone is 6 hours off UTC.

If you're unsure what your UTC time is, you can find it at the Greenwich Mean Time website at `wwp.greenwichmeantime.com`. GMT is essentially the same thing as UTC. WordPress provides some major city names in the Timezone drop-down menu to help make it a bit easier to select your correct time zone. For those of you who live in areas that recognize daylight saving time, your WordPress blog will automatically update and make that adjustment when the time comes.

Timezone	Chicago ▾ *UTC time is* `2012-06-24 15:15:54` *Local time is* `2012-06-24 10:15:54` *Choose a city in the same timezone as you.* This timezone is currently in daylight saving time. Standard time begins on: `November 4, 2012 2:00 am`.
Date Format	⦿ June 24, 2012 ○ 2012/06/24 ○ 06/24/2012 ○ 24/06/2012 ○ Custom: `F j, Y` June 24, 2012 Documentation on date and time formatting.
Time Format	⦿ 10:15 am ○ 10:15 AM ○ 10:15 ○ Custom: `g:i a` 10:15 am
Week Starts On	Monday ▾

Figure 3-10:
Choose
Date and
Time
settings
for your
WordPress
blog.

✔ **Date Format:** Select how you want to display the date. The default format is *F j, Y* (F = the full month name; j = the two-digit day; Y = the four-digit year), which gives you the output of June 24, 2012. Select a different format by clicking the circle to the left of the option.

✔ **Time Format:** Select how you want to display the time. The default format is *g:i a* (g = the two-digit hour; i = the two-digit minute; a = lowercase a.m. or p.m.), which gives you the output of 10:15 a.m. Select a different format by clicking the circle to the left of the option. You can also customize the date display by selecting the Custom option and entering your preferred format in the text box provided; find out how at

    codex.wordpress.org/Formatting_Date_and_Time.

✔ **Week Starts On:** From the drop-down menu, choose the day the week starts in your calendar. The display of the calendar in the sidebar of your blog is optional. If you choose to display the calendar, you can select the day of the week you want your calendar to start with.

Finally, set your language preference by clicking the Language drop-down menu and selecting from the several different language options provided by WordPress. This language is the language that your blog is primarily written in.

Click the Save Changes button at the bottom of any page where you set new options. If you don't click Save Changes, your settings aren't saved, and WordPress reverts to the previous options.

Setting your public profile: Tell us a little about yourself

The next set of options you need to update is your profile. In this area, you configure your personal settings to individualize your WordPress blog and tell the world a little more about yourself. This blog is, after all, about you, and this is your opportunity to brag and promote!

To get started telling the world about yourself, follow these steps:

1. **Hover your mouse pointer over the Users menu item in the navigation menu.**

2. **Click the My Profile link on the Users menu.**

   The My Public Profile page opens, as shown in Figure 3-11.

You can adjust all sorts of personal settings to let your visitors get to know you better. You can be liberal with the information you share, or be as stingy as you want. It's *your* blog, after all.

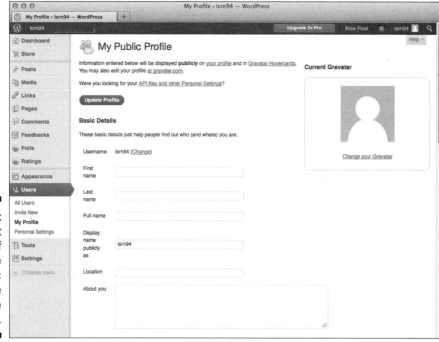

Figure 3-11:
Brag about yourself on the My Public Profile page on the Dashboard.

Choose carefully the information you share on your blog, especially if you have a public blog on WordPress — public blogs can (and are) viewed by a worldwide audience! If you don't want people to know your real name, use a nickname. If you don't want to share a picture of yourself for fear of shattering computer monitors worldwide, you can choose not to upload any picture at all or to upload a picture of something that reflects the essence of you. (You can post a picture of a book if you're an avid reader, a picture of a camera if you're a photographer, and so on.)

Make your blog your own. Stake your claim and mark your territory in this section!

Basic Details

In the first section of the My Public Profile page, you can see seven settings for your blog, only six of which you can change:

- ✔ **Username:** This displays your current username; you can change your username by clicking the nearby Change link.
- ✔ **First Name:** Type your first name in the text box provided.
- ✔ **Last Name:** Type your last name in the text box provided.
- ✔ **Full Name:** Type your full name in the text box provided.
- ✔ **Display Name Publicly As:** Type in the name you would like displayed publicly.
- ✔ **Location:** Type your location in the text box provided.
- ✔ **About You:** In this section, you can provide a little biography, as well as change the password for your blog. Figure 3-11 shows this section in detail.

Contacts

In the Contacts section of the My Public Profile page, you can add different types of contact information and make them public on your profile. Followers of the blog use this information to keep in touch with you and ask you questions. Here's what's included (you don't need to fill in all this information):

- ✔ **Home Phone, Work Phone, Mobile Phone:** Type these phone numbers if you so desire.
- ✔ **Public Email:** Type your e-mail address in the text box.
- ✔ **AIM, Live Messenger, Yahoo!, ICQ, Jabber:** If you want to share this information, enter your identities in the appropriate text boxes.
- ✔ **GTalk and Skype:** Type your Google Talk and Skype names in the text boxes if you'd like to share them.

Photos

To include several different photographs on your WordPress.com profile, click the Add Photo Through Gravatar button to upload photos from your computer. Any photos you add in this section will be displayed on your Profile page on WordPress.

Links

Add any links to websites that you'd like to have listed on your Profile page. For example, if you have several different websites other than the one you're creating on WordPress, you can add the links to those websites here so that they appear on your public profile for people to visit.

To add links, simply type the link URL in the URL text box, and the name of the page in the Title text box. Then click the Add Link button. You can edit and delete links in this area of the My Public Profile page anytime you want.

Verified external services

Verified external services are online services such as social networking and social bookmarking sites that you use in addition to your WordPress blog. WordPress wants you to include your online identities with these services because, in the words of WordPress, "they help people to confirm that you are in fact who you say you are." Your verified external services will be listed on your public profile. The different types of external services available in this section include

- ✔ Blogger
- ✔ Facebook
- ✔ Flickr
- ✔ foursquare
- ✔ FriendFeed
- ✔ Goodreads
- ✔ Google Profiles
- ✔ LinkedIn
- ✔ MySpace
- ✔ Posterous
- ✔ TripIt
- ✔ Tumblr
- ✔ Twitter

✔ Vimeo

✔ WordPress

✔ Yahoo!

✔ YouTube

Current Gravatar

Want to show the world your pretty picture? In the Current Gravatar section of the My Public Profile page, you can upload a picture of yourself or an image that represents you. This image is called a *gravatar*. This section is located on the right side of the My Public Profile page (refer to Figure 3-11).

The picture/avatar that you insert into your WordPress blog is used in several ways:

✔ **The WordPress Blogs of the Day page (**`botd.wordpress.com/top-posts`**):** This page lists the top posts from the top blogs of the day. If your blog is included in this list, a smaller version of the picture you've uploaded to your profile appears next to the listing.

✔ **The Freshly Pressed:** Also called a "fresh" post, this appears on the main page at `wordpress.com`, under the Freshly Pressed tab. If the WordPress spotlight shines in your direction, your picture is displayed here for your own 15 minutes of WordPress fame.

✔ **The WordPress directory (by topic) of its community blogs:** This directory is called the Tags page (`wordpress.com/tags`). Bloggers on WordPress can tag their posts with keywords that help define the topics of their posts; WordPress collects all those tagged posts and sorts them by name on the Tags page.

✔ **On Tag pages:** This blogging page (`wordpress.com/tag/blogging`) allows you to find the most recent posts that WordPress bloggers have made on the topic of blogging. If your blog appears in this directory, a thumbnail of your picture appears, as well.

Follow these steps to insert a picture or avatar into your profile:

1. **Choose the image you want to attach to your profile and save it to your computer.**

   Upload an image that's at least 128 pixels wide and 128 pixels tall. Later in these steps, you see how you can crop a larger image to the perfect size.

2. **In the Current Gravatar section of the My Public Profile page, click the Change Your Gravatar link.**

   The Gravatar.com window appears. Click the Upload a New Image from Your Computer link. The Select File from Your Computer window opens.

3. **Click the Browse button and select an image from your computer.**

4. **Click the Next button.**

   No matter what size image you chose, the Gravatar.com page allows you to crop your image to the correct size and lets you decide which part of your image to use for your picture display. When you click the Next button, the Crop Your Photo page appears, and you can crop your chosen picture to the desired size. See Figure 3-12.

5. **Use the crop tool to highlight the area of the picture that you want to remain after cropping.**

   In Figure 3-12, the box with a dotted line outlines the part of the image I've chosen to use. This dotted outline indicates the size the picture will be when I'm done cropping it. You can move that dotted box around to choose the area of the image you want to use as your avatar. The Gravatar.com crop tool gives you two previews of your cropped image on the right side of the window: Small Preview and Large Preview.

6. **Click the Crop and Finish! button.**

   The Choose a Rating page opens, where you can choose a rating for your new Gravatar.

Figure 3-12:
Using the WordPress image-cropping interface.

7. **Choose a rating.**

   The rating system works very much like the movie rating system we're all familiar with: G, PG, R, and X. A *G* rating means that your Gravatar is suitable for all ages, whereas an *X* rating means that your Gravatar contains some unmentionables that you would not want any kids to see.

8. **Choose an e-mail address.**

   If you have more than one e-mail address associated with your WordPress account, you can assign your Gravatar to a particular e-mail address so that your Gravatar images appear on any blog you comment on, provided that you use your assigned e-mail address to do so.

   When you're done, you get a message from Gravatar.com that says `Your new Gravatar is now being applied.`

9. **Click the X in the upper-right corner of the window to return to the Profile page on your WordPress Dashboard.**

   The My Public Profile page now displays your newly uploaded Gravatar. Visit this page again, anytime, to change your Gravatar.

Setting your preferences

WordPress gives you the capability to set a few different preferences based on your individual tastes for publishing, proofreading, and passwords. On the WordPress Dashboard, click the Personal Settings link in the Users menu to load the Personal Settings page. Here, you have several different options available to you.

Personal Options

This section gives you the opportunity to configure some basic settings for how you would like to manage your WordPress.com site, including the display color of the Dashboard, use of keyboard shortcuts, text messaging, and more.

- ✔ **Fun:** Select this box to tell WordPress to set up all of the options for you. This is called Fun Mode because WordPress sets random configurations for the Personal Settings, so you may be surprised with what you get.

- ✔ **Instant Feedback:** Select this box to have WordPress display instant feedback details on your posts after you publish them. Information displayed includes things like social media sharing and tips for improving your posts.

- ✔ **Admin Color Scheme:** This option changes the colors on your WordPress Dashboard, which uses the Gray color scheme by default. The other option is Blue — the choice is yours!

✔ **Keyboard Shortcuts:** These shortcuts are designed to save you time navigating through the different areas of the Dashboard. Click the More Information link to read about how you can use keyboard shortcuts on your WordPress Dashboard.

✔ **Text Messaging:** Interact with your blog from your mobile phone by signing up for it here. Click the Text Messaging Settings link in this section and enter your mobile phone number. WordPress sends you an activation code, and after it's activated, you can do things such as log in, moderate comments, create new posts, and more — all from your mobile phone. (Text messaging in WordPress is currently available only in the United States.)

✔ **Twitter API:** Enable this option to connect to WordPress using the Twitter program of your choice. This option also allows you to follow other blogs via Twitter and to post status updates to the WordPress blog of your choice from Twitter. More information, including recommendations for Twitter programs for your desktop and mobile phone, can be found on the WordPress website here: `http://support.wordpress.com/twitter-api`.

✔ **Browser Connection:** You can select whether to use the HTTPS connection when visiting your WordPress Dashboard. *HTTPS* (Hypertext Transfer Protocol over Secure Sockets Layer) refers to a secure browser connection called *SSL-encrypt*, which protects your Internet connection and keeps out potential hackers.

✔ **Interface Language:** The Interface Language option refers to the language that you want to set for the Dashboard only. Don't confuse this setting with the Language option on the General Settings page, which determines the language you publish your blog in. If you want to view the settings on your WordPress Dashboard in Italian but want your published blog to appear in English, set the Interface Language option on the Personal Settings page to Italian and the Language option on the General Settings page to English. Capiche?

✔ **Primary Blog:** This option is the URL of your primary WordPress blog. Because WordPress allows you to have several blogs under one account, if you have more than one blog, a drop-down menu appears here, and you can use it to choose the blog you want to set as your primary blog.

✔ **Proofreading:** WordPress allows you to proofread your blog posts and page content. This section gives you several different options to choose from, such as

- Biased language

- Clichés

- Duplicate words

- Double negatives

- Jargon

- Redundant phrases

Click the link that says *Learn more* (about these options) to read about how the proofreader can help you publish better content on your blog. You can also select the box next to the words Use Automatically Detected Language to Proofread Posts and Pages to be sure that WordPress auto-detects your language preferences when proofreading.

✔ **Additional Post Content:** Select the box next to the words Help Me Find Related Content (Images, Links, Related Articles, and Tags) to Use in My Posts, and WordPress will include relevant, related content for you to refer to when writing and publishing new posts.

Account Details

In this section, you manage WordPress.com account items such as your username, password, e-mail, and website URL.

✔ **Username:** Your WordPress username is displayed here. Click the Change link to change your username.

✔ **E-mail:** Your e-mail address is displayed here. You can leave it as is or change it whenever you want.

✔ **Website:** The URL address for your WordPress blog is displayed here; you can change it if you want. This is the link that's attached to your name throughout your blog, such as when you leave comments.

✔ **New Password:** When you want to change the password for your blog, type your new password in the first text box. To confirm your new password choice, type it again in the second text field.

Directly below the two New Password text boxes is a password helper. WordPress assists you in creating a secure password by giving you a tip about the password you have chosen. WordPress alerts you if the password is too short or not secure enough (by telling you that it's *Bad*).

When you create a new password, use a combination of letters, numbers, and symbols to make it hard for anyone to guess what it is (for example, *Aty89!#4j*). When you create a password that WordPress thinks is a good one, it says the password is Strong.

Change your password frequently. I can't recommend this practice strongly enough. Some people on the Internet make it their business to hijack blogs for their own malicious purposes. If you change your password monthly, you lower your risk by keeping the hackers guessing.

When you finish setting all the options on the Personal Settings page, don't forget to click the Save Changes button to save your changes.

Chapter 4

Writing and Managing Your Blog

*T*he first chapter in this part (Chapter 3) covers the signup process and a few important settings and options that you configure when you first log in to your new WordPress blog. Now it's time to make a blogger out of you. In this chapter, I show you the tools you need to write your first post. When you understand the process, the blogging world is right at your fingertips.

This chapter also shows you the basics of categorizing your posts and links, uploading images to your blog posts, setting discussion and reading options for your blog, using static pages, and managing your users and authors. I don't have the space in this chapter to cover every option available, but I hit the high points of what you need to know.

Ready? Set? Blog!

On the Dashboard, click the Add New link on the Posts menu to display the Add New Post page where you write, organize, and publish your first post. Start by thinking up a name for your post and entering it in the Enter Title Here text box, shown in Figure 4-1.

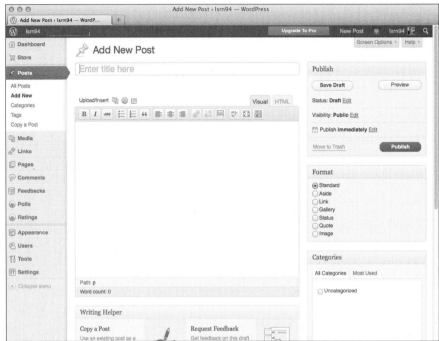

Figure 4-1:
Add your
post from
this page.

You can make the name snappy and fun if you want, but don't be cryptic. Use titles that give your readers a basic idea of what they're about to read in the posts. No set of hard-and-fast rules exists when it comes to creating titles for your blog posts, of course. Have fun with your title, and let it reflect your personality and writing style. After giving your post a title, write the content of your post in the Post text box.

The area in which you write your post is in Visual Editing mode, as indicated by the Visual tab above the text. Visual Editing mode is how WordPress provides WYSIWYG (What You See Is What You Get) options for formatting. Rather than embedding HTML code within your post, you can simply type your post, highlight the text you'd like to format, and click the buttons, shown in Figure 4-1, that appear above the box in which you type your post.

If you've ever used a word processing program such as Microsoft Word, you'll recognize many of these buttons:

- ✔ **Bold:** Embeds the `<strong> </strong>` tag to emphasize the text in bold (example: **bold text**).
- ✔ **Italics:** Embeds the `<em> </em>` tag to emphasize the text in italics (example: *italic text*).

- ✔ **Strikethrough:** Embeds the `<strike> </strike>` tag to put a line through your text (example: `strikethrough text`).

- ✔ **Unordered List:** Embeds the `<ul><li> </li></ul>` tag to create an unordered, or bulleted, list.

- ✔ **Ordered List:** Embeds the `<ol><li> </li></ol>` tag that creates an ordered, or numbered, list.

- ✔ **Blockquote:** Inserts the `<blockquote> </blockquote>` tag to indent the selected paragraph or section of text.

- ✔ **Align Left:** Inserts the `<p align="left"> </p>` tag to align the selected paragraph or section of text against the left margin.

- ✔ **Align Center:** Inserts the `<p align="center"> </p>` tag to position the selected paragraph or section of text in the center of the page.

- ✔ **Align Right:** Inserts the `<p align="right"> </p>` tag to align the selected paragraph or section of text against the right margin.

- ✔ **Insert/Edit Link:** Applies the `<a href=" "> </a>` tag to the selected text to create a hyperlink.

- ✔ **Unlink:** Removes a hyperlink from selected text.

- ✔ **Insert More Tag:** Inserts the `<!--more-->` tag to split the display on your blog page. It publishes the text written above this tag with a Read More link, which takes the user to a page with the full post. This feature is good for really long posts.

- ✔ **Toggle Spellchecker:** This is a perfect tool for you if you make spelling errors while you type. Use it to check your spelling before you post.

- ✔ **Toggle Full Screen Mode:** Expands the Post text box to occupy the full height and width of your browser screen. Use this tool to use the WordPress Distraction-Free Writing feature to focus on writing without being distracted by all the other options on the page. To bring that Post text box back to its normal state, click the Toggle Full Screen Mode button again, and voilà — it's back to normal.

- ✔ **Show/Hide Kitchen Sink:** Displays a new formatting menu, providing options for underlining, font color, custom characters, undo and redo, and so on — a veritable kitchen sink full of options. I saw this option and thought, "Wow! WordPress does my dishes, too!" Unfortunately, the option's name is a metaphor to describe the advanced formatting options available with the Visual Editor.

If you'd rather embed your own HTML and skip the Visual Editor, click the HTML tab to the right of the Visual tab above the Post text box. If you type HTML in your post — using a table or embedding video files, for example — click the HTML tab before you insert that code. If you don't, the Visual Editor formats your code, and it most likely looks nothing like you intended it to.

You can skip to the "Publishing your post" section, later in this chapter, for information on publishing your post to your blog, or continue with the following sections to discover how to include images in, and refine the options for, your post.

WordPress.com has a nifty autosave feature that saves your work while you're typing and editing a new post. If your browser crashes, or you accidentally close your browser window before you save your post, the post is there when you get back.

Inserting media files into your post

Pictures, images, video, and audio files can greatly enhance the content of a post by adding visual and/or auditory effects to go along with the words that you've written. Look right above the formatting buttons on the Add New Post page (refer to Figure 4-1), and you see an Upload/Insert toolbar. Have a look again; it's pretty small, but it's there! The Upload/Insert toolbar has a few small buttons:

- ✔ Add Media
- ✔ Add Poll
- ✔ Add a Custom Form

As of this writing, if you don't purchase blog space upgrades for your account, you can upload only image (`.jpg`, `.jpeg`, `.png`, `.gif`), document (`.pdf`, `.doc`, `.docx`), presentation (`.ppt`, `.odt`, `.pptx`, `.pps`, `.ppsx`), and spreadsheet (`.xls`, `.xlsx`) files. If you purchase a space upgrade, you can upload other files — audio (`.mp3`, `.mp4a`, `.wav`) and video (`.avi`, `.mp4`, `.mpg`, `.mov`, `.wmv`) files. Chapter 5 has information on the upgrades available for your WordPress blog.

Adding an image

Adding an image or photo to your post is easy. Start by clicking the Add Media button, which is the first button on the Upload/Insert toolbar. The Add Media window opens, letting you choose images from your hard drive or from the web. See Figure 4-2.

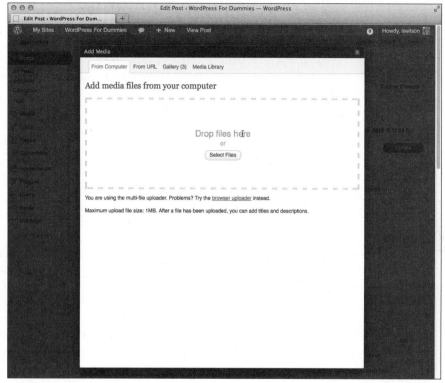

Figure 4-2:
Add media
to your post
with the
WordPress.
com media
uploader.

To add an image from the web after you click the Add Media button, follow
these steps:

1. **Click the From URL tab.**

2. **Type the URL (Internet address) of the image in the Image URL
   text box.**

   Type the full URL, including the `http` and `www` portion of the address.
   You can find the URL of any image on the web by right-clicking it and
   selecting Properties.

3. **Type a title for the image in the Image Title box.**

   Give the image a title so you can easily identify the image later when
   using the Media Library. A title also assists in search engine optimization because WordPress inserts a `<title>` tag in the HTML markup
   that looks like this: `title="`*your image title here*`"`, which helps
   search engines identify the type of content on your page.

4. **(Optional) Type a description of the image in the Alternate Text box.**

   The Alternate Text, also referred to as the ALT tag, is shown only if a browser is unable to show the image itself. It provides a text description of the image; additionally, search engines read ALT tags easily, which helps them categorize your site in their search engine directory.

5. **(Optional) Type a description of the image in the Image Caption box.**

   The caption displays underneath the images on your blog after your post is published.

6. **Choose your alignment option by selecting the None, Left, Center, or Right radio button.**

7. **Type a link or choose not to link the image:**

   - *None:* Choose this option if you don't want to link the image to anything.

   - *Link to Image:* Choose this option if you want to link the image to its individual URL, or you can type any URL to link an image to another website or page.

8. **Click the Insert into Post button.**

To add an image from your hard drive after you click the Add Media button, follow these steps:

1. **Click the From Computer tab (refer to Figure 4-2).**

2. **Click the Select Files button.**

   A dialog box opens, letting you choose an image from your hard drive.

3. **Choose an image or multiple images to upload.**

4. **Click Open.**

   The image uploads to your web server from your computer. WordPress displays a progress bar on the upload and displays an image options box when the upload is finished.

5. **Edit the details for the image(s) by filling in the fields in the Add Media box:**

   - *Title:* Type a title for the image.

   - *Alternate Text:* ALT tags help search engines find and list your site in their directories. Type a description of the image if you can.

   - *Caption:* Type a caption for the image (such as **This is a flower from my garden**).

   - *Description:* Type a description of the image.

   - *Link URL:* Type the URL you want the image linked to. Whatever option you choose from the following three options determines where your readers go when they click the image you've uploaded:

None: Choose this if you don't want the image to be clickable.

File URL: Readers can click through to the direct image itself.

Post URL: Readers can click through to the post that the image appears in. You can type your own URL in the Link URL text box.

- *Alignment:* Choose None, Left, Center, or Right.
- *Size:* Choose Thumbnail, Medium, Large, or Full Size.

6. **Click the Edit Image button, shown in Figure 4-3, to edit the appearance of the image.**

   Figure 4-4 shows the following image editor options:

   - *Crop:* Click this button to cut the image down to a smaller size.
   - *Rotate counter-clockwise:* Click this button to rotate the image to the left.
   - *Rotate clockwise:* Click this button to rotate the image to the right.
   - *Flip vertically:* Click this button to flip the image upside down, and back again.
   - *Flip horizontally:* Click this button to flip the image from right to left, and back again.
   - *Undo:* Click this button to undo any changes you've made.
   - *Redo:* Click this button to redo image edits that you've made.
   - *Scale Image:* Click this link to see a drop-down menu that you can use to set a specific width and height for the image.

7. **Click the Insert into Post button.**

   The HTML code needed to display the image within your published post is inserted automatically. The Add Media window closes and returns you to the Add New Post page. Alternatively, you can click the Save All Changes button to save the options you've set for the image(s) and then return at a later date to insert the image(s) in your post, without having to reset those options again.

Along with inserting just one image into your post, you can use the media uploader to insert a full gallery of images. Go through the steps I outline in this section to upload images, but don't click the Insert into Post button. Instead, click the Gallery tab at the top of the Add Media window (refer to Figure 4-2).

You can configure the options (as explained in Step 5 of the preceding steps) for each image by clicking the Show link to the right of the image. When you're done, click the Insert Gallery into Post button. A short piece of code is inserted that looks like this: `[gallery]`. That piece of code tells WordPress to display your gallery of images inside the post you are about to publish.

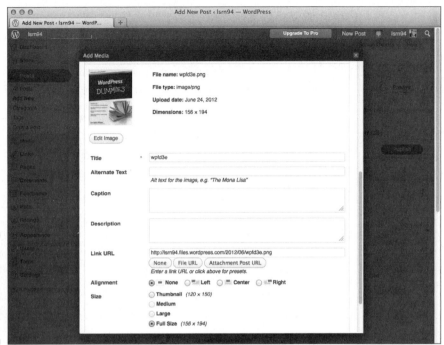

Figure 4-3:
Setting
options for
the image
after you
upload it.

Figure 4-4:
Edit the
details for
your image.

The interface that WordPress.com uses for file upload is Flash based. Adobe Flash contains a specific set of multimedia technologies programmed to handle media files on the web. Some browsers and operating systems aren't configured to handle Flash-based applications. If you experience difficulties with the media uploader, WordPress gives you a handy alternative method. In the media uploader (refer to Figure 4-2), click the Browser Uploader link to upload files in an interface that is not Flash based.

Using audio, video, and other media files

The Upload/Insert toolbar (refer to Figure 4-1) contains two other buttons:

✔ **Add Poll:** You can automatically set up an account with WordPress. com's sister company, Polldaddy, to create and insert polls on your WordPress.com blog.

✔ **Add a Custom Form:** You can add a contact form that gives your visitors the capability to send you an e-mail directly from your website by simply filling out a form and clicking Send. You can create forms with your desired fields and insert them into a post or page to display on your site.

How do media files differ from image, video, and audio files? Media files include Microsoft PowerPoint presentation files (.ppt), Microsoft Word documents (.doc), and Adobe Portable Document Format files (.pdf). Although these types of files can also contain images, video, and audio files, you can use the media uploader to upload these files to your WordPress.com account so that you can display and link to them on your blog.

WordPress.com gives you 3 GB of disk space for your free blog, and though it would take a lot of files to use up that amount of space, if you upload large image files, that space can go a lot quicker than you think. Keep the actual file size of the images you upload in mind when you upload media; you can eat up that disk space before you know it.

Refining your post options

After you write the post, you can choose a few extra options before you publish it for the entire world to see. These settings are applied only to the post you're working on; they don't apply automatically to any of your future or past posts. You can find these options (see Figure 4-5) underneath and to the right of the Post text box.

If you don't see the modules for the options I list in this section, click the Screen Options tab at the top-right side of your Dashboard window and enable the display options.

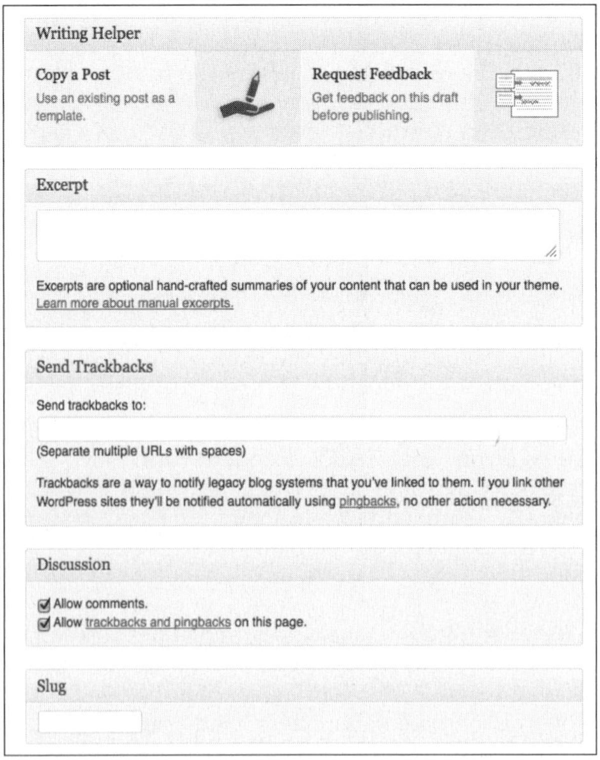

Figure 4-5:
Several
options for
your blog
post.

Here are all the options:

- ✔ **Writing Helper:** WordPress wants you to be successful in your writing, so it provides two options to help you meet your writing goals:

  - *Copy a Post:* Click this link to display a listing of posts you've already written on your blog and select one to use as a template for formatting.

  - *Request Feedback:* Want to get feedback on your post before you publish it? Click the Request Feedback link and enter the e-mail addresses of the person (or people) you'd like to e-mail your draft to so that you can elicit their feedback before you publish it.

- ✔ **Excerpt:** *Excerpts* are short summaries of your posts. Many bloggers use snippets to show teasers of their blog posts, thereby encouraging the reader to click the Read More link to read posts in their entirety. Type your short summary in the Excerpt box. Excerpts have no word limit, but the idea is to keep them short and sweet.

✔ **Send Trackbacks:** If you want to send a trackback to another blog, enter that blog's Trackback URL in the Send Trackbacks To text box. You can send trackbacks to more than one blog; just be sure to separate trackback URLs with spaces.

✔ **Discussion:** Decide whether to allow readers to submit feedback through the comment system and whether to allow pingbacks and trackbacks by selecting the boxes here or leaving them blank. *Pingbacks* differ slightly from trackbacks in that the software handles them more like comments; trackbacks are generally kept separate from comments.

✔ **Slug:** A slug is what WordPress calls the *permalink,* or URL address, of an individual post or page on your blog. By default, WordPress adopts the title of your blog post to use as a portion of the URL, or slug, for your post, but you can customize it in the Slug box if you'd like (for example, if you want a shorter URL with posts that have really long titles).

✔ **Author:** For multiauthor blogs, you can use a drop-down menu to select the person listed as the official author of an individual blog post.

✔ **Likes and Shares:** WordPress.com allows other WordPress.com members to Like and Share posts across its global network, and your blog is no exception. However, if you don't want your readers to Like or Share your blog posts within the network, you can disable Likes and Shares in this section by deselecting the check boxes.

✔ **Publish:** These are the publishing options for your blog post. I cover these options in detail in the next section, "Publishing your post."

✔ **Format:** Some of the themes on WordPress.com support *Post Formats,* which are different types of posts such as video posts, photo galleries, and *asides* (small, short status updates rather than long, full posts), that have special formatting and styling. If you are using a theme with Post Formats, you see a module on the right side of the Add New Post page titled Format (refer to Figure 4-1) where you can select the type of format you'd like to use.

✔ **Categories:** You can file your posts in different categories to organize them by subject. (See more about organizing your posts in the "Organizing Your Blog by Subject" section, later in this chapter.) Select the box to the left of the category name you want to use. Don't see the category you need listed here? Click the Add New Category link at the bottom of the Categories box and you can add a new category.

✔ **Tags:** Tags are a nice feature of WordPress.com because they allow you to add searchable and archived keywords for your posts in small subtopics. Type your chosen tags (or keywords) in the Tags box. Tags can be single words or several words; just make sure to separate tags with commas (for example, enter **books, movies, pop culture, entertainment**).

> ✔ **Featured Image:** When uploading images to your blog posts, you can select one image to serve as a Featured Image for your post, and it displays as a thumbnail on your blog in areas such as archive listings and search results. Use the Featured Image module to assign the title to an image, if you are using one (or more).

When you finish setting the options for your post, don't navigate away from this page because your options haven't been fully saved. You need to scroll back up to the top and click the Save Draft button on the top-right side of the page. Before you do that, however, check out the next section, which discusses publishing options for your new blog post.

Publishing your post

You have given your new post a title and written the content of your new blog post. Maybe you even added an image or other type of media file to your blog post and configured the tags, categories, and other options. Now the question is: To publish? Or not to publish (yet)?

WordPress.com gives you three options for saving or publishing your post when you're done writing it. Figure 4-6 shows the Publish section located on the right side of the Add New Post page.

Figure 4-6:
Check out these options in the Publish section before publishing your post.

> Publish
>
> (Save Draft)   Preview
>
> Status: **Draft**
>
> [Draft   ▾] (OK) Cancel
>
> Visibility: **Public**
> ● Public
>   ☐ Stick this post to the front page
> ○ Password protected
> ○ Private
> (OK) Cancel
>
> 📅 Publish **immediately**
> [06-Jun ▾] [24] , [2012] @ [10] : [41]
> (OK) Cancel
>
> Move to Trash   **Publish**

The Publish menu offers three options:

> ✔ **Status:** Click the Edit link next to the Status option, and a new drop-down menu appears with the following options shown in Figure 4-6. (***Note:*** The figure displays a `Cancel` link, however that link says `Edit` before you click it.)

- *Pending Review:* Select this option to set the post status as Pending; the post shows up in your list of drafts next to a Pending Review header. This option lets the administrator of the blog know that contributors have entered posts that are waiting for administrator review and approval (helpful for blogs with multiple authors).

- *Draft:* Select this option to save the post but not publish it to your blog. Your post is saved in draft form, allowing you to return to it later.

Click OK when you're done to save your settings.

✔ **Visibility:** Click the Edit link next to the Visibility option and a new menu appears with the following options shown in Figure 4-6; again, the link says `Edit` before you click it.

- *Public:* Choosing this option publishes your post to your blog for the entire world to see. Select the Stick This Post to The Front Page check box if you want to publish this post to the very top of your blog and keep it there until you come back and edit the status later.

- *Password Protect This Post:* You can password-protect a post by entering a password in this field. (***Note:*** The text field appears after you select the option to password protect the post.) When you do, you can share the password with only the readers you want to let read that post. This feature is perfect for those times when you'd love to make a blog post about all the stupid things your boss did today but don't want your boss to see it. This feature also hides the post from search engines so that it doesn't show up in search results.

- *Private:* This option allows you publish a post privately, which means the only person who can read the post is you — it is completely hidden from public view. I've known some writers who use their blogs for private journal entries, so this option would be helpful in that regard.

Click OK when you're done to save your settings.

✔ **Publish Immediately:** Click the Edit link next to the Publish Immediately option. (Figure 4-6 displays a `Cancel` link; however, that link says `Edit` before you click it.) A new menu appears where you can set the date (or time stamp) of the post and publish it right away. The date settings here allow you to set a date in the future for the post to publish, or you can back-date a post to publish on a date in the past.

Click OK when you are done to save your settings.

When you have chosen a publishing status, click the Publish button. WordPress saves your publishing-status option. Successfully published blog posts show up on the front page of your blog.

If you want to publish your blog post right away, skip the drop-down menu options and click the Publish button, which sends your new blog post to your blog in all its glory. If you click Publish and for some reason don't see the post you just published to the front page of your blog, you probably left the Publish Status drop-down menu set to Unpublished. Look for your new post among the draft posts.

Organizing Your Blog by Subject

Categorizing your posts in WordPress provides an organizational structure for your blog. Each blog post assigned to a category is grouped with other posts in the same category. When your blog is a few months old, this structure creates a nice topical directory of posts for you and your readers.

Category lists generally appear in two places on your blog, letting your readers find all your posts by subject very easily. Almost all WordPress themes list categories within the blog post itself. Most themes also provide a list of your categories in the sidebar of your blog so that your readers can click a topic of interest.

Each category in a WordPress.com blog has its own RSS feed, making it easy for your readers to subscribe to a feed and keep updated on what you have to say in your blog about a certain topic.

Creating categories and subcategories

A brand-new WordPress blog has only one category: *Uncategorized,* but you can add as many categories as you want and can manage those categories on the Categories page on your Dashboard, as shown in Figure 4-7.

You can create new categories (and categories within those categories) by following these steps:

1. **Click the Categories link on the Posts submenu.**

   The Categories page opens (refer to Figure 4-7).

2. **Under the Add New Category heading, type the name of your category in the Name text box.**

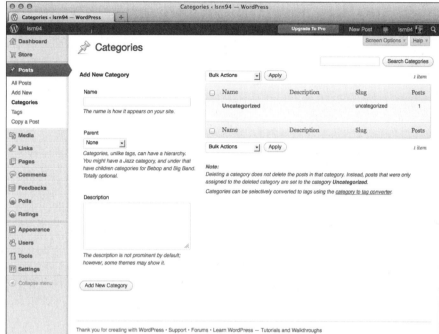

Figure 4-7:
Add as
many
categories
as you
want on the
Dashboard's
Categories
page.

3. Leave the Parent drop-down menu set to the default option (None).

The Parent drop-down menu allows you to create subcategories. If you have a main category called Books, for example, Books appears in the Parent drop-down menu. To create a subcategory of the Books category, follow Steps 1 and 2 and then choose Books from the Parent drop-down menu.

4. (Optional) Enter a description of the category in the Description text box.

Do this step now so that later on you'll know what you were thinking of when you created this category. A short summary will do. (Also, some WordPress themes are coded to display the category description in the sidebar of your blog.)

5. Click the Add New Category button.

Categories you create now aren't set in stone. You can edit or delete them by revisiting the Categories page and clicking the name of the category you want to edit. The Edit Category page opens, and you can edit the category name, category parent, and description.

Filing posts in categories and subcategories

The preceding section tells you how to create categories and subcategories. When you create those categories and subcategories, you don't ever have to re-create them — they are always there for you to assign your blog posts to.

To assign existing posts to a category, follow these steps:

1. **Click All Posts in the Posts menu.**

   The Posts page appears in your browser window, displaying a list of posts you've made.

2. **Click the name of the post you want to categorize.**

   The Edit Post page opens, displaying your post content and saved options.

3. **In the Categories section to the right of the Post text box, select the check box next to the category or subcategory (you can select more than one category and subcategory) that you want to assign to the post.**

   You can also use the Categories section before you publish a new post to assign it to the categories you'd like.

4. **Scroll to the top of the Edit Post page and click the Update button.**

   WordPress refreshes the Edit Post page, displaying the post you just edited; it reflects the changes you just made.

Creating and Categorizing Your Blogroll

A *blogroll* is a list of links that you display on your blog. In this section, I show you how to add and manage the links in your blogroll.

To view your default blogroll, click the Links menu on the Dashboard navigation menu. The Links page opens, and you see the default links already included in your WordPress blog. See Figure 4-8.

If you want to remove a link from your blogroll, select the box to the left of the link name; select Delete from the Bulk Actions drop-down menu at the top of the page, and click the Apply button (refer to Figure 4-8).

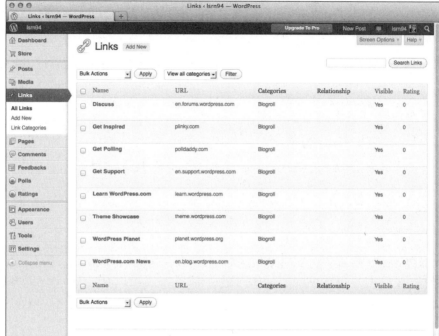

Creating link categories

WordPress lets you have an unlimited number of link categories on your blog. Link categories, which function similarly to the post categories discussed in the previous section, provide you a way of separating your blogrolls (or list of links) into topical categories.

By default, WordPress sets up a link category for you called — by no coincidence — Blogroll. To add a new category, click the Link Categories link on the Links menu to open the Link Categories page on your Dashboard.

You add a new link category the same way you add new post categories (see the "Creating categories and subcategories" section, earlier in this chapter).

Adding new links to your blogroll

To add a new link to your blogroll, click the Links subtab and then click the Add New link. The Add New Link page opens, as shown in Figure 4-9.

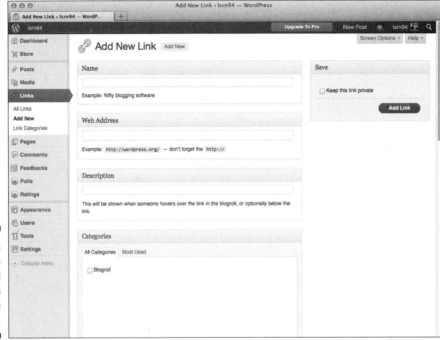

Figure 4-9:
Add a link to
your blogroll
by using this
tool from
WordPress.

Follow these steps to add your new link:

1. **In the Name text box, type the name of the website you're adding.**

2. **In the Web Address text box, type the website's URL, making sure to include the** `http://` **part.**

3. **(Optional) In the Description text box, type a short description of the website.**

4. **In the Categories box, select the check box to the left of the category you want this link to appear in.**

5. **(Optional) Select the target for your link in the Target box.**

   The target tells your browser how you want this link to load in your visitor's browser window after the visitor clicks it. You have three choices:

   • *_blank:* Loads the link in a new browser window

   • *_top:* Loads the link in the top frame (if your site is designed with frames)

   • *None:* Loads the link in the same browser window (the default setting, should you choose to overlook this step)

The third option — None — is my preference and recommendation. I like to let my visitors decide whether they want a bunch of new browser windows to open every time they click a link on my site.

6. **(Optional) Select the Link Relationship (XFN) option and define why you're providing this link.**

   XFN, or XHTML Friends Network, allows you to indicate the relationship you have with the people you are linking to by defining how you know, or are associated with, them. Table 4-1 lists the different relationships you can assign to your links.

7. **(Optional) Select advanced options for your link in the Advanced box:**

   - *Image Address:* This option associates an image with the link, and some WordPress themes display the image on your site along with the link. Type the URL for the image in the Image Address box. For this purpose, you need to know the direct URL to the image (for example, `http://yourdomain.com/images/image.jpg`).

   - *RSS Address:* Type the RSS feed URL for the blog you are linking to. WordPress displays the link to the site's RSS feed alongside the link that appears on your site. Not all WordPress themes accommodate this feature.

   - *Notes:* Type your notes in the Notes box. These notes aren't displayed on your site, so feel free to leave whatever notes you need to further define the details of this link. A month from now, you may not remember who this person is or why you linked to her, so you can add notes to remind yourself.

   - *Rating:* Use the Rating drop-down menu to rate this link from 0 to 10, 0 being the worst and 10 being the best. Some WordPress themes display your blogroll in the order you rate your links, from best to worst.

8. **Scroll to the top of the page, and click the Add Link button.**

   Your new link is saved and a blank Add New Link page opens, ready for you to add another new link to your blogroll(s). Additionally, in the Save section at the top right, you can choose to keep this link private; this option, if selected, keeps the link from being displayed publicly on your blog. The link would be kept protected and for your eyes only.

Table 4-1	Link Relationships (XFN) Defined
Link Relationship	*Description*
Identity	Select this check box if the link is to a website you own.
Friendship	Select the option (Contact, Acquaintance, Friend, or None) that most closely identifies the relationship.
Physical	Select this check box if you've met the person you're linking to face to face. Sharing pictures over the Internet doesn't count — this selection identifies a person you've physically met.
Professional	Select one of these check boxes if the person you're linking to is a co-worker or colleague.
Geographical	Select Co-Resident if the person you're linking to lives with you. Or select Neighbor or None, depending on which option applies to your relationship with the person.
Family	If the blogger you're linking to is a family member, select the option that tells how the person is related to you.
Romantic	Select the option that applies to the type of romantic relationship you have with the person you're linking to. Do you have a crush on him? Is she your creative muse? Is he someone you consider to be a sweetheart? Select the option that most closely identifies the romantic relationship, if any.

You can find more information on XFN at `http://gmpg.org/xfn`.

Revisit the Manage Links page anytime you want to add a new link, edit an old link, or delete an existing link. You can create an unlimited amount of blogroll categories to sort your blogrolls by topics. I know one blogger who has 50 categories for his links, so the options are limitless.

Managing and Inviting Users

What's a blog without blog users? Of course, your WordPress.com blog always has at least one user: you. To see your list of users, click the Users link in the navigation menu. The Users page opens and the Users menu expands to show three different links:

- Authors & Users
- Your Profile (See Chapter 3 for information on the Profile page.)
- Invites

Managing authors and users

The Users page tells you about all the users on your blog. It lists each user's username, name, e-mail address, role on your blog, and number of posts made to your blog.

To manage user roles, you need to understand the distinct differences among the roles. The following list explains the type of access each role provides:

- **Follower:** This default role is assigned to anyone not logged in or anyone who leaves a comment. Followers receive e-mail updates whenever you update your blog with new content, but they don't have any editing privileges.

- **Contributor:** A Contributor can upload files and write/edit/manage her own posts. When a Contributor writes a post, however, that post is saved as a draft to await administrator approval; Contributors can't publish their posts. This feature is a nice way to moderate content written by new authors.

- **Administrator:** An Administrator has the authority to change any of the Administration options and settings in the WordPress blog. You, as the account owner, are listed as an Administrator already. You can also assign other users as Administrators.

- **Editor:** In addition to having the access and permissions of an Author, an Editor can moderate comments, manage categories, manage links, edit pages, and edit other Authors' posts. Editors can also read and edit private posts.

- **Author:** In addition to having the access and permissions of a Contributor, an Author can publish his own posts without administrator approval. Authors can also delete their own posts.

WordPress lets you have an unlimited number of users and authors on one blog, which is a nice feature if running a multiauthor blog is something you'd like to do.

To change a user's role, follow these steps:

1. **Click the All Users link in the Users submenu.**

   Locate the name of the user that you'd like to edit.

2. **Select the check box next to the username.**

3. **From the Change Role To drop-down menu at the top the page, choose the role you want to assign; then click the Change button.**

   The Users page refreshes with the new role assignment applied.

To view all the posts made by an author, click the number that appears below the Posts column for that user.

Inviting friends to WordPress.com

Now that you've experienced the fun, ease, and excitement of having your very own WordPress.com blog, why not tell your friends so that they can tell their friends, and their friends can tell their friends, and so on?

Click the Invite New link in the Users submenu to load the Invite New Users to Your Blog page, as shown in Figure 4-10. This page gives you the tools you need to add new users to your blog, and by *user,* WordPress means simply a person who is a member of your blog as a contributor, an author, an editor, or an administrator. You can have an unlimited amount of users on one WordPress blog.

Enter up to ten e-mail addresses for people you'd like to invite to your blog, assign a user role, add an optional message to them, and click the Send Invitation button. If the person you invite already has a WordPress.com account, your blog is added to their Dashboard after they accept your invitation. If you enter someone who doesn't have a WordPress.com account yet, WordPress sends that person an invitation to become a member, along with instructions on how to sign up. (The WordPress people have thought of everything, haven't they?)

At the bottom of the Invite New Users to Your Blog page, in the Past Invitations section, you can review users you've previously invited to your blog and their current status (whether or not they've accepted your invite and the date they accepted it).

Follow these instructions to invite as many people as you want to join WordPress.com:

1. **Click the Invite New link in the Users menu.**

   The Invite New Users to Your Blog page opens.

2. **In the Usernames or Email Addresses box, enter either a user's WordPress.com username (if that user already has an account) or enter the prospective member's e-mail address.**

3. **Select the appropriate role in the Role drop-down menu.**

4. **Type a special note to the user in the Message text box.**

   This message appears in the e-mail that the user receives.

5. **Click the Send Invitation button to send the invitation to the prospective member via e-mail.**

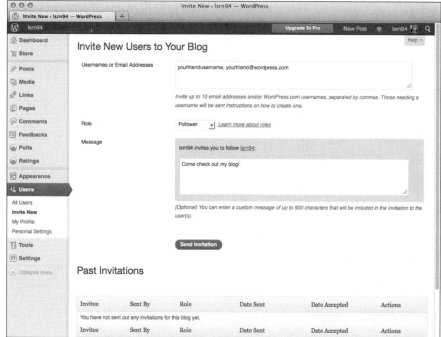

Figure 4-10:
WordPress.
com Invite
New page.

When you complete these steps, WordPress sends you confirmation that the invitation was sent.

Managing Comments and Comment Spam

Comments provide a great way for readers to interact with you, and vice versa. Readers of your blog can post comments by using the comment form that appears on the same page as each of the published posts on your blog. You need to be able to control the comments that appear, however, and I tell you how to do that in this section.

Setting discussion options for your blog

Click the Discussion link on the Settings submenu. On the Discussion Settings page, you can set the options (such as notification settings) for your posts, determine how comments and comment spam are handled, and specify whether you want to use avatars on your blog. The Discussion Settings page has six settings that you can configure for your blog, each of which I discuss in the following sections.

When you're done setting up your options, click the Save Changes button at the bottom of the page to make the changes take effect. You can revisit this page as often as needed so that you can keep your settings current and to your liking.

Default Article Settings

The Default Article Settings section is where you tell WordPress.com how to handle post notifications. Three options are available to you:

- ✓ **Attempt to Notify Any Blogs Linked to from the Article:** Enabled by default, this option makes your blog send a notification, via a ping, to any site you've linked to in your blog post. This feature is very similar to a trackback (which I discuss in Chapter 2) and can slow the process of posting just a bit because of the time it takes for your blog to talk to another blog to let it know that you're talking about it.

- ✓ **Allow Link Notifications from Other Blogs (Pingbacks and Trackbacks):** Enabled by default, this option tells WordPress that you want your blog to be notified via pings and trackbacks that other people have linked to you. WordPress lists any ping and trackback notifications on your site as comments in the Comments section. If you deselect this option, your ears may tingle, but you won't know when other people are talking about, or linking to, you on other blogs.

- ✓ **Allow People to Post Comments on the Article:** Enabled by default, this option lets people leave comments on your blog.

Other Comment Settings

The Other Comment Settings tell WordPress how to handle comments:

- ✓ **Comment Author Must Fill Out Their Name and Email:** Enabled by default, this option requires everyone who comments on your blog to fill in the Name and Email field when leaving a comment. This option is very helpful in combating comment spam. See Chapters 2 and 10 for information on comment spam. Deselect this check box to disable this option.

- ✓ **Users Must Be Registered and Logged in to Comment:** Not enabled by default, this option allows you to accept comments on your blog from only those people who have registered and are logged in as a user on your blog. If a user is not logged in, he or she sees a message that says: `You must be logged in in order to leave a comment.`

- ✓ **Automatically Close Comments on Articles Older Than *X* Days:** Select the box next to this option to tell WordPress that you want comments on older articles to be automatically closed. Fill in the text box provided with the number of days you would like to wait before WordPress closes comments on older articles.

This is a very effective anti-spam technique that many bloggers use to limit the comment and trackback spam on their blogs.

- ✔ **Enable Threaded (Nested) Comments *X* Levels Deep:** This drop-down menu allows you to choose the level of threaded comments you'd like to have on your blog. The default is 3; you can choose up to 10 levels. Instead of all comments being displayed on your blog in chronological order (as it is by default), nesting them allows you and your readers to reply to comments within the comment itself.

- ✔ **Break Comments into Pages with *X* Comments Per Page:** Fill in the text box with a number of comments you want to display on one page. Setting a limit is very helpful for blogs that receive a large number of comments. It lets you break the long string of comments into several pages, which makes it easier to read and helps speed up the load time of your site because the page isn't loading such a large number of comments simultaneously.

- ✔ **Comments Should Be Displayed with the Older/Newer Comments at the Top of Each Page:** Use the drop-down menu to select Older or Newer. Selecting Older displays the comments on your blog in the order of oldest to newest. Selecting Newer displays comments from newest to oldest.

Email Me Whenever

The four options in the Email Me Whenever section include

- ✔ Anyone posts a comment
- ✔ A comment is held for moderation
- ✔ Someone Likes one of my posts
- ✔ Someone reblogs one of my posts
- ✔ Someone follows my blog

The e-mail feature settings tell WordPress that you want to receive an e-mail anytime anyone leaves a comment on your blog, when a comment awaits your moderation, or when someone Likes or subscribes to your blog. The e-mail feature can be very helpful, particularly if you don't visit your blog daily. Everyone likes to get comments on their blog posts, and it's good to be notified when it happens so that you can revisit that post, respond to your readers, and keep the conversation active. All four options in this section are enabled by default; you can easily disable any, or all, of them by deselecting the check box to the left of each option.

Before a Comment Appears

The two options in the Before a Comment Appears section tell WordPress how you want WordPress to handle comments before they appear in your blog:

✔ **An Administrator Must Always Approve the Comment:** Selecting this option holds every new comment on your blog in the moderation queue until you log in and approve it. This feature is particularly helpful if you want to review the content of comments before they're published to your blog.

✔ **Comment Author Must Have a Previously Approved Comment:** When this box is selected, the only comments approved and published on your blog are those left by commenters who are already approved by you. Their e-mail addresses are stored in the database, and WordPress runs a check on their e-mails. If the e-mail address matches a previously approved comment, the new comment is published automatically. If no match occurs, WordPress places the comment in the moderation queue, awaiting your approval. This measure is yet another feature that helps prevent comment spam.

Comment Moderation

In the Comment Moderation section, you can set options to specify what types of comments are held in the moderation queue to await your approval. Frequently, comment spammers try to spam your blog with a *ton* of links in the hope of promoting their own sites through your comment form. You can set the number of links allowed in a comment before it's tossed into the moderation queue to await approval. The default is 2. Give that a try, and if you're getting lots of spam comments with multiple links, you may want to revisit this page and increase that number.

You can set keywords, URLs, e-mail addresses, or IP addresses to be flagged for moderation in the text box below the link setting. Check out the sidebar "A case for moderation over blacklisting" for an example of how moderation helps you distinguish the real spam.

By default, WordPress.com automatically discards spam on older posts on your blog. You can switch this option off by checking the Don't Discard Spam on Old Posts box at the top of this section.

Comment Blacklist

In contrast to the Comment Moderation list, the Comment Blacklist is a list of words, URLs, e-mail addresses, and IP addresses that you want to flat-out ban from ever making it to your blog. Items placed here don't even make it into your Comment Moderation queue; they're filtered as spam by the system and completely disregarded. The words I placed in my Blacklist are not family friendly and have no place in a nice book like this.

A case for moderation over blacklisting

One popular topic that comment spammers like to spam with is Viagra; they fill their comments with links to sites where you can purchase Viagra. Really, if you wanted to know about those sites, wouldn't you seek them out? Well, that's beside the point. If you're getting a lot of Viagra spam, you can enter **Viagra** in the Comment Moderation list rather than in the Comment Blacklist because you may actually receive a legitimate comment with the word *Viagra* in it that you would like to approve. A visitor to my blog left a comment — "Espresso is Viagra for my brain!" — in response to a post I made about my love for espresso. That comment is legitimate but got thrown into my moderation queue because I have that term in my Comment Moderation list.

Are you getting the feeling that comment spam is a real issue for bloggers? It's huge — probably bigger than you imagine it to be. Much of the comment-spam prevention is done behind the scenes, so you don't even see half of what's going on. All the options on the Discussion Settings page are geared toward decreasing or eliminating comment or trackback spam from your blog. If, during the course of your blogging experience on WordPress.com, you find that you're having an issue with spam, you may want to revisit these options and make adjustments.

Comment Reply via Email

Select the box labeled Enable Sending Comment Replies via Email, and WordPress.com not only publishes your comment replies to your readers on your blog, but also sends your reply via e-mail to the reader you're replying to. That e-mail contains the body of your reply and a link back to your blog.

Follow Comments

Select the box labeled Show a 'Follow Comments' Option in the Comment Form if you want to allow the readers of your blog to subscribe to individual comment threads on your blog. When you enable this option, a check box appears in your comments section allowing your readers to opt to receive e-mails every time a new comment is posted to a specific post on your blog. This option also puts a comment subscription management page on your blog that allows readers to view and manage their comment subscriptions. This is a really great tool to keep readers coming back to your blog over and over again, and a great way to keep lively discussions going!

Follow Blog

Select the box labeled Show a 'Follow Blog' Option in the Comment Form if you want to give your readers an easy way to subscribe to your blog via e-mail. With this option enabled, readers who select this option receive an update in their e-mail box every time you publish a new post to your blog. This is a fantastic way to keep your readers informed and coming back to your blog time and time again for more of your great published content.

Avatars

Avatars are photos or images that represent your commenters (and you) on your blog. You can choose to display avatars on your blog by selecting the Show Avatars option. You can also set the maximum rating for the avatars; it's much like the movie rating system we're all used to. If your site is family-friendly, you probably don't want to display R- or X-rated avatars on your blog. You can select G, PG, R, or X ratings for the avatars that display on your blog. You can also select an image to use as the default avatar for those users who do not yet have avatars assigned to their e-mail.

For WordPress.com users, the avatars displayed are the images that users uploaded to their profiles (see Chapter 3). Users who are not registered with WordPress can still display an avatar when they comment on your blog by signing up for one at `http://gravatar.com`.

Comment Form

The text field here displays `Leave a Reply` by default, and it's the prompt your readers see on your blog that encourages them to leave a comment. You can leave this as is, or you can type your own prompt in this box to change the wording that displays in your comment area.

Viewing comments

Open the Comments page by clicking the Comments link on the Dashboard navigation menu. The Comments page shows all the comments on your blog from the very first day you started. Here you can view the comments, edit them, mark them as spam, or flat-out delete them.

If you set your Comments options so that comments aren't published until you approve them, you can approve comments in this section as well. To do this, of course, you have to have comments on your blog, and if your blog is new, you may not have any yet. Figure 4-11 shows what a comment looks like in this area.

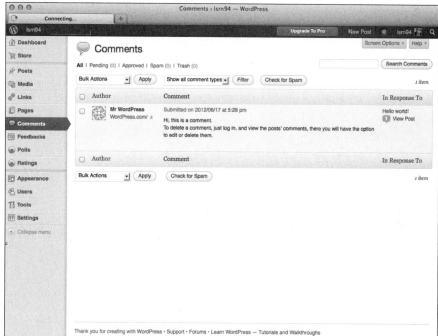

Figure 4-11: Looking at comments on the Comments page on the Dashboard.

To manage a comment, find one that you want to edit, delete, unapprove (that is, remove it from your blog page), or mark as spam. If you need to, you can find a specific comment by using the search feature. Just type a keyword in the search box located in the top-right corner of the page and click the Search Comments button.

When you find the comment you want to manage, hover your mouse over the comment. Six different links appear beneath the comment text as follows:

- **Approve or Unapprove:** If the comment hasn't been approved, the Approve link appears here. Click Approve to publish the comment to your blog. If the comment is approved, click the Unapprove link to . . . well, unapprove it. This link puts the comment back into the moderation queue.

- **Reply:** This link drops a text box down on the same page to allow you to reply to the comment right from the Comments page.

- **Quick Edit:** This link accomplishes the same as the Edit link, except that instead of taking you to a new Edit Comment page on your Dashboard, it drops down a Quick Edit text box that allows you to do a fast edit right on the same page.

✔ **Edit:** Clicking this link takes you to the Edit Comment page, where you can edit the text of the comment if you need to (correcting typos, anyone?).

✔ **Spam:** This link tells WordPress that this comment is spam and removes it from your blog.

✔ **Trash:** This link deletes the comment from your blog.

Creating a Static Page

You can create pages on your blog that are treated differently from posts. These pages, called *static pages,* appear as separate pages on your blog rather than as posts within your blog. You use nearly the same process of writing a static page as you do to write a post. You can easily create an unlimited number of static pages, which can serve as nice complements to your overall site content.

You can use this feature to write, for example, an About page, on which you give all the wild and wooly details about yourself. If you use the Page Sidebar widget, the pages you create are listed in your sidebar; you can also add pages to the main navigation menu. (See Chapter 5 for more about widgets and menus.)

You can create static pages by logging on to your WordPress Dashboard and following these steps:

1. **Click the Add New link in the Pages menu.**

   The Add New Page screen appears, and you can compose your static page.

2. **Type the title of your page in the Title text box.**

3. **Type the body of your page in the Page text box.**

   You can use the Visual Text Editor and insert media files into your page by using the same techniques discussed in the "Ready? Set? Blog!" section, earlier in this chapter.

4. **Set the options for your page by using the option boxes below the Page text box.**

   To display these boxes, click the white arrow to the left of each option title. The following options appear:

   • *Discussion:* By default, the Allow Comments and Allow Pings boxes are selected. Deselect them if you don't want to allow comments or pings.

   • *Parent:* Choose the page's parent from the drop-down menu if you want to make the static page a subpage of another page you've created.

- *Template:* If the WordPress.com theme you're using has page templates available, choose the template you want to use from this drop-down menu.

- *Order:* Enter a number in the text box that reflects the order in which you want this page to display on your site. If you want this page to be the third page listed, for example, enter **3**.

5. **Scroll back to the top of the page and choose options from the Publish Status drop-down menu.**

   These options are the same as the Publish Status options available when you're writing a new blog page. I cover the available options in the "Ready? Set? Blog!" section, earlier in this chapter.

6. **Click the Save or Publish button when you're done to save your work.**

Your static pages aren't included in your Recent Posts list, in categories, or in your monthly archive. Figure 4-12 shows an example of a static page on the Edit Page section of the Dashboard.

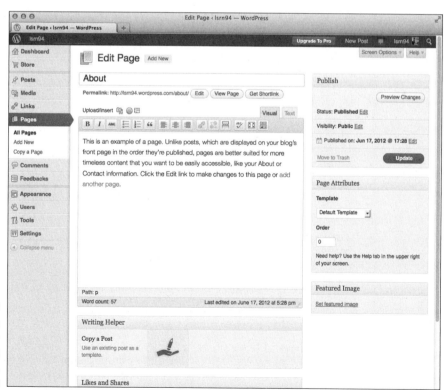

Figure 4-12:
Edit your static pages here.

Setting Up Your Front Page

On the Reading Settings page (click the Reading link in the Settings menu), you can set how many blog posts show up on the front page of your blog and/or change your front page to display a static page rather than your most recent blog posts. (See the preceding section, "Creating a Static Page.") You can also determine how many blog posts your readers can see in your RSS feed. Figure 4-13 shows the available options.

The Reading Settings page gives you control of the settings that let you make these decisions for your blog:

- **Front Page Displays:** This setting determines what appears on the front page of your site.

   - *Your Latest Posts:* Select this option if you want your blog posts to display on the front page of your blog.

   - *A Static Page:* Select this option if you want a static page instead of a listing of your recent blog posts to display on the front page of your site.

   - *Front Page:* If you choose to display a static page, choose from this drop-down menu which page to display.

   - *Posts Page:* If you choose to display a static page, use this drop-down menu to tell WordPress which page to display your posts on.

- **Blog Pages Show at Most:** If you choose to display your blog posts on your front page, this step is where you set the number of blog posts to display per page. Figure 4-13 shows that I decided to display ten posts on my front page.

- **Syndication Feeds Show the Most Recent:** This setting determines how many posts show in your RSS feed at one time. See Chapter 2 for details on RSS.

- **For Each Article in a Feed, Show:** Indicate here which portion of each article you want to show in your feed:

   - *Full Text:* Select this radio button if you want the entire text of each post to be displayed in your RSS feed.

   - *Summary:* Select this radio button if you want only excerpts of your posts to be displayed in your RSS feed.

- **To Infinity and Beyond:** Select this option to tell WordPress to automatically display more posts once the reader gets to the very bottom of your site. WordPress detects when the readers reach the end of the page and automatically displays the next seven posts on your blog.

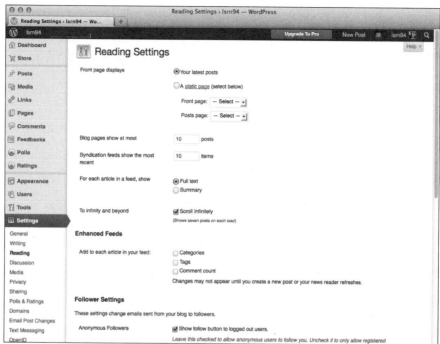

Figure 4-13:
The Reading
Settings
page.

✔ **Enhanced Feeds:** Here, you have the option of showing several more details about your blog in your RSS feed:

- Categories

- Tags

- Comment Count

✔ **Follower Settings:** When people subscribe to your blog for the first time, an e-mail is sent to them welcoming them to your blog. The text box in the E-mail Settings area provides default text for that e-mail. You can change this text to suit your needs.

When you change any settings in the Reading Settings page, click the Save Changes button in the bottom-left corner to save your preferences.

Publishing a Public or Private Blog

This section describes three very simple options, and the option you choose lets you determine how you want to deal with publicity on your blog. Figure 4-14 shows your choices. To access the privacy options for your blog, click the Privacy link on the Settings menu. You can choose one of these three options in the Privacy Settings page:

✔ **Allow Search Engines to Index this Site:** Select this option if you want to freely allow search engines to visit your blog and include its content in their search directories.

✔ **Ask Search Engines Not to Index this Site:** Select this option if you don't want search engines to visit and include your site in their directories. This option is helpful if you want normal (read: human) visitors but don't want the publicity that search engines provide.

✔ **I Would Like My Site to be Private, Visible Only to Users I Choose:** Select this option if you want to make your blog available only to the people you choose. This option keeps your blog completely private and away from prying eyes — except for those users you allow.

When you select and save this option, WordPress.com provides a form in which you can enter the WordPress.com usernames for the people you want to invite to view your private blog. (With WordPress.com, you can add up to 35 users at no cost; you can pay an annual fee to add more.)

When you finish making your decision, be sure to click the Save Changes button to have the changes take effect.

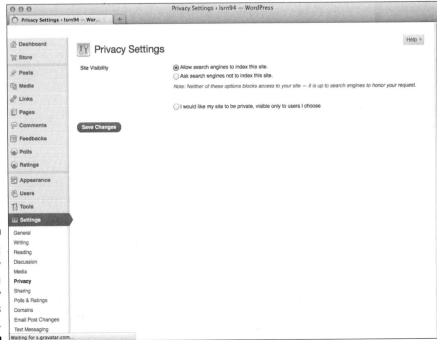

Figure 4-14:
Site Visibility
options in
the Privacy
Settings
page.

Publicizing through Social Media

WordPress gives you the ability to easily integrate your WordPress blog with various social networks, like Facebook, Twitter, and LinkedIn, for example. Click the Sharing link in the Settings submenu on your Dashboard to load the Sharing Settings page.

In the Sharing section, connect your blog to popular social networks to automatically share your new posts with your friends within that network. WordPress allows you to share your blog on the following networks:

- Facebook
- Twitter
- Yahoo!
- Messenger Connect
- LinkedIn

Click the icon for the social network you want to connect to and follow the steps provided to authorize your WordPress blog with that network.

Making sharing easy

Users of social media like to share the interesting content they find around the web with their friends on other social media sites, and the Sharing feature on WordPress.com gives you the tools that make it easy for your readers to share links to your content in different ways:

- **Email:** Allows readers to e-mail your blog content to a friend
- **Print:** Allows readers to print your blog posts
- **Digg:** Allows readers to share your content on the Digg social media site at http://digg.com
- **Facebook:** Allows readers to share your content on the Facebook social media site at http://facebook.com
- **LinkedIn:** Allows readers to share your content on the LinkedIn social media site at http://linkedin.com
- **Reddit:** Allows readers to share your content on the Reddit social media site at http://reddit.com

- ✔ **StumbleUpon:** Allows readers to share your content on the StumbleUpon social media site at `http://stumbleupon.com`

- ✔ **Tumblr:** Allows readers to share your content on the Tumblr social media site at `http://tumblr.com`

- ✔ **Twitter:** Allows readers to share your content on the Twitter social media site at `http://twitter.com`

- ✔ **Pinterest:** Allows readers to share your photos and graphics on the Pinterest social media website at `http://pinterest.com`

- ✔ **Press This:** Gives readers a button to click to easily use the WordPress. com Press This feature, allowing them to post links to your content on their own WordPress.com blog

- ✔ **Google +1:** Allows readers to share your content on the Google+ social media site at `http://plus.google.com`

By default, Email, Twitter, and Facebook services are already enabled. And in the Sharing Buttons sections, you can select the different social networks for your readers to share your content on. To enable any other service, click its button in the Available Services section and drag and drop it into the Enabled Services section. After you've done that, small, convenient buttons display within each blog post on your site; your visitors can click these buttons to share your content with their friends on their own social networks.

Like button

If you're a Facebook user, as I am, you'll find that the WordPress Like feature is very similar to the Facebook Like feature that you use within your Facebook account to indicate that you Like a friend's Facebook status.

On the bottom of the Sharing Settings page you can set your preference for WordPress.com Likes — select whether you want them turned on for all posts (by default), or turned on per post (so that you determine the placement of the WordPress.com Like on a per-post basis). This feature does exactly what it says: It displays a Like button on your blog posts, allowing readers to click it and Like your posts within the WordPress.com network.

You can disable the WordPress Like feature at any time. Also, you can disable the Like feature on a per-post basis. This means that you can enable it globally, but disable it on individual posts if you publish a post that you don't want people to be able to Like.

Interaction Through SMS (Text Messaging)

Enabling the text messaging feature in WordPress allows you to take your blog with you wherever you go by interacting with your blog via your mobile phone through SMS/text messaging. Click the Text Messaging link in the Settings submenu to load the Text Messaging Settings page on your Dashboard and enter your ten-digit mobile phone number in the fields provided. Then click the Send Activation button. WordPress sends a code to your phone, via text message. Enter that code in the field provided on the Text Messaging Settings page on your Dashboard to complete the steps required to enable text messaging.

With text messaging enabled, you can perform the following functions on your WordPress blog through your mobile phone:

- ✔ **Receive comment notifications and moderate comments:** With comment notifications sent to your mobile phone, WordPress provides a comment moderation ModCode for each comment. To approve the comment, reply with a text message that says: **Approve 10** (where *10* is the ModCode provided by WordPress for that comment). To unapprove the comment, text back with a message that says: **Unapprove 10**.

- ✔ **Reply to comments:** When you receive a new comment notification, you can reply to the comment via text message by using the ModCode and replying with something like: **Reply 10 Thanks for your comment!** (where *10* is the ModCode provided by WordPress for that comment.)

- ✔ **Publish new posts:** You're limited when publishing a new post via text message because you're limited to 160 characters or less. So, the post you make via text message is more like a status update than a full blog post. To create a new post via text message, send a text message to 77377 that says something like: **POST I am posting via SMS!**

All texts from WordPress come from the shortcode 77377, so when you send text messages to your blog, 77377 is the shortcode to use in place of a standard phone number.

You can text **HELP** to 77377 to obtain additional help for the use of text messaging with WordPress. You can also text **STOP** to 77377 to disable the text messaging feature on your WordPress blog.

Establishing Trust Relationships with OpenID

OpenID is a third-party, Internet-community identification system that allows an Internet user to create an online identity that she can use anywhere on the web where OpenID is supported. OpenID is commonly used with larger sites that receive a lot of traffic and public comments. With WordPress.com, you already have an OpenID identity.

On the WordPress Dashboard, click the OpenID link on the Settings menu to see the OpenID Trusted Sites page, which tells you what your OpenID is. (It's usually your main WordPress.com domain: for example, `http://1srn94.wordpress.com`.) You can also add the URLs of what you consider to be trusted sites. After you enter the URL of a trusted site and click the Add Site button, you aren't asked whether you trust the site when you attempt to log in to it. In a nutshell, this setting means that you can use your WordPress.com OpenID to log in to any website that supports OpenID.

Chapter 5

Enhancing Your Blog with Themes, Widgets, and Upgrades

You don't want your blog to look identical to everyone else's, do you? Although WordPress.com doesn't give you the vast array of design options that you'd have by hosting your own blog, you do have some flexibility.

The great thing about the WordPress hosted service is how easily you can change your theme to one of the alternative designs available. What's not so hot is that you can't create your own custom theme. As I note later in this chapter, you can pay a fee to customize the CSS of the template you choose to use, but you need to be familiar with CSS to use this upgrade — and again, you're limited to customizing only the templates that WordPress provides.

Most of the themes available on WordPress.com are free; however, a handful of Premium themes cost anywhere from $30 to $75 and have extended features that make them different from the free themes.

In this chapter, you discover the WordPress.com themes that let you choose a design and format for your blog. You have some fabulous themes to choose among, all created by WordPress users. At this writing, 170 themes are available. You also explore the fun of using sidebar widgets to rearrange how you show off your blogroll, category and monthly archive lists, and page lists.

This chapter also discusses enhancing your blog with custom CSS (Cascading Style Sheets), choosing a domain name, and increasing the amount of hard drive space on your WordPress.com account through its upgrade feature (for a fee).

Changing Your Blog's Look

It's time to choose a theme for your WordPress.com blog. In this case, the word *theme* is synonymous with the words *design* and *template*. All three words describe the very same things: the visual layout and appearance of your blog.

Follow these steps to find your theme:

1. **On the Dashboard, click the Themes link on the Appearance menu.**

   A page full of themes appears along with a thumbnail image of each theme so you get a basic idea of what it looks like. Figure 5-1 shows the Browse Themes area of this page.

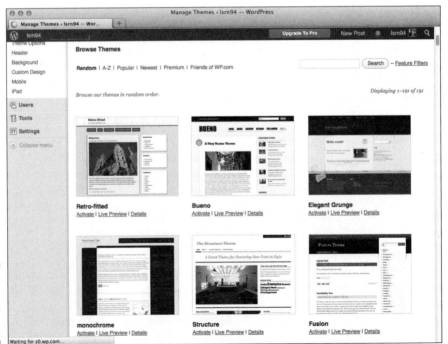

Figure 5-1:
Choose a
look for
your blog.

2. **Scroll through the themes and when you find one you like, click the thumbnail image associated with it or the Live Preview link for more options.**

   What happens next is pretty nifty! A new page pops up showing you a preview of what your own blog would look like with that particular theme and any options you set. You can also just click the Activate link to use the theme immediately with its default options, or click the Details link to see more information about the theme.

   You can page through the list of available themes by using the handy menu links under Browse Themes at the top of the page. You can browse by the following: Random, Alphabetical (A-Z), Popular, Recently Added, Premium, and Friends of WP.com. You can also search for themes by clicking the Feature Filters link to the right of the search button to filter your theme choices by color, columns, width, and features.

3. **Click the Activate link in the top-left corner of the theme you're previewing to activate the theme on your own blog, or click the Cancel link in the top-left corner if you decide that you'd rather not use that theme.**

No, really — it's just that easy. If you get tired of your theme, go to the Themes link and click a different theme name, and you're done.

In the introduction to this chapter, I tell you about the Premium themes at WordPress.com. Some of the themes you find on the Themes page on your Dashboard may be marked Premium, and WordPress.com requires payment from you before you can use them.

Enhancing Your Theme with Features

Several different features and tools are available within your WordPress.com account that enable you to individualize your site with the look and features that you need. Among your choices are everything from menus to fonts and backgrounds to social media features and tools to enhance the look and functionality of your WordPress.com blog.

Adding navigation menus

WordPress helps you easily add navigation menus to your theme with a feature called Menus. This feature enables you to build your own custom menu of links by adding links to any pages, posts, categories, or custom links you'd like. Click the Menus link under the Appearance menu to load the Menus page shown in Figure 5-2. On the Menus page, you can build your custom menu by adding links from Posts, Pages, Categories, or Custom links on the left side of the Menu page to the menu interface on the right side of the page. Follow these steps to make it happen:

1. **Click the Menus link in the Appearance menu on your Dashboard.**

    The Menus page opens on your WordPress Dashboard.

2. **Type a name in the Menu Name box and click the Create Menu button.**

    The Menus page is reloaded with a message that tells you your new menu has been created.

3. **Assign the new menu to the Theme Locations area.**

    Most themes have a defined location for the main navigation menu for your site. Figure 5-2 shows the Primary Menu drop-down list under the Theme Locations section. For your primary navigation menu, click the drop-down list in the Theme Locations section and choose the menu you just created to assign it as the Primary Menu for your site; then click the Save button.

4. **Add links to your newly created menu.**

    You can add links to the new menu you just created in three ways (the items in this list are shown in Figure 5-2):

    - *Custom Links:* In the URL field, type the URL of the website that you want to add (for example, **http://www.google.com**). Then type the name of the link that you want displayed in your menu in the Label field (for this URL, type **Google**). Then click the Add to Menu button.

    - *Pages:* Click the View All link to display a list of all the published page(s) on your site. Select the check box next to the page names you would like to add to your menu. Then click the Add to Menu button.

    - *Categories:* Click the View All link to display a list of all the categories you created on your site. Select the check box next to the category names you would like to add to the menu. Then click the Add to Menu button.

5. **Review your menu choices on the right side of the page.**

    When you add new menu items, the column on the right side of the Menus page populates with your menu choices. In Figure 5-2, I've populated my menu with Home and About links.

6. **Edit your menu choices, if needed.**

    Click the down arrow to the right of the menu link name to edit the information of each individual link in your new menu.

7. **Save your menu before leaving the Menus page.**

    Click the Save Menu button under Menu Settings on the top-right side. A message confirming the save appears.

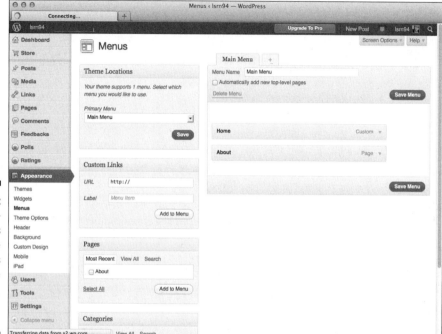

Figure 5-2:
Add naviga-
tion menus
with the
Menus
page on the
WordPress.
com
Dashboard.

Changing the background color and image

Almost every theme in the WordPress.com theme library supports the
Background feature, which allows you to use the handy Background tool
to change the background color and/or image that displays on your website. Visit the Custom Background page on your Dashboard by clicking the
Background link under the Appearance menu and then follow these steps to
make changes to the background color and/or image for your site:

1. **Click the Background link under the Appearance menu.**

   The Custom Background page loads on the Dashboard.

2. **To change the background color, type the hexadecimal color code in
   the Background Color text box.**

   If you don't know what hex code you want to use, click the Select a
   Color link, and click a color within the provided color wheel shown in
   Figure 5-3.

TIP

A hexadecimal (or *hex*) code represents a certain color. Hex codes always start with a hash symbol (#) and have six letters and/or numbers to represent a particular color, for example, #d5d6d7.

3. **To use an image file for the background, upload an image from your computer.**

Click the Browse button under the Choose an Image from Your Computer text, and select a file from your computer. Then click the Upload button.

4. **Change the display options for your new background image.**

- *Position:* Select Left, Center, or Right to set the screen position of the background image on your website.

- *Repeat:* Select No Repeat, Tile, Tile Horizontally, or Tile Vertically in the drop-down menu to set the image repeat behavior of the background image on your website.

- *Attachment:* Select Scroll to set the background image to scroll down the page or select Fixed to set the background image in a static position (so it doesn't scroll down the page).

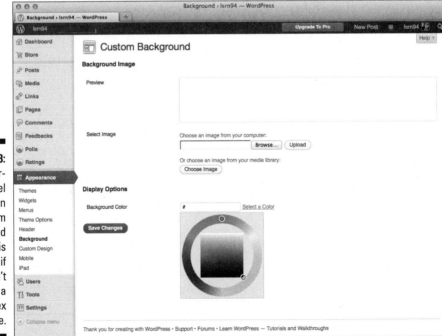

Figure 5-3:
The color-wheel selector on the Custom Background page is helpful if you don't know a color's hex code.

5. Save your changes.

Click the Save Changes button before navigating away from the Custom Background page. Otherwise, your new settings aren't saved.

Creating an iPad-friendly display

The mobile web is all the rage today: Visitors to your site use every type of device from desktop computers to laptops, tablets, and mobile phones. WordPress.com gives you a nifty interface to create an iPad-friendly theme for your blog, which helps create a beautiful application-like experience for anyone browsing your website on an iPad. Follow these steps to enable and configure the iPad feature on your WordPress.com blog:

1. Click the iPad link under the Appearance menu.

The Onswipe iPad Settings page displays in your browser window shown in Figure 5-4.

Figure 5-4:
Make your site mobile-friendly with the Onswipe iPad Settings page on your WordPress.com Dashboard.

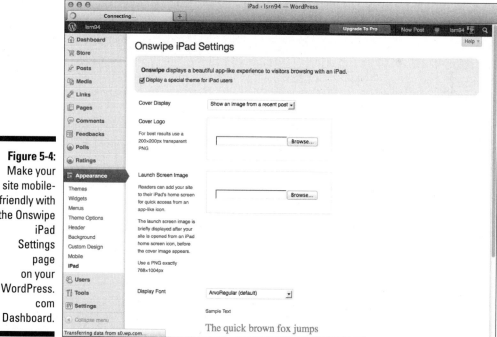

   2. **If it's not already selected, click the Display a Special Theme for iPad Users check box to select it.**

      This feature is actually enabled by default. You can disable this feature at any time by deselecting this check box.

   3. **Select an image (or not) for the cover display by choosing one of the options in the Cover Display drop-down menu.**

      You have three choices here:

      - No Cover

      - Show an Image from a Recent Post

      - Use the Launch Screen Image

   4. **Click the Browse button to select an image from your computer to use as the cover logo on the cover display for iPad users.**

      The recommended dimensions for the logo image are 200 pixels wide by 200 pixels high. Additionally, WordPress recommends using a transparent PNG image (or an image without a background color) for best display results.

   5. **Click the Browse button to select an image from your computer to use as the launch screen image for iPad users.**

      iPad users can easily add your site to their iPad home screen for ready access via an app-like icon. WordPress recommends using a transparent PNG image that's exactly 768 pixels wide by 1004 pixels high.

   6. **Using the drop-down menu in the Display Font section, choose the font you would like to use for display on iPad browsers.**

      You can choose from several fonts here and you can always change your font selection by revisiting this page and making your edits.

   7. **Select an accent color.**

      WordPress provides you with nine color selections shown as color circles on the Onswipe iPad Settings page. Select your preferred accent color by clicking that color's circle.

   8. **Click the Save Changes button.**

      The Onswipe iPad Settings page reloads with a message that tells you that your settings have been saved.

With the Onswipe iPad feature enabled and your configurations saved, readers of your blog who use iPads can now have an enjoyable experience browsing your site.

Changing the header image

Several themes in the WordPress.com library support the Custom Header feature, which allows you to change the image displayed in the header (or top) of your site through the use of a friendly interface on your WordPress Dashboard. Click the Header link under the Appearance menu to load the Custom Header page where you have eight premade images to choose from, along with the capability to upload your own header image.

With the Twenty Eleven theme, WordPress did all the hard work for you. Including a custom header image on a blog that uses the Twenty Eleven theme is pretty darn easy, whether you use your own header image or one of eight existing images that WordPress provides for you.

To use existing header images, follow these steps:

1. **Click the Header link in the Appearance menu on your Dashboard.**

   The Your Header Image page appears.

2. **Choose from one of eight header images.**

   Scroll down to the bottom of the page and select one of the cool header images that WordPress provides by clicking the circle to the left of your chosen image.

3. **Click the Save Changes button.**

   The header image you chose is now saved. When you view your website, you see it displayed at the top.

To upload a new header image, follow these steps:

1. **Click the Browse button under the Upload New Header Image title. Select the image from your computer; then click Open.**

   WordPress automatically resizes your header image to 1000 pixels wide and 288 pixels high — so for best results, start with an image that meets those dimensions, at a minimum.

2. **Click Upload.**

   Your image uploads to your web server. The Crop Header Image page appears where you can crop the image and adjust which portion of the header image you would like displayed. See Figure 5-5.

3. **Click the Crop and Publish button.**

   The Header Image page appears, and your new header image is now displayed.

4. **View your website.**

   Your new header image is now displayed at the top of your website.

Figure 5-5:
These dotted lines indicate the area of the header to be displayed.

In themes that don't have the custom header image feature, you can easily define a background image for the header image using CSS (see Chapter 13).

Using the Custom Design upgrade

WordPress.com themes give users another option for customizing the design of their theme: the Custom Design upgrade. Click the Custom Design link in the Appearance menu and you see that, for $30.00 per year, you have access to other customization tools such as:

- ✔ **Fonts:** Personalize the display of fonts on your site with Typekit (http://typekit.com), which is an external service that allows you to use real fonts of your choice for display on your WordPress.com site. Typekit provides you with a choice of hundreds of fonts in its font library, but you need to sign up for a Typekit account to use its fonts on your WordPress.com site.

- ✔ **Colors:** Change the colors of your theme instantly using WordPress color palettes.

- ✔ **CSS:** Gain full control over the CSS (Cascading Style Sheet) for your theme with this option (Chapter 13 contains additional information on CSS).

Widget Wonder: Adding Handy Tools to Your Sidebar

WordPress widgets are very helpful tools built in to the WordPress.com application. They allow you to easily arrange the display of content in your blog sidebar, such as your blogroll(s), recent posts, and monthly and category archive lists. With widgets, you can arrange and display the content in the sidebar of your blog without having to know a single bit of PHP or HTML.

Selecting and activating widgets

Click the Widgets link on the Appearance menu on the Dashboard. The Widgets page displays the available widgets shown in Figure 5-6. This feature is a big draw because it lets you control what features you use and where you place them — all without having to know a lick of code.

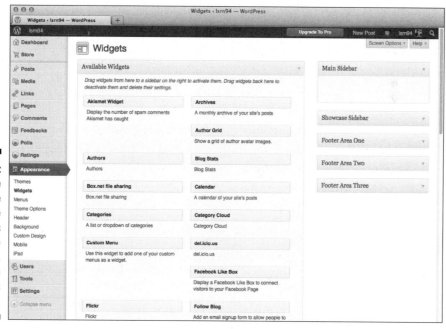

Figure 5-6:
Choose from the available widgets on the WordPress. com Widgets page.

On the left side of the Widgets page, within the Available Widgets box, is a listing of all widgets available for your WordPress blog.

On the right side of the Widgets page are separate boxes called Widget Areas that are available for the display of different widgets on your blog. Widget Areas are defined by the theme you've chosen to use on your site. Some themes have only one Widget Area available; other themes have several.

To add a new widget to your sidebar, follow these steps:

1. **Choose the widget you want to use.**

   The widgets are listed in the Available Widgets section, and you may have to scroll to see them all. For the purpose of these steps, choose the Recent Posts widget.

2. **Click the widget name.**

   Drag and drop the widget into your desired Widget Area on the right side of the page. After you release your mouse button and drop the widget in the Widget Area, your site updates automatically. In other words, the contents of the widget (in this case, a listing of recent posts on your blog) now appear on your site.

3. **Click the arrow to the right of the widget title.**

   Click the arrow on the Recent Posts widget to expand the widget and view the widget options. Each widget has different options that you can configure. The Recent Posts widget, for example, lets you configure the title and the number of posts to display in the Recent Posts listing on your site. See Figure 5-7.

4. **Select your options and click the Save button.**

   The options you've set are now saved. Click the Close link to collapse the widget options.

5. **Arrange your widgets in the order you want them to appear on your site by clicking a widget and dragging it above or below another widget.**

   Repeat this step until your widgets are arranged the way you want them.

To remove a widget from your sidebar, click the arrow to the right of the widget title to open the options menu. Then click the Delete link. WordPress removes the widget from the Widget Area on the right side of this page and places it back in the Available Widgets list.

After you select and configure all your widgets, visit the front page of your website and you see that your blog's sidebar matches the content (and order of the content) that you've arranged in the sidebar on the Widgets page. How cool is that? You can go back to the Widgets page and rearrange the items, as well as add and remove items, to your heart's content.

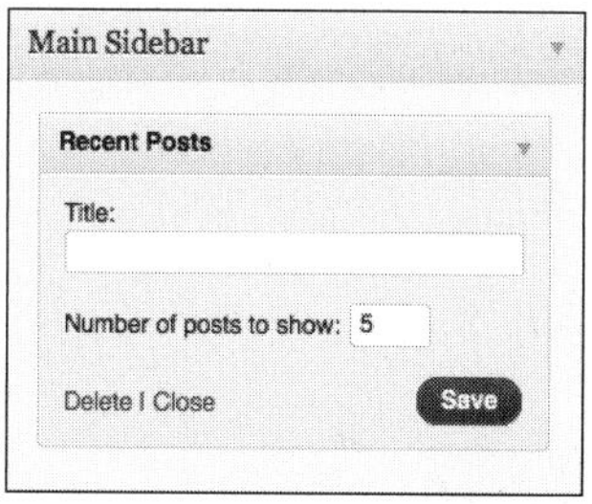

Figure 5-7:
Configuring
widget
options.

Main Sidebar ▾

Recent Posts ▾

Title:

Number of posts to show: 5

Delete I Close   Save

Using Text widgets

The Text widget in WordPress.com is a little different from the rest of the widgets on the Widgets page. Add the Text widget just as you would any other, using the steps in the preceding section. After you have it settled in the sidebar, click the arrow to the right of the widget title. A text box drops down to let you type text or HTML code to insert a hyperlink or include an image file. See Figure 5-8.

WordPress.com users can't, by default, monetize their blogs within their network. This means that you can't run any type of advertisement services such as Google AdSense, Yahoo!, or text ad links. I mention this here because many users think they can use the Text widget to include the ad code (JavaScript, PHP, or others) that advertisement services provide them to display ads on their site. WordPress doesn't allow it; therefore programming code such as JavaScript and PHP doesn't work in the WordPress.com Text widget. WordPress.com allows some light advertising in only very special circumstances, and it has a program called WordAds that users can opt into — but currently it's open to sites that have moderate to high traffic and appropriate content on their site. You can read more about WordPress.com's advertising policy here:

```
http://en.support.wordpress.com/advertising
```

You have no real options to configure for the Text widget, but you can use this simple text box for several things. Here are a couple of examples of what you can use a Text widget for:

- Type a short paragraph of text, such as a bio.
- Insert the HTML code to display an image in your sidebar. (See Chapter 13 for some information on basic HTML codes you can use.)

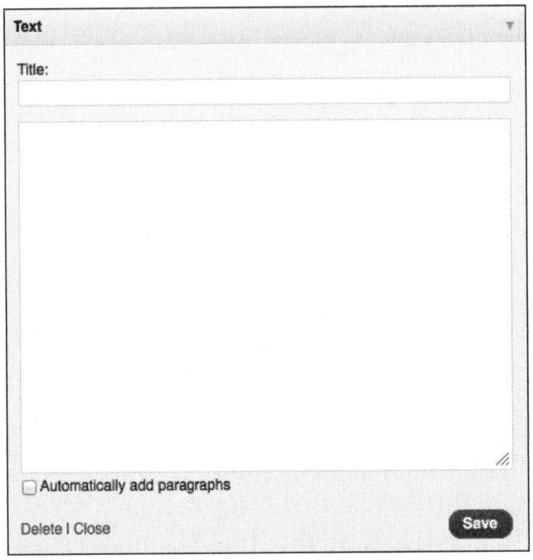

Text ▾

Title:

☐ Automatically add paragraphs

Delete | Close   **Save**

Figure 5-8:
Type text or
HTML code
into the
Text widget
text box.

The Text widget accepts basic HTML that you can use to do things like insert an image, a hyperlink, or a list of items. You may need to brush up on some HTML markup to make that happen, but the next section gives you some basic methods to get you started.

Inserting images

You may want to insert an image in your Text widget. The HTML markup to insert an image looks like this:

```
<img src="/path/to/image-file.jpg" alt="Image File Name" />
```

I break down this code for you in easy snippets to help you understand what's at work here:

- ✔ `<img src=`: This is the HTML markup that tells the browser that the website is looking for an image file.

- ✔ `"/path/to/image-file.jpg"`: This is the actual directory path where the web browser can find the physical image file. For example, if you upload an image to your web server in the `/wp-content/uploads` directory, the physical path for that image file would be `/wp-content/uploads/image-file.jpg`.

The easiest way to include an image is to use the media uploader to upload your image, then copy the file URL and paste it as the path in this HTML markup code.

✔ `alt="Image File Name"`: The alt tag is part of the HTML markup and provides a description for the image that search engines pick up and recognize as keywords. The alt tag description also displays as text on browsers that can't, for some reason, load the image file. For example, if the server load time is slow, the text description loads first to at least provide visitors with a description of what the image is.

✔ `/>`: This HTML markup tag closes the initial `<img src=` tag, telling the web browser when the call to the image file is complete.

Inserting hyperlinks

At times, you may want to insert a link (commonly referred to as a *hyperlink*) within the Text widget. A hyperlink is a line of text that's anchored to a web address (URL) so that when visitors on your website click the text, it takes them to another website, or page, in their browser window. The HTML markup to insert a hyperlink looks like this:

```
<a href="http://wiley.com">Wiley Publishing</a>
```

To break down that markup, here's a simple explanation:

✔ `<a href=`: This is the HTML markup that tells the browser that the text within this tag should be hyperlinked to the web address provided in the next bullet point.

✔ `"http://wiley.com"`: This is the URL that you want the text to be anchored to. The URL needs to be surrounded by quotes, which defines it as the intended anchor, or address.

✔ `">`: This markup closes the previously opened `<a href=` HTML tag.

✔ `Wiley Publishing`: In this example, this is the text that is linked, or anchored, by the URL. This clickable text displays on your website.

✔ `</a>`: This HTML markup tag tells the web browser that the hyperlink is closed. Anything that exists between `<a href="..">` and `</a>` is hyperlinked, or clickable, through to the intended anchor, or web address.

Commonly, designers use URLs to link words to other websites or pages. However, you can also provide hyperlinks to files like PDF (Adobe Acrobat), DOC (Microsoft Word), or any other file type.

Inserting lists

You may need to provide a clean-looking format for lists of information that you publish on your website. With HTML markup, you can easily provide lists that are formatted depending on your needs.

Ordered lists are numbered sequentially, such as a step list of things to do, like this:

1. Write my book chapters.

2. Submit my book chapters to my publisher.

3. Panic a little when the book is released to the public.

4. Breathe a sigh of relief when public reviews are overwhelmingly positive!

Ordered lists are easy to do in a program like Microsoft Word, or even in the WordPress post editor because you can use the What You See Is What You Get (WYSIWYG) editor to format the list for you. However, if you want to code an ordered list using HTML in a Text widget, it's a little different. My preceding step-list sample looks like this when using HTML markup:

```
<ol>
<li>Write my book chapters.</li>
<li>Submit my book chapters to my publisher.</li>
<li>Panic a little when the book is released to the public.</li>
<li>Breathe a sigh of relief when public reviews are overwhelmingly positive!</
            li>
</ol>
```

The beginning `<ol>` tells a web browser to display this list as an ordered list, meaning that it's ordered with numbers starting with the number 1. The entire list ends with the `</ol>` HTML tag, which tells the web browser that the ordered list is now complete.

Between the `<ol>` and `</ol>` are list items designated as such by the HTML markup `<li>`. Each list item starts with `<li>` and ends with `</li>`, which tells the web browser to display the line of text as one list item.

If you fail to close any open HTML markup tags — for example, if you start an ordered list with `<ol>` but fail to include the closing `</ol>` at the end — it messes up the display on your website. The web browser considers anything beneath the initial `<ol>` to be part of the ordered list until it recognizes the closing tag `</ol>`.

Unordered lists are very similar to ordered lists, except instead of using numbers, they use bullet points to display the list, like this:

✔ Write my book chapters.

✔ Submit my book chapters to my publisher.

✔ Panic a little when the book is released to the public.

✔ Breathe a sigh of relief when public reviews are overwhelmingly positive!

The HTML markup for an unordered list is just like the unordered list, except instead of using the `<ol>` tag, use the `<ul>` tag (*ul* stands for *unordered list*):

```
<ul>
<li>Write my book chapters.</li>
<li>Submit my book chapters to my publisher.</li>
<li>Panic a little when the book is released to the public.</li>
<li>Breathe a sigh of relief when public reviews are overwhelmingly positive!</
         li>
</ul>
```

Both the ordered and unordered lists use the list item tags `<li>` and `</li>`. The only difference between the two lists is in the first opening and last closing tags. Ordered lists use `<ol>` and `</ol>`, whereas unordered lists use `<ul>` and `</ul>`.

Using the RSS widget

The RSS widget lets you display content from another blog in your sidebar. If I wanted to display a list of recent posts from another blog that I have somewhere else, for example, I would use the RSS widget to accomplish this task. Follow these steps to add the RSS widget to your blog:

1. **Add the RSS widget to your selected Widget Area on the Widgets page.**

   Follow the steps in the "Selecting and activating widgets" section, earlier in this chapter, to add the widget.

2. **Click the drop-down arrow to the right of the RSS widget's name.**

   A box drops down, displaying the different options you can configure for the RSS widget.

3. **In the Enter the RSS URL Here text box, type the RSS URL of the blog you want to add.**

   You can usually find the RSS Feed URL of a blog listed in the sidebar.

4. **Type the title of the RSS widget.**

   This title is what appears in your blog above the links from this blog. If I wanted to add the RSS feed from my personal blog, for example, I would type **Lisa Sabin-Wilson's blog**.

5. **Select the number of items to display.**

   The drop-down menu here gives you a choice of 1–20. Choose the number of items from the RSS feed that you would like to display on your site.

6. **(Optional) Select the Display the Item Content check box.**

   Selecting this check box tells WordPress that you also want to display the content of the feed (usually, the content of the blog post from the feed URL). If you want to display only the title, leave the check box unselected.

7. **(Optional) Select the Display Item Author, If Available check box.**

   Select this option if you want to display the author's name along with the item's title.

8. **(Optional) Select the Display Item Date check box.**

   Select this option if you want to display the date the item was published, along with the item title.

9. **Click the Save Changes button.**

   WordPress saves all the options you just set and reloads the Widgets page with your RSS widget intact.

Figure 5-9 shows my WordPress.com blog displaying the content from my personal blog in the sidebar. I used the RSS widget to make this happen!

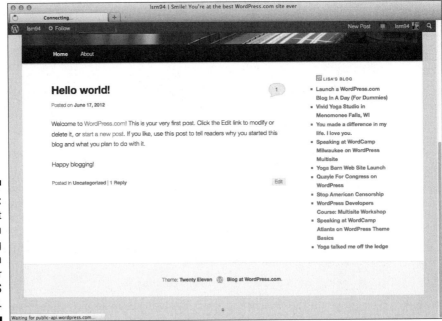

Figure 5-9:
Content from another blog shown in my sidebar via the RSS widget.

Upgrading Your WordPress Account (For a Fee)

Although WordPress.com is a free service, it offers enhancements for a fee. WordPress.com calls these items *upgrades,* and you can purchase the upgrades from within your WordPress.com Dashboard. Click the Store link on the Dashboard navigation menu to display the Store page shown in Figure 5-10.

Following is a list of the current upgrades you can purchase to enhance your WordPress.com account with the prices reflecting the annual cost:

- ✔ **Add A Domain:** This upgrade allows you to add your own domain name to your WordPress.com account; see the next section, "Naming Your Domain." This service costs $5 for the domain registration and $13 for the domain mapping.

- ✔ **VideoPress:** This upgrade allows you to upload, store, and share your videos from your WordPress.com account. This service covers the storage space that your video files take up on the WordPress.com servers. It costs $60 per year.

- ✔ **Custom Design:** This upgrade lets you customize the Cascading Style Sheets (CSS) and use Custom Fonts for the theme you're currently using in the WordPress.com system. Recommended for users who understand the use of CSS, this upgrade costs $30 per year.

- ✔ **Space Upgrades:** With the free WordPress.com blog, you have 3GB of hard drive space for use in your upload directory. The various space upgrades add more, letting you upload more files (images, videos, audio files, and so on). Currently you can add

  - 10GB for $20 per year
  - 25GB for $50 per year
  - 50GB for $90 per year
  - 100GB for $160 per year
  - 200GB for $290 per year

- ✔ **No Ads:** For the cost of $30 per year, you can ensure that your WordPress.com blog is ad-free. Occasionally, WordPress.com does serve ads on your blog pages to try to defray the costs of running a popular service. If you'd rather not have those ads appearing on your blog, pay for the No Ads upgrade and you'll be ad-free!

- ✔ **Site Redirect:** You can pay WordPress.com to add a forwarder on your WordPress.com blog address if you change blog addresses or domain name. The forwarder automatically forwards your visitor's browser to your new domain name, or blog address, seamlessly. The cost is $13 per year.

✔ **Guided Transfer:** Sometimes WordPress.com users transfer their site to their own hosting account using the (self-hosted) WordPress.org software, which provides them with a great deal more control and flexibility. If transferring your WordPress.com account is something you'd rather not do yourself, you can hire WordPress.com to do it for you for the price of $129.

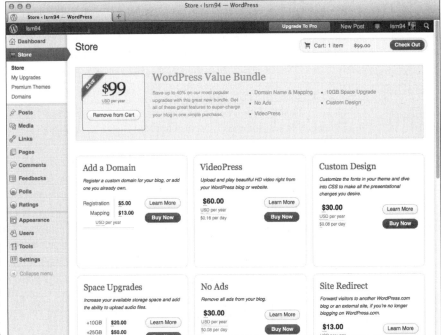

Figure 5-10: Visit the WordPress. com Store page for upgrades.

WordPress.com Value Bundle

WordPress makes several of their Pro features available in one convenient bundle called their Value Bundle. For $99 per year, you can upgrade your WordPress account to include the following premium features: one domain name of your choice or domain mapping for a domain that you already own, VideoPress, Custom Design, 10GB space upgrade, and the No Ads option for your WordPress account. This bundle provides you with some of the more popular upgrade features that WordPress has available and is an easy way to take advantage of some savings to include these premium features on your account.

Naming Your Domain

The URL for your WordPress.com blog is `http://blogaddress.wordpress.com`, with *blogaddress* being the blog address you chose for your WordPress.com blog. My blog address is `lsrn94`; therefore, my WordPress.com domain is `http://lsrn94.wordpress.com`.

WordPress.com lets you use your own domain name for your WordPress.com blog. Using the Domains feature in WordPress.com is not free, however. At this writing, this feature costs $5 for the domain registration and $13 for the domain mapping.

When you have your domain registered, go to your WordPress.com Dashboard, click the Domains link in the Store menu to display the Domains page, and type your domain name in the Add a Domain text box shown in Figure 5-11. Then follow the prompts to fully set up your domain name.

When you configure your domain name correctly, your domain name points to your WordPress.com blog.

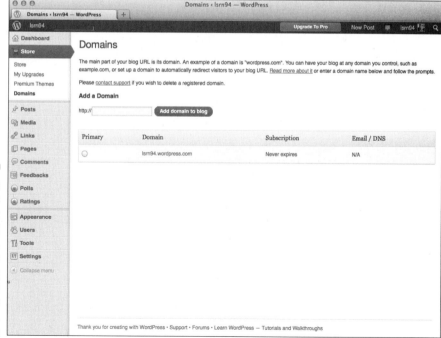

Figure 5-11: Use your own domain in WordPress.com by upgrading on the Domains page.

Part III
Self-Hosting with WordPress.org

The 5th Wave   By Rich Tennant

"Tell the boss you-know-who is talking smack in his blog again."

In this part . . .

In this part, I show you how to dig into the guts of WordPress.org. I tell you how to get your own domain name and web host, and I walk you through the installation procedure and features of the Dashboard that you'll want to know about when you're getting started.

Chapter 6

Setting Up Blogging Base Camp

. . . .

. . . .

*B*efore you can start blogging with WordPress.org, you have to set up your base camp. Doing so involves more than simply downloading and installing the WordPress software. You also need to establish your *domain* (your blog address) and your *web-hosting service* (the place that houses your blog). Although you initially download your WordPress software onto your hard drive, your web host is where you install it.

Obtaining a web server and installing software on it are much more involved projects than simply obtaining an account with the hosted version of WordPress that's available at WordPress.com (covered in Part II). You have to consider many factors in this undertaking, as well as cope with a learning curve, because setting up your blog through a hosting service involves using some technologies that you may not feel comfortable with at first. This chapter takes you through the basics of those technologies, and by the last page of this chapter, you'll have WordPress successfully installed on a web server with your own domain name.

Establishing Your Domain

You've read all the hype. You've heard all the rumors. You've seen the flashy blogs on the web powered by WordPress. But where do you start?

The first steps toward installing and setting up a WordPress blog are making a decision about a domain name and then purchasing the registration of that name through a domain registrar. A *domain name* is the *unique* web address that you type in a web browser's address bar to visit a website. Some examples of domain names are WordPress.org and Google.com.

Domain names: Do you own or rent?

In reality, when you "buy" a domain name, you don't really own it. Rather, you're purchasing the right to use that domain name for the period of time specified in your order. You can register a domain name for one year or up to ten years. Be aware, however, if you don't renew the domain name when your registration period ends, you lose it — and most often, you lose it right away to someone who preys on abandoned or expired domain names. Some people keep a close watch on expiring domain names, and as soon as the buying window opens, they snap up the names and start using them for their own websites in the hope of taking full advantage of the popularity that the previous owners worked so hard to attain for those domains.

I emphasize the word *unique* because no two domain names can be the same. If someone else has registered the domain name you want, you can't have it. With that in mind, it sometimes takes a bit of time to find a domain that isn't already in use and is available for you to use.

Understanding domain name extensions

When registering a domain name, be aware of the *extension* that you want. The `.com`, `.net`, `.org`, `.info`, `.me`, `.us`, or `.biz` extension that you see tacked onto the end of any domain name is the *top-level domain extension*. When you register your domain name, you're asked to choose the extension you want for your domain (as long as it's available, that is).

A word to the wise here: Just because you have registered your domain as a `.com` doesn't mean that someone else doesn't, or can't, own the very same domain name with a `.net`. So if you register MyDogHasFleas.com, and it becomes a hugely popular site among readers with dogs that have fleas, someone else can come along and register MyDogHasFleas.net and run a similar site to yours in the hope of riding the coattails of your website's popularity and readership.

You can register your domain name with all available extensions if you want to avert this problem. My business website, for example, has the domain name EWebscapes.com; however, I also own EWebscapes.net, EWebscapes.biz, and EWebscapes.info.

Considering the cost of a domain name

Registering a domain costs you anywhere from $3 to $30 per year depending on what service you use for a registrar and what options (such as privacy options and search-engine submission services) you apply to your domain name during the registration process.

When you pay the domain registration fee today, you need to pay another registration fee when the renewal date comes up again in a year, or two, or five — however many years you chose to register your domain name for. (See the "Domain names: Do you own or rent?" sidebar.) Most registrars give you the option of signing up for a service called Auto Renew to automatically renew your domain name and bill the charges to the credit card you set up on that account. The registrar sends you a reminder a few months in advance, telling you it's time to renew. If you don't have Auto Renew set up, you need to log in to your registrar account before it expires and manually renew your domain name.

Registering your domain name

Domain registrars are certified and approved by the Internet Corporation for Assigned Names and Numbers (ICANN). Although hundreds of domain registrars exist today, the ones in the following list are popular because of their longevity in the industry, competitive pricing, and variety of services they offer in addition to domain name registration (such as web hosting and website traffic builders):

- **Go Daddy:** http://GoDaddy.com
- **NamesDirect:** http://namesdirect.com
- **Network Solutions:** http://networksolutions.com
- **Register.com:** http://register.com

No matter where you choose to register your domain name, here are the steps you can take to accomplish this task:

1. **Decide on a domain name.**

   Doing a little planning and forethought here is necessary. Many people think of a domain name as a *brand* — a way of identifying their websites or blogs. Think of potential names for your site; then you can proceed with your plan.

2. **Verify the domain name's availability.**

In your web browser, enter the URL of the domain registrar of your choice. Look for the section on the registrar's website that lets you enter the domain name (typically, a short text field) to see whether it's available. If the domain name isn't available as a `.com`, try `.net` or `.info`.

3. **Purchase the domain name.**

Follow the domain registrar's steps to purchase the name using your credit card. After you complete the checkout process, you receive an e-mail confirming your purchase, so use a valid e-mail address during the registration process.

The next step is obtaining a hosting account, which I cover in the next section.

Some of the domain registrars have hosting services that you can sign up for, but you don't have to use those services. Often you can find hosting services for a lower cost than most domain registrars offer. It just takes a little research.

Finding a Home for Your Blog

When you have registered your domain, you need to find a place for it to live: a web host. Web hosting is the second piece of the puzzle that you need before you begin working with WordPress.org.

A *web host* is a business, group, or individual that provides web server space and bandwidth for file transfer to website owners who don't have it. Usually, web hosting services charge a monthly or annual fee — unless you're fortunate enough to know someone who's willing to give you server space and bandwidth for free. The cost varies from host to host, but you can obtain quality web hosting services for $3 to $10 per month to start.

Web hosts consider WordPress to be a *third-party application*. What this means to you is that the host typically won't provide technical support on the use of WordPress (or any other software application) because support isn't included in your hosting package. To find out whether your chosen host supports WordPress, always ask first. As a WordPress user, you can find WordPress support in the official forums at `http://wordpress.org/support`.

Several web-hosting providers also have WordPress-related services available for additional fees. These services can include technical support, plugin installation and configuration, and theme design services.

Web-hosting providers generally provide (at least) these services with your account:

- ✔ Hard drive space
- ✔ Bandwidth (transfer)
- ✔ Domain e-mail with web mail access
- ✔ File Transfer Protocol (FTP) access
- ✔ Comprehensive website statistics
- ✔ MySQL database(s)
- ✔ PHP

Because you intend to run WordPress on your web server, you need to look for a host that provides the minimum requirements needed to run the software on your hosting account, which are

- ✔ PHP version 5.2.4 (or greater)
- ✔ MySQL version 5.0 (or greater)

The easiest way to find out whether a host meets the minimum requirements for running the WordPress software is to check the FAQ (Frequently Asked Questions) section of the host's website, if it has one. If not, find the contact information for the hosting company and fire off an e-mail requesting information on exactly what it supports.

Getting help with hosting WordPress

The popularity of WordPress has given birth to services on the web that emphasize the use of the software. These services include WordPress designers, WordPress consultants, and — yes — web hosts that specialize in using WordPress.

Many of these hosts offer a full array of WordPress features, such as an automatic WordPress installation included with your account, a library of WordPress themes, and a staff of support technicians who are very experienced in using WordPress.

Here is a list of some of those providers:

- ✔ **Bluehost:** http://ewebscapes.com/bluehost
- ✔ **HostGator:** http://ewebscapes.com/hostgator

✔ **Page.ly:** `http://page.ly`

✔ **WP Engine:** `www.wpengine.com`

✔ **ZippyKid:** `http://zippykid.com`

A few web-hosting providers offer free domain name registration when you sign up for hosting services. Research this topic and read their terms of service because that free domain name may come with conditions. Many of my clients have gone this route only to find out a few months later that the web-hosting provider has full control of the domain name, and they aren't allowed to move that domain off the host's servers either for a set period (usually, a year or two) or for eternity. It's always best to have the control in *your* hands, not someone else's, so try to stick with an independent domain registrar, such as Network Solutions.

Dealing with disk space and bandwidth

Web hosting services provide two very important things with your account:

✔ Disk space

✔ Bandwidth transfer

Think of your web host as a garage that you pay to park your car in. The garage gives you the place to store your car (disk space). It even gives you the driveway so that you, and others, can get to and from your car (bandwidth). It won't, however, fix your rockin' stereo system (WordPress or any other third-party software application) that you've installed — unless you're willing to pay a few extra bucks for that service.

Managing disk space

Disk space is nothing more complicated than the hard drive on your own computer. Each hard drive has the capacity, or space, for a certain amount of files. An 80GB (gigabyte) hard drive can hold 80 GB of data — no more. Your hosting account provides you a limited amount of disk space, and the same concept applies. If your web host provides you 10GB of disk space, that's the limit on the file size that you're allowed to have. If you want more disk space, you need to upgrade your space limitations. Most web hosts have a mechanism in place for you to upgrade your allotment.

Starting out with a self-hosted WordPress blog doesn't take much disk space at all. A good starting point for disk space is between 3 and 5GB of storage space. If you find that you need additional space, contact your hosting provider for an upgrade.

Choosing the size of your bandwidth pipe

Bandwidth refers to the amount of data that is carried from point A to point B within a specific period (usually, only a second or two). I live out in the country — pretty much the middle of nowhere. The water that comes to my house is provided by a private well that lies buried in the backyard somewhere. Between my house and the well are pipes that bring the water to my house. The pipes provide a free flow of water to our home so that everyone can enjoy their long, hot showers while I labor over dishes and laundry, all at the same time. Lucky me!

The very same concept applies to the bandwidth available with your hosting account. Every web-hosting provider offers a variety of bandwidth limits on the accounts it offers. When I want to view your website in my browser window, the bandwidth is essentially the "pipe" that lets your data flow from your "well" to my computer and appear on my monitor. The bandwidth limit is kind of like the pipe connected to my well: It can hold only a certain amount of water before it reaches maximum capacity and won't bring the water from the well any longer. Your bandwidth pipe size is determined by how much bandwidth your web host allows for your account — the larger the number, the bigger the pipe. A 50MB bandwidth limit makes for a smaller pipe than does a 100MB limit.

Web hosts are pretty generous with the amount of bandwidth they provide in their packages. Like disk space, bandwidth is measured in gigabytes (GB). Bandwidth provision of 10–50GB is generally a respectable amount to run a website with a blog.

Websites that run large files — such as video, audio, or photo files — generally benefit from more disk space (as compared with sites that don't have large files). Keep this point in mind when you're signing up for your hosting account: If your site requires big files, you need more space. Planning now will save you a few headaches down the road.

Transferring Files from Point A to Point B

This section introduces you to the basic elements of File Transfer Protocol (FTP). FTP is a method you use to move files from one place to another — for example, from your computer to your web hosting account. This method is referred to as *uploading.* The capability to use FTP with your hosting account is a given for almost every web host on the market today.

Using FTP to transfer files requires an FTP client. Many FTP clients are available for download. Following are some good (and free) ones:

- **Cyberduck (for Mac users):** `http://cyberduck.ch`
- **FileZilla:** `http://sourceforge.net/projects/filezilla`
- **FTP Explorer:** `www.ftpx.com`
- **SmartFTP:** `www.smartftp.com/download`
- **WS_FTP:** `www.ipswitch.com/_download/wsftphome.asp`

Earlier in this chapter, in "Finding a Home for Your Blog," you find out how to obtain a web hosting account. Your web host gives you a username and password for your account, including an FTP IP address. (Usually, the FTP address is the same as your domain name, but check with your web host because addresses may vary.) It is this information — the username, password, and FTP IP address — that you insert into the FTP program to connect it to your hosting account.

Figure 6-1 shows my FTP client connected to my hosting account. The directory on the left is the listing of files on my computer; the directory on the right shows the listing of files on my hosting account.

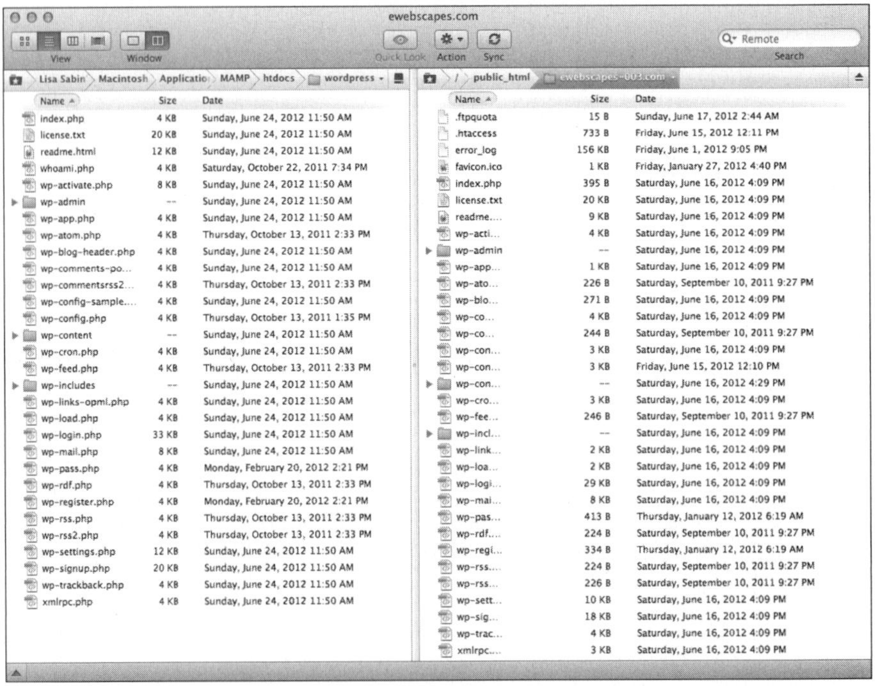

Figure 6-1: Using an FTP client makes file transfers easy.

FTP clients make it easy to transfer files from your computer to your hosting account by using a drag-and-drop method. Simply click the file on your computer that you want to transfer, drag it over to the side that lists the directory on your hosting account, and drop it. Depending on the FTP client you're working with, you can refer to its user manuals or support documentation for detailed information on how to use the program.

Installing WordPress

By the time you're finally ready to install WordPress.org, you should have done the following things:

✔ Purchased the domain name registration for your account

✔ Obtained a hosting service on a web server for your blog

✔ Established your hosting account's username, password, and FTP address

✔ Acquired an FTP client for transferring files to your hosting account

If you missed doing any of these items, you can go back to the beginning of this chapter to read the portions you need.

Using SimpleScripts to install WordPress

SimpleScripts is a very popular script installer that several web-hosting providers make available to their clients. SimpleScripts contains different types of scripts and programs that you can install on your hosting account, notably, the WordPress software.

This section of the book makes a few assumptions about your hosting environment:

✔ Your hosting provider has SimpleScripts available for your use.

✔ Your hosting account has an account management interface called cPanel.

Using SimpleScripts to install WordPress is a pretty quick process; just follow these steps:

1. **Log in to the cPanel for your hosting account.**

   Typically, you browse to `http://yourdomain.com/cpanel` to bring up the login screen for your cPanel. Enter your specific hosting account username and password in the login fields and click OK.

2. **Look for the SimpleScripts link/icon and click it.**

   The SimpleScripts page loads in your browser window and displays a list of available scripts as shown in Figure 6-2.

3. **Click the WordPress link under the Blogs menu.**

   In Figure 6-2, on the left side of the page, you see a menu header labeled Blogs and a WordPress link underneath. Click that link, and the Install WordPress page, shown in Figure 6-3, loads in your browser window.

Figure 6-2:
The Simple Scripts script installer page within cPanel.

Figure 6-3:
The
WordPress
Installation
Page in
Simple
Scripts.

4. **Click the Install button.**

   The Installation Preferences Page shown in Figure 6-4 displays in your web browser.

5. **Select the WordPress version to install in the first drop-down list.**

   You can select any available version; however, I recommend selecting the most recent available stable version of WordPress to make sure you have the latest copy of the software installed on your site. The stable version will be labeled as such in the drop-down list.

6. **Choose the WordPress installation location from the Install on Domain drop-down menu.**

   If you have more than one domain on your account, those domains are shown in the drop-down menu.

7. **Type the directory name for installation in the appropriate text field.**

   Leave this text field empty to install WordPress in the root directory (http://yourdomain.com) or enter the name of the directory you want to install WordPress into (for example, http://yourdomain.com/wordpress). The directory you type in the text field should not exist on your web server; if it does, SimpleScripts tells you that WordPress cannot be installed.

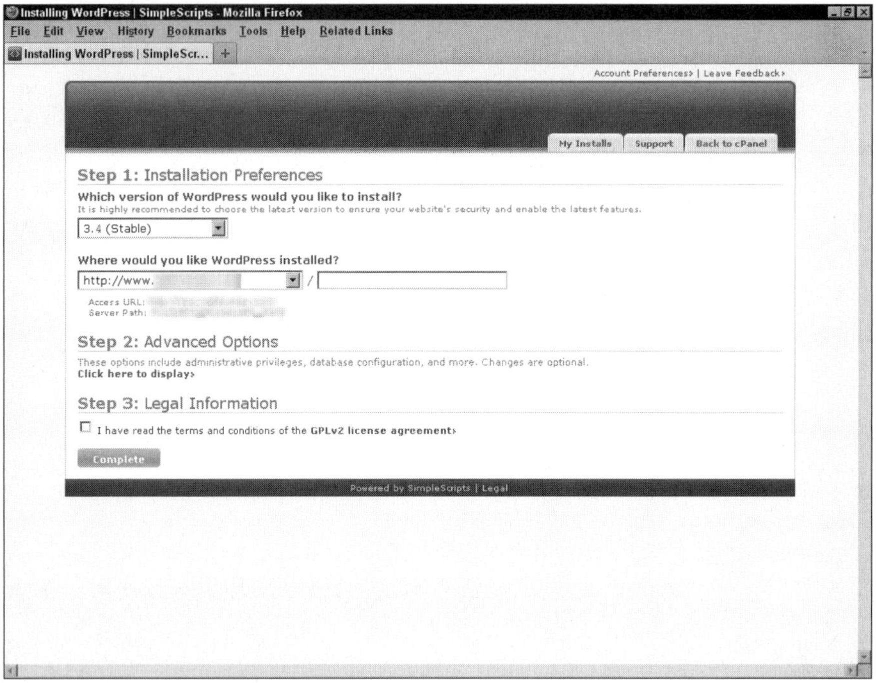

Figure 6-4:
Installation
Preferences
page for
WordPress
in Simple
Scripts.

8. **Open the Advanced Options.**

   You may have to scroll further down the page from what you see in Figure 6-4 to view the Advanced Options. Click the Click Here to Display link in the Advanced Options section (Step 2 — Figure 6-4) and provide the following information:

   • *(Optional) Type the desired title for your blog in the My Blog text field.* This is the name of your blog and can be changed later on your WordPress Dashboard (Chapter 7).

   • *Type your desired username in the Username text field.*

   • *Type your desired password in the Password text field.*

   • *Select the Automatically Create a New Database option to have the SimpleScripts application create a database for you.*

9. **Indicate you have read the terms and conditions of the GPLv2 license agreement.**

   Select the check box next to the words: `I have read the terms and conditions of the GPLv2 license agreement` to indicate that you've read the license. (Click the GPLv2 license agreement link to view and read the agreement, if desired.)

10. **Click the Complete button.**

   An Installation Progress page loads in your browser window that displays the progress of the installation. When WordPress is successfully installed, you see a message indicating the installation is complete, as well as the display of your installation URL (web address) and your username and password that you use to log in.

Your WordPress installation via SimpleScripts is now complete and you are ready to start using WordPress on your web server. If you installed WordPress using the SimpleScripts method and don't want to review the steps to install WordPress manually, flip to Chapter 7 to begin using WordPress. The next section covers the steps involved in installing WordPress manually using FTP.

Installing WordPress manually

If you have to install WordPress manually, here's where the rubber meets the road — that is, you're putting WordPress's famous five-minute installation to the test. Set your watch and see whether you can meet that five-minute mark.

The famous five-minute installation includes the time it takes to install the software only. It doesn't include the time to

- ✔ Register a domain name
- ✔ Obtain and set up your web-hosting service
- ✔ Download, install, configure, and learn how to use the FTP software

Without further ado, go get the latest version of the WordPress software at `http://wordpress.org/download`.

WordPress gives you two compression formats for the software: `zip` and `tar.gz`. I recommend getting the `.zip` file because it's the most common format for compressed files.

Download the WordPress software to your computer and decompress (unpack or unzip) it to a folder on your computer's hard drive. These steps are the first in the installation process for WordPress. Having the program on your own computer isn't enough, however; you also need to *upload* (transfer) it to your web server account (the one you obtained in "Finding a Home for Your Blog," earlier in this chapter). Before installing WordPress on your web server, make sure that you have a MySQL database set up and ready to accept the WordPress installation. The next section tells you what you need to know about MySQL.

Setting up the MySQL database

The WordPress software is a personal publishing system that uses a PHP-and-MySQL platform, which provides everything you need to create your own blog and publish your own content dynamically without having to know how to program those pages yourself. In short, all your content (options, posts, comments, and other pertinent data) is stored in a MySQL database in your hosting account.

Every time visitors go to your blog to read your content, they make a request that's sent to your server. The PHP programming language receives that request, obtains the requested information from the MySQL database, and then presents the requested information to your visitors through their web browsers.

Every web host is different in how it gives you access to set up and manage your MySQL database(s) for your account. In this section, I use a popular hosting interface called cPanel. If your host provides a different interface, the same basic steps apply; just the setup in the interface that your web host provides may be different.

To set up the MySQL database for your WordPress blog with cPanel, follow these steps:

1. **Log in to the administration interface with the username and password assigned to you by your web host.**

   I'm using the cPanel administration interface, but your host may provide NetAdmin or Plesk, for example.

2. **Locate the MySQL Database Administration section.**

   In cPanel, click the MySQL Databases icon.

3. **Choose a name for your database and enter it in the Name text box.**

   Note the database name because you need it during the installation of WordPress later.

   For security reasons, make sure that your password isn't something that sneaky hackers can easily guess. Usually, I give my database a name that I will easily recognize later. This practice is especially helpful if you're running more than one MySQL database in your account. If I name this database something like *WordPress* or *wpblog,* I can be reasonably certain — a year from now, when I want to access my database to make some configuration changes — that I know exactly which one I need to deal with.

4. **Click the Create Database button.**

   You get a message confirming that the database has been created.

5. **Click the Go Back link or the Back button on your browser toolbar.**

6. **Choose a username and password for your database, enter them in the Add New User text boxes, and then click the Create User button.**

   You get a confirmation message that the username was created with the password you specified.

   Make absolutely sure that you note the database name, username, and password that you set up during this process. You *will* need them in the next section before officially installing WordPress on your web server. Jot them down on a piece of paper, or copy and paste them into a text-editor window; either way, just make sure that you have them immediately handy.

7. **Click the Go Back link or the Back button on your browser toolbar.**

8. **In the Add Users to Database section, choose the user account you just set up from the User drop-down menu; then choose the new database from the Database drop-down menu.**

   The MySQL Account Maintenance, Manage User Privileges page appears in cPanel.

9. **Assign user privileges by selecting the All Privileges check box.**

   Because you're the administrator (owner) of this database, you need to assign all privileges to the new user account you just created.

10. **Click the Make Changes button.**

    A page opens with a confirmation message that you've added your selected user to the selected database.

11. **Click the Go Back link.**

    You go back to the MySQL Databases page.

Uploading the WordPress files

To upload the WordPress files to your host, return to the folder on your computer where you unpacked the WordPress software that you downloaded earlier. You'll find all the files you need (shown in Figure 6-5) in a folder called `/wordpress`.

Using your FTP client, connect to your web server and upload all these files to your hosting account into the root directory.

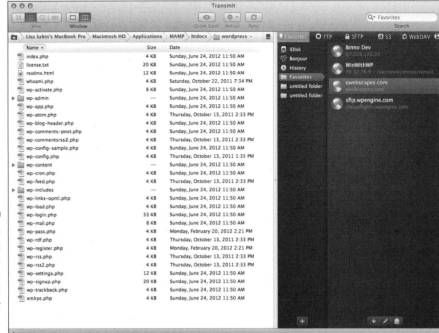

Figure 6-5:
WordPress
software
files to be
uploaded
to your
web server.

If you don't know what your root directory is, contact your hosting provider and ask, "What is my root directory for my account?" Every hosting provider's setup is different. On my web server, my root directory is the `public_html` folder; some of my clients have a root directory in a folder called `httpdocs`. The answer really depends on what type of setup your hosting provider has. When in doubt, ask!

Here are a few things to keep in mind when you're uploading your files:

- ✔ **Upload the *contents* of the `/wordpress` folder to your web server — not the folder itself.** Most FTP client software lets you select all the files and drag 'n' drop them to your web server. Other programs have you highlight the files and click a Transfer button.

- ✔ **Choose the correct transfer mode.** File transfers via FTP have two different forms: ASCII and binary. Most FTP clients are configured to auto-detect the transfer mode. Understanding the difference as it pertains to this WordPress installation is important so that you can troubleshoot any problems you have later:

  - *Binary transfer mode* is how images (such as `.jpg`, `.gif`, `.bmp`, and `.png` files) are transferred via FTP.

  - *ASCII transfer mode* is for everything else (text files, PHP files, JavaScript, and so on).

For the most part, it's a safe bet to make sure that the transfer mode of your FTP client is set to autodetect. But if you experience issues with how those files load on your site, retransfer the files using the appropriate transfer mode.

✔ **You can choose a different folder from the root.** You aren't required to transfer the files to the root directory of your web server. You can make the choice to run WordPress on a subdomain, or in a different folder, on your account. If you want your blog address to be http://your domain.com/blog, you transfer the WordPress files into a folder named /blog.

✔ **Choose the right file permissions.** *File permissions* tell the web server how these files can be handled on your server — whether they're files that can be written to. As a general rule, PHP files need to have a permission (chmod) of 666, whereas file folders need a permission of 755. Almost all FTP clients let you check and change the permissions on the files in case you need to. Typically, you can find the option to change file permissions within the menu options of your FTP client.

Some hosting providers run their PHP software in a more secure format called *safe mode*. If this is the case with your host, you need to set the PHP files to 644. If you're unsure, ask your hosting provider what permissions you need to set for PHP files.

Last step: Running the install script

The final step in the installation procedure for WordPress is connecting the WordPress software you uploaded to the MySQL database. Follow these steps:

1. **Type this URL in the address window of your browser, replacing *your-domain.com* with your own domain name:**

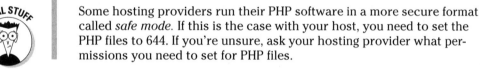

   http://*yourdomain.com*/wp-admin/install.php

   If you chose to install WordPress in a different folder from the root directory of your account, make sure you indicate this fact in the URL for the install script. If you transferred the WordPress software files to a folder called /blog, for example, you would point your browser to the following URL to run the installation: http://*yourdomain.com*/blog/wp-admin/install.php.

   Assuming that you did everything correctly (see Table 6-1 for help with common installation problems), you see the message shown in Figure 6-6.

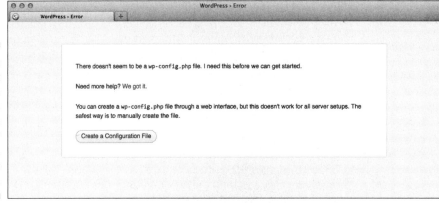

Figure 6-6:
The first
time you
run the
installation
script for
WordPress,
you see this
message.

2. **Click the Create a Configuration File button.**

   The next page that opens is a Welcome to WordPress message, which gives you the information you need to proceed with the installation.

3. **Click the Let's Go button at the bottom of that page.**

4. **Dig out the database name, username, and password that you saved earlier, and use that information to fill in the following fields (shown in Figure 6-7):**

   • *Database Name:* Type the database name you used when you created the MySQL database before this installation. Because hosts differ in configurations, enter either the database name or the database name with your hosting account username appended.

   If you named your database *wordpress,* for example, you would enter that in this text box. Or if your host requires you to append the database name with your hosting account username, you would enter ***username*_wordpress**, substituting your hosting username for *username.* My username is *lisasabin,* so I would enter **lisasabin_wordpress**.

   • *User Name:* Type the username you used when you created the MySQL database before this installation. Depending on what your host requires, you may need to append this username to your hosting account username.

   • *Password:* Type the password you used when you set up the MySQL database. You don't need to append the password to your hosting account username here.

   • *Database Host:* Ninety-nine percent of the time, you'll leave this field set to *localhost.* Some hosts, depending on their configurations, have different hosts set for the MySQL database server. If *localhost* doesn't work, you need to contact your hosting provider to find out the MySQL database host.

- *Table Prefix:* Leave this field set to *wp,* although you can change the table prefix to something completely random to increase security for your site, such as: xyz123_.

5. **When you have all that information filled in, click the Submit button.**

   You see a message that says, `All right, sparky! You've made it through this part of the installation. WordPress can now communicate with your database. If you're ready, time now to run the install!`

6. **Click the Run the Install button.**

   You see another welcome page with a message welcoming you to the famous five-minute WordPress installation process.

7. **Enter or possibly change this information (shown in Figure 6-8):**

   - *Site Title:* Enter the title you want to give your blog. The title you enter isn't written in stone; you can change it later.

   - *Username:* This is the name you will use to log in to WordPress. By default, the username is admin, and you can leave it that way. However, for security reasons, it's recommended practice to change your username to something unique to you.

   - *Password:* Type your desired password in the first text box. Then type it again in the second text box to confirm that you've typed it correctly. If the two versions of your password don't match, WordPress alerts you with an error message. If you don't enter a password, one will automatically be generated for you.

Figure 6-7: At this step of the WordPress installation, enter the database name, username, and password.

For security reasons (and so that other people can't make a lucky guess), passwords should be at least seven characters long and use as many different characters in as many combinations as possible. Use a mixture of uppercase and lowercase letters, numbers, and symbols (such as ! " ? $ % ^ &).

- *Your E-mail:* Enter the e-mail address you want to use to be notified of administrative information about your blog. You can change this address later, too.

- *Allow My Blog to Appear in Search Engines Like Google and Technorati:* By default, this check box is selected, which lets the search engines index the content of your blog and include your blog in search results. To keep your blog private and out of the search engines, deselect this check box.

8. **Click the Install WordPress button.**

   The WordPress installation machine works its magic and creates all the tables within the database that contain the default data for your blog. WordPress displays the login information you need to access the WordPress Dashboard. Make note of this username and password before you leave this page. Scribble it down on a piece of paper or copy it into a text editor such as Notepad.

Figure 6-8: Information needed to finish the WordPress installation.

After you click the Install WordPress button, you receive an e-mail with the login information and login URL. This information is handy if you're called away during this part of the installation process. So go ahead and let the dog out, answer the phone, brew a cup of coffee, or take a 15-minute power nap. If you somehow get distracted away from this page, the e-mail sent to you contains the information you need to successfully log in to your WordPress blog.

9. **Click the Log In button to log in to WordPress.**

If you happen to lose this page before clicking the Log In button, you can always find your way to the login page by entering your domain followed by the call to the login file (for example, `http://yourdomain.com/wp-login.php`).

You know that you're finished with the installation process when you see the login page as shown in Figure 6-9. Check out Table 6-1 if you experience any problems during this installation process; it covers some of the common problems users run in to.

So do tell — how much time does your watch show for the installation? Was it five minutes? Stop by my blog sometime (`http://lisasabin-wilson.com`), and let me know whether WordPress stood up to its famous five-minute-installation reputation. I'm a curious sort.

The good news is — you're done! Were you expecting a marching band? WordPress isn't that fancy . . . yet. Give them time, though; if anyone can produce it, the folks at WordPress can.

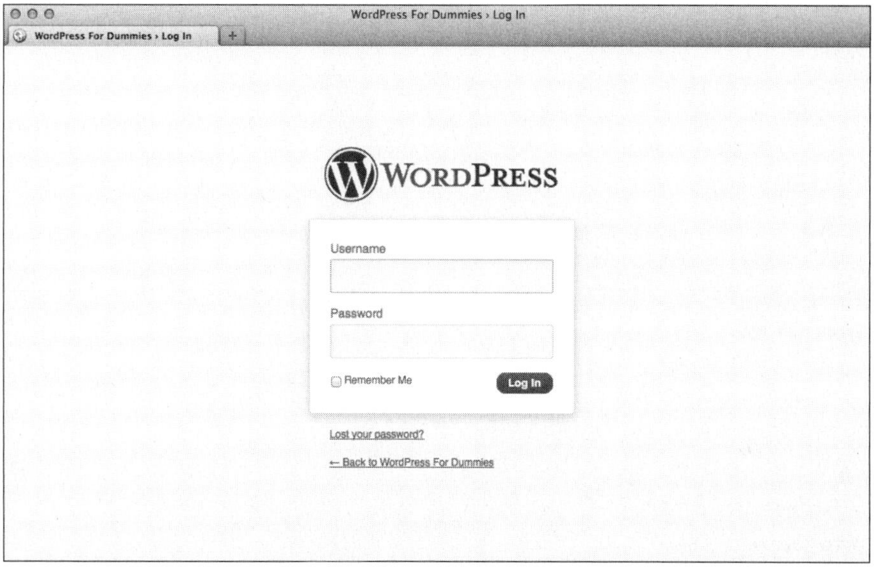

Figure 6-9:
You know you've run a successful WordPress installation when you see the login page.

WordPress For Dummies › Log In

WORDPRESS

Username

Password

☐ Remember Me   **Log In**

Lost your password?

← Back to WordPress For Dummies

Table 6-1	Common WordPress Installation Problems	
Error Message	*Common Cause*	*Solution*
Error Connecting to the Database	The database name, username, password, or host was entered incorrectly.	Revisit your MySQL database to obtain the database name, username, and password, and re-enter that information.
Headers Already Sent Error Messages	A syntax error occurred in the `wp-config.php` file.	Open the `wp-config.php` file in a text editor. The first line should contain only this line: `<?php`. The last line should contain only this line: `?>`. Make sure that those lines contain nothing else — not even white space. Save the file changes.
500: Internal Server Error	Permissions on PHP files are set incorrectly.	Try setting the permissions (`chmod`) on the PHP files to 666. If that change doesn't work, set them to 644. Each web server has different settings for how it lets PHP execute on its servers.
404: Page Not Found	The URL for the login page is incorrect.	Double-check that the URL you're using to get to the login page is the same as the location of your WordPress installation (such as `http://yourdomain.com/wp-login.php`).
403: Forbidden Access	An `index.html` or `index.htm` file exists in the WordPress installation directory.	WordPress is a PHP application, so the default home page is `index.php`. Look in the WordPress installation folder on your web server. If there is an `index.html` or `index.htm` file in there, delete it.

Let me be the first to congratulate you on your newly installed WordPress blog! When you're ready, log in and familiarize yourself with the Dashboard, which I describe in Chapter 7.

Chapter 7

Understanding the WordPress.org Dashboard

*W*ith WordPress.org successfully installed, you can explore your new blogging software. This chapter guides you through the preliminary setup of your new WordPress blog using the Dashboard. When you blog with WordPress, you spend a lot of time on the Dashboard, which is where you make all the exciting, behind-the-scenes stuff happen. In this panel, you find all the settings and options that enable you to set up your blog just the way you want it. (If you still need to install and configure WordPress, check out Chapter 6.)

Feeling comfortable with the Dashboard sets you up for a successful entrance into the WordPress blogging world. Expect to tweak your WordPress settings several times throughout the life of your blog. In this chapter, as I go through the various sections, settings, options, and configurations available to you, understand that nothing is set in stone. You can set options today and change them at any time.

Logging On to the Dashboard

I find that the direct approach (also known as jumping in) works best when I want to get familiar with a new software tool. To that end, just follow these steps to log in to WordPress and take a look at the guts of the Dashboard:

1. **Open your web browser and type the WordPress login-page address (or URL) in the address box.**

   The login-page address looks something like this (exchange that `.com` for a `.org` or a `.net` as needed):

   `http://www.`*`yourdomain`*`.com/wp-login.php`

   If you installed WordPress in its own folder, include that folder name in the login URL. If you installed WordPress in a folder ingeniously named `wordpress`, the login URL becomes

   `http://www.`*`yourdomain`*`.com/wordpress/wp-login.php`

2. **Type your username in the Username text box and your password in the Password text box.**

   In case you forget your password, WordPress has you covered. Click the Lost Your Password link (located near the bottom of the page), enter your username and e-mail address, and then click the Submit button. WordPress resets your password and e-mails the new password to you.

   After you request a password, you receive two e-mails from your WordPress blog. The first e-mail contains a link that you click to verify that you requested the password. After you verify your intentions, you receive a second e-mail containing your new password.

3. **Select the Remember Me check box if you want WordPress to place a cookie in your browser.**

   The cookie tells WordPress to remember your login credentials the next time you show up. The cookie set by WordPress is harmless and stores your WordPress login on your computer. Because of the cookie, WordPress remembers you the next time you visit. Also, because this option tells the browser to remember your login, I don't advise checking this option on public computers. Avoid selecting Remember Me when you're using your work computer or a computer at an Internet café.

   Note: Before you set this option, make sure that your browser is configured to allow cookies. (If you aren't sure how to do this, check the help documentation of the Internet browser you're using.)

4. **Click the Log In button.**

After you log in to WordPress, you see the Dashboard page.

Navigating the Dashboard

You can consider the Dashboard to be a Control Panel of sorts because it offers several quick links and areas that provide information about your blog, starting with the actual Dashboard page shown in Figure 7-1.

You can change how the WordPress Dashboard looks by changing the order of the modules that appear on it (for example, Right Now and Recent Comments). You can expand (open) and collapse (close) the individual modules by clicking your mouse anywhere within the gray title bar of the module. This feature is really nice because you can use the Dashboard for just those modules that you use regularly. The concept is easy: Keep the modules you use all the time open and close the ones that you use only occasionally — you can open those modules only when you really need them. You save space and can customize your Dashboard to suit your own needs.

When you view your Dashboard for the very first time, all the modules appear in the expanded (open) position by default (refer to Figure 7-1).

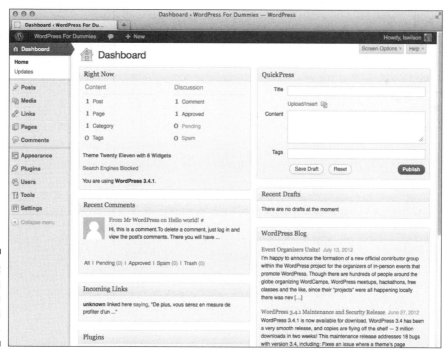

Figure 7-1:
Log on to the WordPress Dashboard.

The navigation menu on the WordPress Dashboard appears on the left side of your browser window. When you need to get back to the main Dashboard page, click the Dashboard link at the top of the navigation menu found on any of the pages within your WordPress Dashboard.

In the following sections, I cover the Dashboard page as it appears when you log on to your WordPress Dashboard for the very first time; later in this chapter, I show you how to configure the appearance of your Dashboard so that it best suits how you use the available modules.

Right Now

The Right Now module on the Dashboard shows what is going on in your blog right now, right this very second! Figure 7-2 shows the expanded Right Now module in my brand-spanking-new WordPress blog.

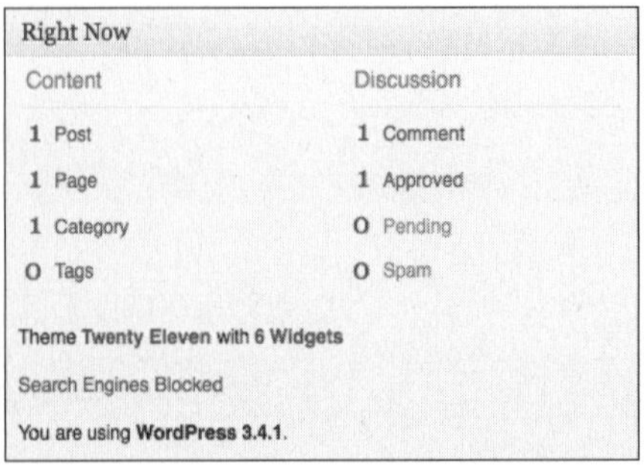

Figure 7-2:
The Right
Now mod-
ule on the
Dashboard
expanded
to see the
available
features.

Right Now		
Content		Discussion
1 Post		1 Comment
1 Page		1 Approved
1 Category		0 Pending
0 Tags		0 Spam
Theme Twenty Eleven with 6 Widgets		
Search Engines Blocked		
You are using **WordPress 3.4.1**.		

The Right Now module shows the following default:

✔ **The number of posts you have:** This number reflects the total number of posts you have in your WordPress blog; I have 1 post on my blog. The number is blue, which means it's a link that you can click. When you do, you go to the Edit Posts page, where you can edit the posts on your blog. I cover editing posts in Chapter 8.

✔ **The number of pages:** This is the number of pages on your blog, which changes as you add or delete pages. (*Pages,* in this context, refer to the static pages you have created in your blog.) Figure 7-2 shows that my blog has 1 page.

Clicking this link takes you to the Edit Pages page, where you can view, edit, and delete your pages. (Find the difference between WordPress posts and pages in Chapter 8.)

✔ **The number of categories:** This is the number of categories you have on your blog, which changes as you add and delete categories. Figure 7-2 shows that I have 1 category for my blog.

Clicking this link takes you to the Categories page, where you can view, edit, and delete your categories; or add brand new ones. (For details about the management and creation of categories, see Chapter 8.)

✔ **The number of tags:** This is the number of tags you have in your blog, which changes as you add and delete tags. Figure 7-2 shows that I have 0 tags.

Clicking this link takes you to the Tags page, where you can add new tags and view, edit, and delete your tags. (You can find more information about tags in Chapter 8.)

✔ **The number of comments:** This is the total number of comments on your blog. Figure 7-2 shows that I have 1 Comment, 1 Approved, 0 Pending, and 0 marked as Spam.

Clicking any of these four links takes you to the Edit Comments page, where you can manage the comments on your blog. I cover the management of comments in the "Comments" section, later in this chapter.

The last section of the Dashboard's Right Now module shows the following information:

✔ **Which WordPress theme you're using:** Figure 7-2 shows that I'm using the theme Twenty Eleven. The theme name is a link that takes you to the Manage Themes page, where you can view and activate themes on your blog.

✔ **How many widgets you've added to your blog:** This is the number of WordPress widgets you're using in your blog. Figure 7-2 shows that I have 6 widgets in use. The number 6 is a link that takes you to the Widgets page, where you can change your widget options by editing them, moving them, or removing them. (I cover widgets in detail in Chapter 5, if you want to check that out. Although that chapter is in the WordPress.com part of this book, the method of using sidebar widgets is the same for self-hosted WordPress.org blogs.)

✔ **Search Engines Blocked:** This is displayed only if you have indicated that you would like to block your blog from search engines in the privacy settings, covered later in this chapter.

✔ **The version of WordPress you're using:** This is the last statement in the Right Now section. Figure 7-2 shows that I'm using WordPress version 3.4.1. This version announcement will change if you are using an older version of WordPress. When WordPress software is upgraded, this statement tells you that you're using an outdated version of WordPress and encourages you to upgrade to the latest version.

Recent Comments

The next module is called Recent Comments. Within this module, you find

- ✔ **Most recent comments published to your blog:** WordPress displays a maximum of five comments in this area.

- ✔ **The author of each comment:** The name of the person who left the comment appears above it. This section also displays the author's picture (or avatar), if she has one.

- ✔ **A link to the post the comment was left on:** The post title appears to the right of the commenter's name. Click the link and you go to that post on the Dashboard.

- ✔ **An excerpt of the comment:** This is a snippet of the comment this person left on your blog.

- ✔ **Comment management links:** When you hover over the comment with your mouse cursor, five links appear underneath the comment. These links give you the opportunity to manage those comments right from your Dashboard: The first link is Unapprove, which appears only if you have comment moderation turned on. (Find out more about moderating comments in the "Comments" section, later in this chapter.) The other four links are Reply, Edit, Spam, and Trash.

- ✔ **View links:** These links appear at the bottom of the Recent Comments module, where you can click All, Pending, Approved, Spam, and Trash.

You find even more information on managing your comments in the "Comments" section, later in this chapter.

Incoming Links

The next module visible on the Dashboard is Incoming Links. It lists all the blog-savvy people who wrote a blog post that links to your blog. When your blog is brand new, you won't see any incoming links listed in this section. Don't despair, however; as time goes on, you will see this listing of links fill up as more and more people discover you and your inspired writings!

In the meantime, the Incoming Links module shows the following message: `This dashboard widget queries Google Blog Search so that when another blog links to your site it will show up here. It has found no incoming links ... yet. It's okay — there is no rush.` The phrase *Google Blog Search* is a link; when you click it, you go to the Google Blog Search directory, which is a search engine for blogs only.

The following steps show you how to edit the Incoming Links module:

1. **Hover your mouse pointer over the title of the Incoming Links module, and a new link labeled *Configure* appears directly to the right of the title. Click that link.**

   Now you can change the settings of the Incoming Links module. See Figure 7-3.

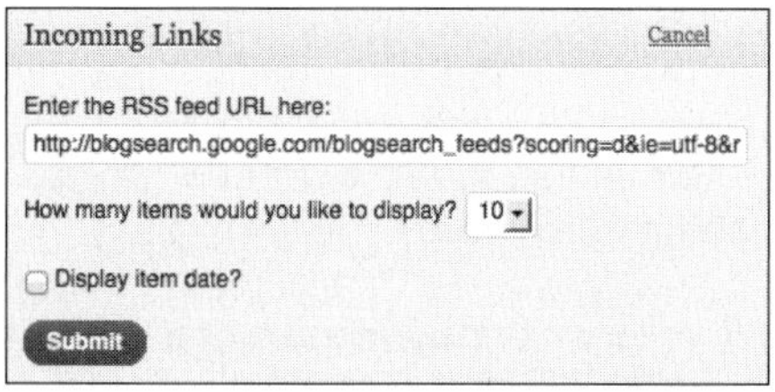

Figure 7-3:
Change
the set-
tings of the
Incoming
Links
module by
clicking the
Configure
link.

2. **Add a URL in the Enter the RSS Feed URL Here box.**

   You can enter the URL of any RSS feed you want to display incoming links to your site. Examples of feeds you can use include the following:

   - Technorati (`http://technorati.com`)
   - Yahoo! Search (`http://search.yahoo.com`)
   - Social Mention (`www.socialmention.com`)

   You're not restricted to using the Google Blog Search engine (`http://blogsearch.google.com`) to provide your Incoming Links information.

3. **Specify how many items you want to display.**

   The default number is 5, but making a different choice from the How Many Items Would You Like to Display drop-down menu lets you display up to 20 items (incoming links).

4. **Specify whether to display the item date.**

   Check the Display Item Date check box if you want each incoming link to display the date the link was created. If you don't want the date to display, leave that box unchecked.

5. **Click the Submit button to save all your preferences.**

   Clicking Submit resets the Incoming Links module with your new settings saved.

Plugins

I cover the management and use of WordPress plugins in detail in Chapter 10; however, for the purposes of this section, I discuss the functions of the Plugins module on the Dashboard so that you know what to do with it now!

The Plugins module includes three titles of WordPress plugins linked to its page within the WordPress Plugin Directory. The Plugins module pulls information via RSS feed from the official WordPress Plugin Directory at `http://wordpress.org/extend/plugins`. This module displays a plugin from two different plugin categories in the official WordPress Plugin Directory: Most Popular and Newest Plugins.

The Plugins module doesn't have an Edit link, so you can't customize the information that it displays. Use this box to discover new plugins that can help you do fun and exciting things with your blog.

The Plugins module does have a very exciting feature that you can use to install, activate, and manage plugins on your blog. Just follow these steps to make it happen:

1. **Click the Install link next to the title of the plugin.**

   The Plugin Information pop-up window opens. It displays the various bits of information about the plugin you've chosen, such as title, description, version, author, date last updated, and the number of times the plugin was downloaded.

2. **Click the Install Now button.**

   This button is at the top right of the Plugin Information page.

   The Plugin Information pop-up window closes, and the Install Plugins page on your WordPress Dashboard opens where you see a confirmation message that the plugin has been downloaded, unpacked, and successfully installed.

3. **Specify whether to install the plugin or proceed to the Plugins page.**

   Two links are shown under the confirmation message:

   - *Activate Plugin:* Click this link to activate the plugin you just installed on your blog.

   - *Return to Plugins Page:* Click this link to go to the Manage Plugins page.

   I cover the installation and activation of WordPress plugins in further depth in Chapter 10.

4. **Click the Dashboard link to return to the Dashboard.**

   The Dashboard link is located at the top of the left-side navigation menu on every page of your WordPress Dashboard.

QuickPress

The QuickPress module is a handy form that allows you to write, save, and publish a blog post right from your WordPress Dashboard. The options are similar to the ones I cover in the section on writing posts in Chapter 8.

Recent Drafts

If you're using a brand new WordPress blog and this is a new installation, the Recent Drafts module displays the message: There are no drafts at the moment. That's because you haven't written any drafts. As time goes on, however, and you've written a few posts in your blog, you may save some of those posts as Drafts — to be edited and published at a later date. Those drafts show up in the Recent Drafts module.

WordPress displays up to five drafts and displays the title of the post, the date it was last saved, and a short excerpt. Click the View All link to go to the Manage Posts page where you can view, edit, and manage your blog posts. Check out Chapter 8 for more information.

WordPress Blog

When you first install WordPress, the WordPress Blog module is by default populated with the two most recent updates from the official WordPress blog at http://wordpress.org/news. You see the title of the last post, the date it was published, and a short excerpt of the post. Click a title and you go directly to that post on the WordPress blog.

Following the updates of the WordPress Blog is very useful, and I highly recommend it because every single time you log in to your WordPress Dashboard, a glance at this section informs you about any news, updates, or alerts from the makers of WordPress. You can find out about any new versions of the software, security patches, or other important news regarding the software you are using to power your blog.

Although I recommend that you keep the WordPress Blog updates in this section, the WordPress platform lets you change this box to display posts from another blog of your choosing. You can accomplish this change by following these steps:

1. **Hover your mouse pointer over the WordPress Blog module title. Click the Configure link shown to the right of the WordPress Blog title.**

   The module changes to display several options to change the information contained in the box. See Figure 7-4.

```
WordPress Blog                              Cancel

Enter the RSS feed URL here:
http://wordpress.org/news/feed/

Give the feed a title (optional):
WordPress Blog

How many items would you like to display?  2 ▾

☑ Display item content?

☐ Display item author if available?

☑ Display item date?

  Submit
```

2. **Type your preferred RSS feed in the Enter the RSS Feed URL Here box.**

3. **Type your preferred title in the Give the Feed a Title (Optional) box.**

4. **Specify the number of items you want to display.**

   The default number is 2, but you can display up to 20 by making a different choice from the How Many Items Would You Like to Display drop-down menu.

5. **Specify whether you want to display the item's content.**

   Item content refers to the text content of the post. If you don't select the Display Item Content check box, WordPress doesn't display an excerpt of the post — only the post title.

6. **Specify whether you want to display the name of the person who wrote the post.**

   Leave the Display Item Author If Available box deselected if you don't want the author's name displayed.

7. **Specify whether you want to display the date.**

   Leave the Display Item Date box deselected if you don't want the date displayed.

8. **Click the Submit button to save your changes.**

   The Dashboard page refreshes with your new changes. Click the title of the box to collapse it.

If you change your mind, click the Cancel link shown to the right of the WordPress Blog title. Clicking Cancel discards any changes you made and keeps the original settings intact.

The title of the WordPress Blog module changes to the title you chose in Step 3. Figure 7-5 shows that I changed the title to Lisa's Blog.

Figure 7-5:
The
WordPress
Blog module
changes
based on
the options
you set.

> **Lisa's Blog**
>
> Launch a WordPress.com Blog In A Day (For Dummies) May 22, 2012
> Happy to announce the release of my latest project for Wiley Publishing. The For Dummies division is launching a new series called "...In A Day For Dummies" which are short e-books geared toward helping you learn a new skill "in a day". Wiley Publishing decided to pilot this new series with books on WordPress since it's such a damn popular service (can ya bl [...]
>
> Vivid Yoga Studio in Menomonee Falls, WI May 10, 2012
> I've become the owner of a business that is completely unrelated to WordPress – do you believe it? As a matter of fact – it's completely unrelated to internet publishing or any type of web development or design work at all! Months back, I posted about how I found yoga (or maybe how yoga found me?) and SO much has happened since then! I met a good friend, Mic [...]

Other WordPress News

The Other WordPress News module of the Dashboard pulls in posts from a site called WordPress Planet (http://planet.wordpress.org). By keeping the default setting in this area, you stay in touch with several posts made by folks who are involved in WordPress development, design, and troubleshooting. You can find lots of interesting and useful tidbits if you keep this area intact. Quite often, I find great information about new plugins or themes, problem areas and support, troubleshooting, and new ideas, so I tend to stick with the default setting.

WordPress is all about user experience, however, so you can change the options to specify what displays in this area. You can change the items in this module the same way that you change the options for the WordPress Blog module (see the preceding section).

Arranging the Dashboard to Your Tastes

You can arrange the order of the modules on your Dashboard to suit your tastes. WordPress places a great deal of emphasis on user experience, and a big part of that effort results in your ability to create a Dashboard that you find most useful. Happily, changing the modules that are displayed, and the order in which they're displayed, is easy.

In the following steps, I show you how to move the Right Now module so that it displays on the right side of your Dashboard page:

1. **Hover your mouse pointer over the title bar of the Recent Comments module.**

   When hovering over the box title, your mouse cursor changes to the Move cursor (a cross with arrows on a PC or the hand cursor on a Mac).

2. **Click and hold your mouse button and drag the Recent Comments module to the right side of the screen.**

   As you drag the box, a light-gray box with a dotted border appears on the right side of your screen. That gray box is a guide that shows you where you should drop the module. See Figure 7-6.

3. **Release the mouse button when you have the Recent Comments module in place.**

   The Recent Comments module is now positioned on the right side of your Dashboard page.

   The other modules on the left shift up to fill the space left by the Recent Comments module, and the modules on the right side shift down to make room for the Recent Comments module.

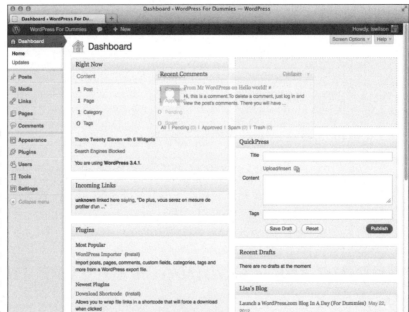

Figure 7-6:
A light-gray box appears as a guide when dragging and dropping modules on the WordPress Dashboard.

4. **(Optional) Click once on the title bar of the Right Now module.**

   The module collapses. Click the title bar again, and the module expands. You can keep that module opened or closed based on your own preference.

Repeat these steps with each module you see on the Dashboard by dragging 'n' dropping them so that they appear in the order you prefer.

When you navigate away from the Dashboard, WordPress remembers the changes you've made. When you return, you still see your customized Dashboard and you don't need to redo these changes.

If you find that your Dashboard contains a few modules you just never use, you can get rid of them altogether by following these steps:

1. **Click the Screen Options button at the top of the Dashboard.**

   The Screen Options menu opens, displaying the title of each module with check boxes to the left of each title.

2. **Deselect the module you want to hide on your Dashboard.**

   The check mark is removed from the box, and the module disappears from your Dashboard. Figure 7-7 shows my customized Dashboard, where I've removed the QuickPress module and moved the Right Now module to the top right.

If you remove a module in the Screen Options and later find that you want it back, you can always revisit the Screen Options panel and re-enable the module by selecting the check box next to the name of the module you want to show on your Dashboard.

Changing the Dashboard layout

I'm almost positive that you and I work differently in terms of how we like our work space laid out. Personally, I like to have one long column of items so that I can scroll through and focus on one area in particular, without having other things to the right and left of my periphery. That's what comes from being someone who is easily distracted.

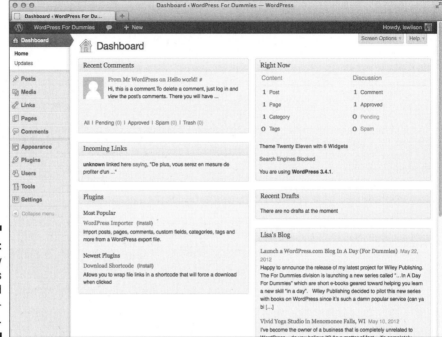

Figure 7-7:
My
WordPress
Dashboard
after I cus-
tomized it.

In the same Screen Options area that you removed modules from in the previous steps, you can also change the format of your Dashboard by choosing to
display one, two, three, or four columns — just follow these few steps:

1. **Click the Screen Options button at the top of the Dashboard.**

   The Screen Options menu opens.

2. **Locate Screen Layout Options.**

   At the bottom of the Screen Options menu is a menu heading titled
   Screen Layout.

3. **Choose the number of columns you want displayed.**

   You have the choice of 1, 2, 3, or 4 columns. Select the radio button
   to the left of the number you want, and your Dashboard displays the
   changes immediately.

4. **Close the Screen Options menu.**

   Click the Screen Options tab again to close the Screen Options menu.

As I mentioned, I like all my stuff in one long column, and you see my own Dashboard from my personal blog in Figure 7-8, where I have chosen to display my Dashboard in a one-column layout. Also note that in Figure 7-8, most of my Dashboard modules are almost all closed. I can expand (open) and collapse (close) them as I need to, based on what I need to see and do within my Dashboard on any given day.

Using the features that enable you to customize your Dashboard, WordPress allows you to create your own, individualized work space that works best for you, based on how you use WordPress. With these features, everyone can customize their own WordPress experience, and it's possible that no two WordPress user experiences are the same — like snowflakes!

Finding inline documentation and help

One thing I really appreciate about the WordPress software is the time and effort put in by the developers to provide users with tons of inline documentation that provides you with several tips and hints right inside the Dashboard. You can generally find inline documentation for just about every WordPress feature you use.

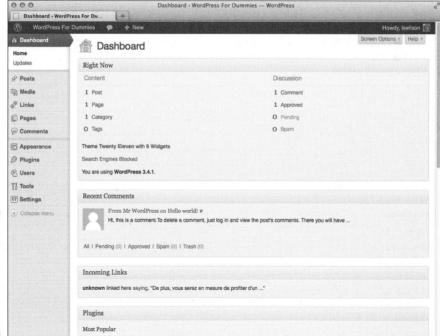

Figure 7-8:
My WordPress Dashboard displays a one-column layout.

Inline documentation are those small sentences and/or phrases that you see alongside, or underneath, a feature in WordPress that give a short but very helpful explanation of what the feature is and serve as guiding tips that correspond with each feature. These tips sometimes even provide basic, recommended settings.

In addition to the inline documentation that you find scattered throughout the Dashboard, you'll also find a helpful tab in the upper-right corner of your Dashboard labeled Help. Click this tab and a panel drops down that contains a lot of text providing documentation relevant to the page you are currently viewing on your Dashboard. For example, if you're viewing the General Settings page, the Help tab drops down documentation relevant to the General Settings page, as shown in Figure 7-9. Likewise, if you're viewing the Add New Post page, clicking the Help tab drops down documentation with topics relevant to the settings and features you find on the Add New Post page within your Dashboard. Just click the Help tab again to close the Help panel when you're done reading it.

The inline documentation and the topics and text you find under the Help tab exist to assist and support you as you experience the WordPress platform to help make it as easy to understand as possible. Other places on the web where you can find help and support for WordPress include the WordPress Support Forums at `http://wordpress.org/support`.

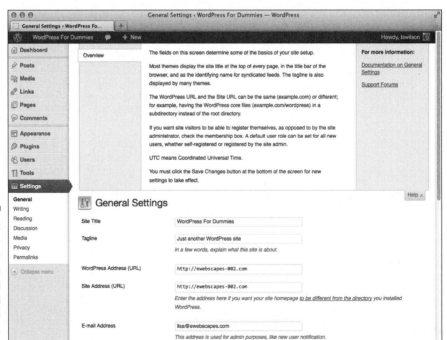

Figure 7-9:
Help documentation shown on the General Settings page on the Dashboard.

Creating your own work space

Throughout the different pages of your WordPress Dashboard, you can apply the customization features that I cover for the main Dashboard page earlier in this chapter. Every section of the WordPress Dashboard is customizable with drag 'n' drop modules, screen options, and inline help and documentation.

Have a look at Figure 7-10, which displays the Add New Post page on the WordPress Dashboard (the Posts page is covered in greater detail in Chapter 8). In the figure, the Screen Options menu shows your options for customization, including the following:

- ✔ Check boxes that you can select to display the Author, Categories, Tags, Comments, and Date of the posts listed on the Posts page

- ✔ A text field for you to input the number of posts you want displayed on the Posts page

Figure 7-11 displays the Help topics on the Posts page when you click the Help tab at the top of the screen to display the inline documentation for the page.

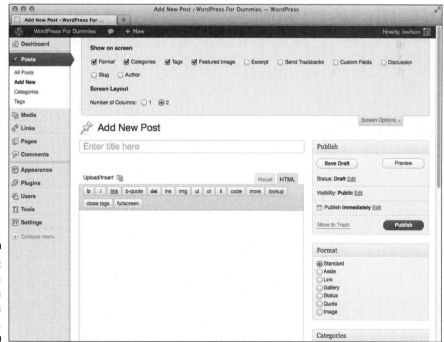

Figure 7-10: Screen Options on the Posts page.

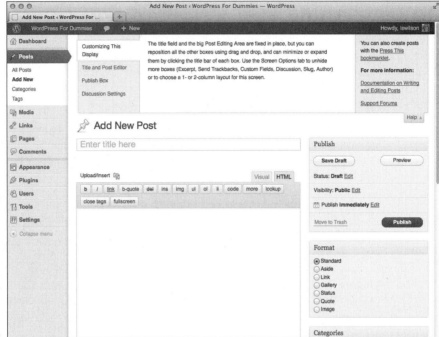

Figure 7-11:
Click the
Help tab on
the Posts
page to
display
inline docu-
mentation.

Another helpful feature in the Help menu on each page of the WordPress
Dashboard is the links that lead you to other areas on the Internet that contain additional help, support topics, and resources for you to learn more
about the various WordPress features.

Setting Options on the Dashboard

The navigation menu is located on the left side of every page within the
WordPress Dashboard. You find it there everywhere you go; like a loyal
friend, it's always there for you when you need it!

The navigation menu is divided into ten different menus (not counting the
Dashboard menu, mentioned previously). Hover your mouse pointer over a
menu, and another menu flies out to the right to reveal the submenu of items.
The submenu items take you to areas within your Dashboard that allow you
to perform tasks such as publishing a new blog post, adding a new link, or
managing your comments.

The settings that allow you to personalize your blog are the first ones that I cover in the next part of this chapter. Some of the menu items, such as creating and publishing new posts, are covered in detail in other chapters, but they're well worth a mention here as well so that you know what you're looking at. (Sections with additional information contain a cross-reference telling you where you can find more in-depth information on that topic in this book.)

Configuring the Settings

At the bottom of the navigation menu is the Settings menu. Hover over the Settings link, and a submenu appears to the right that contains the following links, which I discuss in the sections that follow:

- ✔ General
- ✔ Writing
- ✔ Reading
- ✔ Discussion
- ✔ Media
- ✔ Privacy
- ✔ Permalinks

General

After you install the WordPress software and log in, you can put a personal stamp on your blog by giving it a title and description, setting your contact e-mail address, and identifying yourself as the author of the blog. You take care of these and other settings on the General Settings page.

To begin personalizing your blog, start with your general settings by following these steps:

1. **Click the General link in the Settings menu.**

   The General Settings page appears. See Figure 7-12.

2. **Enter the name of your blog in the Site Title text box.**

   The title you enter here is the one that you've given your blog to identify it as your own. In Figure 7-12, I gave my new blog the title *WordPress For Dummies,* which appears on the blog as well as in the title bar of the viewer's web browser.

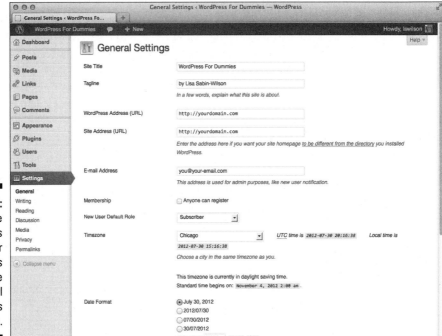

Figure 7-12:
Personalize
the settings
of your
WordPress
blog on the
General
Settings
page.

Give your blog an interesting and identifiable name. You can use *Fried Green Tomatoes,* for example, if you're blogging about the topic, the book, or the movie, or even anything remotely related to the lovely Southern dish.

3. **In the Tagline text box, enter a five- to ten-word phrase that describes your blog.**

   Figure 7-12 shows that my tagline is *by Lisa Sabin-Wilson.* So my blog displays my blog title followed by the tagline: *WordPress For Dummies by Lisa Sabin-Wilson.*

   The general Internet-surfing public can view your blog title and tagline, which various search engines (such as Google, Yahoo!, and MSN) grab for indexing, so choose your words with this fact in mind.

4. **In the WordPress Address (URL) text box, enter the location where you installed your WordPress blog software.**

   Be sure to include the `http://` portion of the URL and the entire path to your WordPress installation — for example, `http://yourdomain.com`. If you installed WordPress in a folder in your directory — in a folder called `wordpress`, for example — you need to include it here. If I had installed WordPress in a folder called `wordpress`, the WordPress address would be `http://yourdomain.com/wordpress`.

5. **In the Site Address (URL) text box, enter the web address where people can find your blog by using their web browsers.**

   Typically, what you enter here is the same as your domain name (`http://yourdomain.com`). If you install WordPress in a subdirectory of your site, the WordPress installation URL is different from the blog URL. If you install WordPress at `http://yourdomain.com/word press/` (WordPress URL), you need to tell WordPress that you want the blog to appear at `http://yourdomain.com` (the blog URL).

6. **Enter your e-mail address in the E-mail Address text box.**

   WordPress sends messages about the details of your blog to this e-mail address. When a new user registers for your blog, for example, WordPress sends you an e-mail alert.

7. **Select a Membership option.**

   Select the Anyone Can Register box if you want to keep registration on your blog open to anyone who wants to register. Keep the box unselected if you'd rather not have open registration on your blog.

8. **From the New User Default Role drop-down menu, choose the role that you want new users to have when they register for user accounts in your blog.**

   You need to understand the differences among the user roles because each user role is assigned a different level of access to your blog, as follows:

   • *Subscriber:* Subscriber is the default role. Assigning this role to new users is a good idea, particularly if you don't know who's registering. Subscribers are given access to the Dashboard page and they can view and change the options in their profiles on the Your Profile and Personal Options page. (They don't have access to your account settings, however — only to their own.) Each user can change his username, e-mail address, password, bio, and other descriptors in his user profile. Subscribers' profile information is stored in the WordPress database, and your blog remembers them each time they visit so that they don't have to complete the profile information each time they leave comments on your blog.

   • *Contributor:* In addition to the access Subscribers have, Contributors can upload files and write, edit, and manage their own posts. Contributors can write posts, but they can't publish the posts; the administrator reviews all Contributor posts and decides whether to publish them. This setting is a nice way to moderate content written by new authors.

   • *Author:* In addition to the access Contributors have, Authors can publish and edit their own posts.

- *Editor:* In addition to the access Authors have, Editors can moderate comments, manage categories, manage links, edit pages, and edit other Authors' posts.

- *Administrator:* Administrators can edit all the options and settings in the WordPress blog.

9. **In the Timezone section, choose your UTC time from the drop-down menu.**

   This setting refers to the number of hours that your local time differs from Coordinated Universal Time (UTC). This setting ensures that all your blog posts and comments left on your blog are time-stamped with the correct time. If you're lucky enough, like me, to live on the frozen tundra of Wisconsin, which is in the Central time zone (CST), you would choose **–6** from the drop-down menu because that time zone is six hours off UTC. WordPress also gives you the names of some of the major cities across the world to make it easier. Just select the name of the major city you live closest to, and chances are, you're in the same time zone as that city.

   If you're unsure what your UTC time is, you can find it at the Greenwich Mean Time website (`http://wwp.greenwichmeantime.com`). GMT is essentially the same thing as UTC.

10. **In the Date Format text box, enter the format in which you want the date to be displayed in your blog.**

    This setting determines the style of the date display. The default format is already selected and displayed for you: **F j, Y** (F = the full month name; j = the two-digit day; Y = the four-digit year), which gives you the date output. This default date format displays the date like this: January 1, 2012.

    Select a different format by clicking the circle to the left of the option. You can also customize the date display by selecting the Custom option and entering your preferred format in the text box provided. If you're feeling adventurous, you can find out how to customize the date format here: `http://codex.wordpress.org/Formatting_Date_and_Time`.

11. **In the Time Format text box, enter the format in which you want the time to be displayed in your blog.**

    This setting is the style of the time display. The default format is already inserted for you: **g:i a** (g = the two-digit hour; i = the two-digit minute; a = lowercase as a.m. or p.m.), which gives you the output of 12:00 a.m.

    Select a different format by clicking the circle to the left of the option. You can also customize the date display by selecting the Custom option and entering your preferred format in the text box provided; find out how at `http://codex.wordpress.org/Formatting_Date_and_Time`.

    You can format the time and date in several ways. Go to `http://us3.php.net/manual/en/function.date.php` to find potential formats at the PHP website.

12. From the drop-down menu, choose the day the week starts in your calendar.

Displaying a calendar in the sidebar of your blog is optional. If you choose to display a calendar, you can select the day of the week you want your calendar to start with.

Click the Save Changes button at the bottom of any page where you set new options. If you don't click Save Changes, your settings aren't saved, and WordPress reverts to the preceding options. Each time you click the Save Changes button, WordPress reloads the current page, displaying the new options that you just set.

Writing

Click the Writing link in the Settings menu; the Writing Settings page opens. See Figure 7-13.

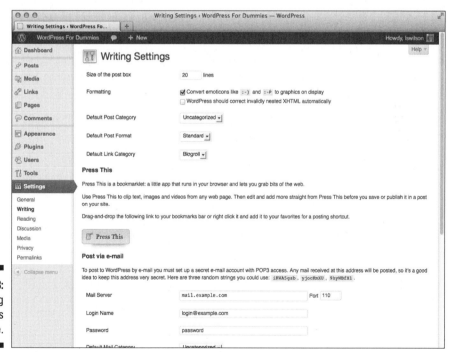

Figure 7-13: The Writing Settings page.

This page lets you set some basic options for writing your posts. Table 7-1 gives you some information on choosing how your posts look and how WordPress handles some specific conditions.

After you set your options, be sure to click the Save Changes button; otherwise, the changes won't take effect.

Table 7-1	Writing Settings Options	
Option	*Function*	*Default*
Size of the Post Box	Determines the size of the text edit box on the Write Post page. The bigger the number, the taller the box.	20 lines
Formatting	Determines whether WordPress converts emoticons to graphics and whether WordPress corrects invalidly nested XHTML automatically. In general, I recommend selecting this option. (You can find more information about valid XHTML code at `http://validator.w3.org/docs/#docs_all`.)	Deselected
Default Post Category	Lets you select the category that WordPress defaults to any time you forget to choose a category when you publish a post.	Uncategorized
Default Post Format	Lets you select the post format that WordPress defaults to anytime you publish a post to your blog. I cover post formats in more detail in Bonus Chapter 1 on the companion website.	Standard
Default Link Category	Lets you select the category that WordPress defaults to anytime you forget to categorize a link.	Blogroll
Press This	A small application to use in your browser that lets you post information and content you find on the web to your blog in a quick and easy fashion. Just drag 'n' drop the Press This button to your browser's bookmark toolbar to use.	N/A
Post via E-mail	Lets you publish blog posts from your e-mail account by letting you enter the e-mail and server information for the account you'll be using to send posts to your WordPress blog.	N/A

Option	Function	Default
Remote Publishing	Lets you enable Atom Publishing Protocol or one of the XML-RPC (XML Remote Procedure Call) publishing interfaces that enable you to post to your WordPress blog from a remote website or desktop publishing application.	Disabled
Update Services **Note:** This option is available only if your blog is made public in the Privacy settings.	Lets you indicate which ping service you want to use to notify the world that you've made updates, or new posts, to your blog. These update services include blogrolling.com and weblogs.com. The default, rpc.pingomatic.com, updates all the popular services simultaneously.	rpc.pingomatic.com

Go to `http://codex.wordpress.org/Update_Services` for comprehensive information on update services.

Reading

The third link in the Settings menu is Reading. See Figure 7-14.

You can set the following options in the Reading Settings page:

- ✔ **Front Page Displays:** Choose what you want to display on the front page of your blog: your latest posts or a static page. You can find detailed information about using a static page for your front page in Bonus Chapter 1 on the companion website for this book.

- ✔ **Blog Pages Show at Most:** Type the maximum number of posts you want to display on each blog page.

- ✔ **Syndication Feeds Show the Most Recent:** In the Posts box, type the maximum number of posts you want to show in your RSS feed at any time.

- ✔ **For Each Article in a Feed, Show:** Select either Full Text or Summary. Full Text publishes the entire post to your RSS feed, whereas Summary publishes only an excerpt. (Check out Chapter 8 for more information on WordPress RSS feeds.)

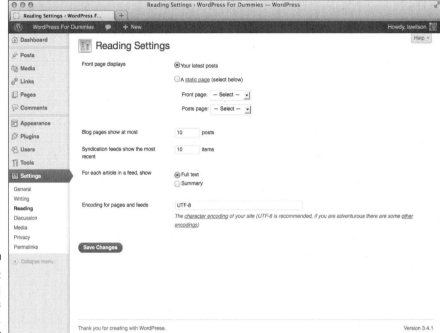

Figure 7-14:
The Reading
Settings
page.

✔ **Encoding for Pages and Feeds:** UTF-8 is the default, and recommended, character encoding for your blog. *Character encoding* is code that handles the storage and transmission of the text from your blog through the Internet connection. Your safest bet is to leave the default setting in place because UTF-8 is the most commonly accepted character encoding and supports a wide range of languages.

Be sure to click the Save Changes button when you've set all your options in the Reading Settings page to make the changes take effect.

Discussion

Discussion is the fourth link in the Settings menu; click it to open the Discussion Settings page; see Figure 7-15. The sections on this tab let you set options for handling comments and publishing posts to your blog.

The following sections cover the options available to you in the Discussion Settings page, which deals mainly with how comments and trackbacks are handled in your blog.

Figure 7-15:
The
Discussion
Settings
page.

Default Article Settings

In the Default Article Settings section, you can tell WordPress how to handle post notifications. Here are your options:

- **Attempt to Notify Any Blogs Linked To from the Article:** Select this box and your blog sends a notification (or *ping*) to any site you have linked to in your blog posts. This notification is also commonly referred to as a *trackback* (I discuss trackbacks in Chapter 2). Clear this box if you don't want these notifications to be sent.

- **Allow Link Notifications from Other Blogs (Pingbacks and Trackbacks):** By default, this box is selected and your blog is open to be notified via a ping or trackback from another blog that has linked to yours. Any trackbacks or pings sent to your blog are listed on your site in the comments section of the blog post. If you deselect this box, your blog won't accept pingbacks or trackbacks from other blogs.

- **Allow People to Post Comments on New Articles:** By default, this box is selected, and people can leave comments on your blog posts. If you deselect this box, no one can leave comments on your blog. (You can override these settings for individual articles — find more information about this in Chapter 8.)

Other Comment Settings

The Other Comment Settings tell WordPress how to handle comments:

- ✔ **Comment Author Must Fill Out Name and E-mail:** Enabled by default, this option requires all commenters on your blog to fill in the Name and E-mail field when leaving a comment. This option is very helpful in combating comment spam. (See Chapters 2 and 10 for information on comment spam.) Deselect this check box to disable this option.

- ✔ **Users Must Be Registered and Logged In to Comment:** Not enabled by default, this option allows you to accept comments on your blog from only those people who have registered and are currently logged in as a user on your blog. If the user is not logged in, he sees a message that says `You must be logged in in order to leave a comment.`

- ✔ **Automatically Close Comments on Articles Older Than *X* Days:** Select the box next to this option to tell WordPress that you want comments on older articles to be automatically closed. Fill in the text box with the number of days you want to wait before WordPress closes comments on older articles.

  This feature is a very effective anti-spam technique that many bloggers use to keep down the comment and trackback spam on their blogs.

- ✔ **Enable Threaded (Nested) Comments *X* Levels Deep:** The drop-down menu allows you to choose the level of threaded comments you'd like to have on your blog. The default is 1; you can choose up to 10 levels. Instead of all comments being displayed on your blog in chronological order (as they are by default), nesting them allows you and your readers to reply to comments within the comment itself.

- ✔ **Break Comments into Pages with *X* Top Level Comments Per Page and the Last/First Page Displayed by Default:** Fill in the text box with a number of comments you want to display on one page. This is very helpful for blogs that receive a large number of comments. It provides you with the ability to break the long string of comments into several pages, which makes those comments easier to read and helps speed up the load time of your site because the page isn't loading such a large number of comments at one time. Also, choose whether you want the first or last page displayed by default from the drop-down menu.

- ✔ **Comments Should Be Displayed with the Older/Newer Comments at the Top of Each Page:** Use the drop-down menu to select Older or Newer. Selecting Older displays the comments on your blog in the order of oldest to newest. Selecting Newer does the opposite: displays the comments on your blog in the order of newest to oldest.

E-mail Me Whenever

The two options in the E-mail Me Whenever section are enabled by default:

✔ **Anyone Posts a Comment:** This option lets you receive an e-mail notification whenever anyone leaves a comment on your blog. Deselect the box if you don't want to be notified by e-mail about every new comment.

✔ **A Comment Is Held for Moderation:** This option lets you receive an e-mail notification whenever a comment is awaiting your approval in the comment moderation queue. (See Chapter 8 for more information about the comment moderation queue.) Deselect this option if you don't want this notification.

Before a Comment Appears

The two options in the Before a Comment Appears section tell WordPress how you want WordPress to handle comments before they appear in your blog:

✔ **An Administrator Must Always Approve the Comment:** Disabled by default, this option keeps every single comment left on your blog in the moderation queue until you, the administrator, log in and approve it. Select this box to enable this option.

✔ **Comment Author Must Have a Previously Approved Comment:** Enabled by default, this option requires comments posted by all first-time commenters to be sent to the comment moderation queue for approval by the administrator of the blog. After comment authors have been approved for the first time, they remain approved for every comment thereafter. WordPress stores their e-mail addresses in the database, and any future comments that match any stored e-mails are approved automatically. This feature is another measure that WordPress has built in to combat comment spam.

Comment Moderation

In the Comment Moderation section, you can set options to specify what types of comments are held in the moderation queue to await your approval.

To prevent spammers from spamming your blog with a *ton* of links, select the Hold a Comment in the Queue If It Contains X or More Links box. The default number of links allowed is 2. Give that setting a try and if you find that you're getting lots of spam comments with multiple links, you may want to revisit this page and increase that number. Any comment with a higher number of links goes to the comment moderation area for approval.

The large text box in the Comment Moderation section lets you type keywords, URLs, e-mail addresses, and IP addresses in comments that you want to be held in the moderation queue for your approval.

Avatars and gravatars: How do they relate to WordPress?

An *avatar* is an online graphical representation of an individual. It's a small graphic icon that people use to visually represent themselves on the web in areas in which they participate in conversations, such as discussion forums and blog comments. *Gravatars* are globally recognized avatars; it's an avatar that you can take with you wherever you go. A gravatar appears alongside blog comments, blog posts, and discussion forums as long as the site you are interacting with is Gravatar enabled. In October 2007, Automattic, the core group behind the WordPress platform, purchased the Gravatar service and integrated it into WordPress so that all could enjoy and benefit from the service. Gravatars are not automatic; you need to sign up for an account with Gravatar before you can assign an avatar to yourself, via your e-mail address. Find out more about Gravatar by visiting `http://gravatar.com`.

Comment Blacklist

In this section, type a list of words, URLs, e-mail addresses, and/or IP addresses that you want to flat-out ban from your blog. Items placed here don't even make it into your comment moderation queue; the WordPress system filters them as spam. Let me just say that the words I have placed in my blacklist are not family friendly and have no place in a nice book like this.

Avatars

The final section of the Discussion Settings page is Avatars. (See the nearby sidebar "Avatars and gravatars: How do they relate to WordPress?" for information about avatars.) In this section, you can select different settings for the use and display of avatars on your site:

1. **In the Avatar Display section, decide how to display avatars on your site.**

   - *Don't Show Avatars:* Choose this option and your blog won't display avatars.

   - *Show Avatars:* Choose this option to have your blog display avatars.

2. **In the Maximum Rating section, set the rating for the avatars that do display on your site.**

   This feature works similarly to the movie rating system you're used to. You can select G, PG, R, and X ratings for the avatars that appear on your site. If your site is family friendly, you probably don't want it to display R- or X-rated avatars.

3. **Choose a default avatar in the Default Avatar section; see Figure 7-16:**

  • Mystery Man

  • Blank

  • Gravatar Logo

  • Identicon (Generated)

  • Wavatar (Generated)

  • MonsterID (Generated)

  • Retro (Generated)

4. **Click the Save Changes button.**

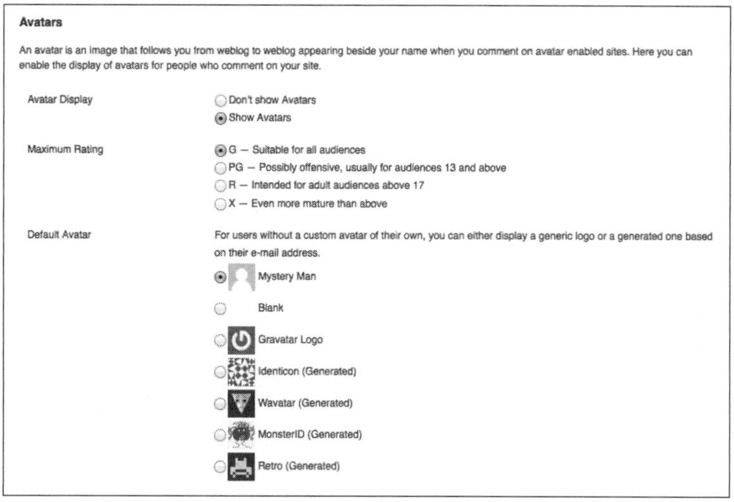

Figure 7-16:
Default avatars you can display in your blog.

Avatars appear in a couple places:

✔ **The Comments page on the Dashboard:** In Figure 7-17, the comment displays the commenter's avatar next to it.

✔ **The comments on individual blog posts to your blog:** Figure 7-18 shows a list of comments on my own personal blog.

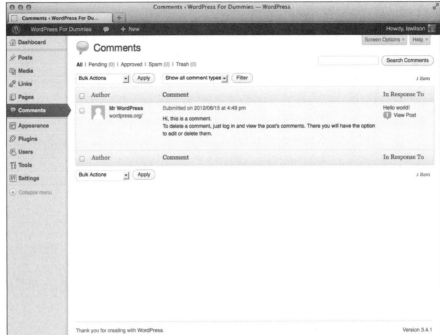

Figure 7-17:
Authors'
avatars
appear
in the
Comments
page on the
WordPress
Dashboard.

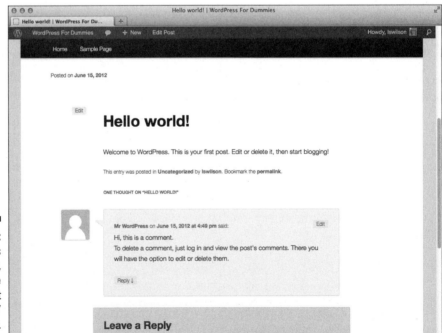

Figure 7-18:
Comments
on a post,
showing the
comment
authors'
avatars.

To enable the display of avatars in comments on your blog, the Comments Template (`comments.php`) in your active theme has to contain the code to display them. Hop on over to Chapter 12 to find out how to do that.

Click the Save Changes button after you've set all your options on the Discussion Settings page to make the changes take effect.

Media

The next link in the Settings menu is Media; click the Media link and the Media Settings page opens. See Figure 7-19.

On the Media Settings page, you can configure the options for how your image files (graphics and photos) are resized for use in your blog.

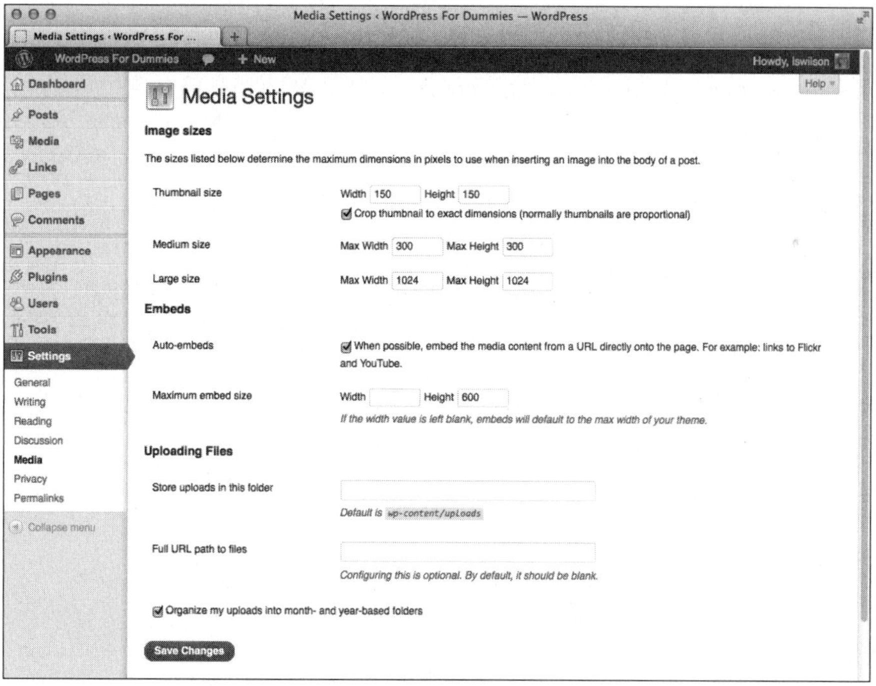

Figure 7-19:
The Media
Settings
page.

The first set of options on the Media Settings page deals with images. WordPress automatically resizes your images for you in three different sizes. The dimensions are referenced in pixels by width and then height. (For example: 150 x 150 means 150 pixels in width by 150 pixels in height.)

✔ **Thumbnail Size:** The default is 150 x 150; enter the width and height of your choice. Select the Crop Thumbnail to Exact Dimensions box to resize the thumbnail exactly to the width and height you specified. Deselect this box and WordPress resizes the image proportionally.

✔ **Medium Size:** The default is 300 x 300; enter the width and height numbers of your choice.

✔ **Large Size:** The default is 1024 x 1024; enter the width and height numbers of your choice.

The second set of options on the Media Settings page deals with embedded links and files, such as video and audio files. If you want your WordPress blog to automatically attach a hyperlink to a text-based URL that you type into your posts or pages, select the box next to When Possible, Embed the Media Content from a URL Directly onto the Page. For Example: Links to Flickr and YouTube. Activating this option means that you don't have to copy and paste the full code given to you by services such as YouTube; instead, you simply paste the hyperlink to the video, and WordPress automatically does the video embedding for you.

Next, set the width and height for the maximum size you want embedded files to be within your post and pages. Embedded items include video players and audio players that display within your post or page.

Finally, the last set of options on the Media Settings page is the Uploading Files section. Here, you tell WordPress where to store your uploaded media files:

✔ **Store Uploads in This Folder:** Type the server path to the folder on your web server where you want to store your file uploads. The default is `wp-content/uploads`. You can specify any folder you want. Just be sure that the folder you specify has permissions (`chmod`) set to 755 so that it's writeable. (See Chapter 6 for more information on setting file permissions.)

✔ **Full URL Path to Files:** You can also type the full URL path to the Uploads folder as an optional setting. (The full URL path would be something like `http://yourdomain.com/wp-content/uploads`.)

✔ **Organize My Files into Month- and Year-Based Folders:** Select this box to have WordPress organize your uploaded files in folders by month and by year. Files you upload in September 2012, for example, would be in the following folder: `/wp-content/uploads/2012/09/`. Likewise, files you upload in December 2012 would be in `/wp-content/uploads/2012/12/`.

This box is selected by default; deselect it if you don't want WordPress to organize your files by month and year.

Be sure to click the Save Changes button to save your configurations!

In Chapter 9, I go into much greater detail on how to insert images into your WordPress posts and pages.

Privacy

The next Settings menu option is Privacy; click it to display the Privacy Settings page.

This page contains only two options, both of which concern visibility on your blog:

- ✔ **Allow Search Engines to Index This Site.** This option is the default setting and means that you are freely allowing search engines to visit your blog and to list you in their search results, and letting your site be indexed in blog archive services such as Technorati.

- ✔ **Ask Search Engines Not to Index This Site.** If you are one of those rare bloggers who *doesn't* want that type of exposure for your blog, but you do want to let normal visitors (read: no search engines) see your blog, select this option.

Generally, you want search engines to be able to find your blog. However, if you have special circumstances, you may want to enforce your privacy settings. I would block search engines, for example, because the site I'm using for the figures in this book is one that I don't want search engines to find. On the main Dashboard, in the Right Now box, is a note that says `Search Engines Blocked`. This note exists only when you have your privacy settings set to block search engines. When you have Privacy On, search engines and other content bots can't find your website.

Be sure to click the Save Changes button after you set all your options on the Privacy Settings page to make the changes take effect.

Permalinks

The next link on the Settings menu is Permalinks. Clicking this link loads the Permalink Settings page. See Figure 7-20.

Each of the posts you create on your blog has a unique URL called a *permalink,* which is a permanent link (URL) for all your blog posts, pages, and archives. I cover permalinks extensively in Chapter 8 by explaining what they are, how you can use them, and how you set the options in this page.

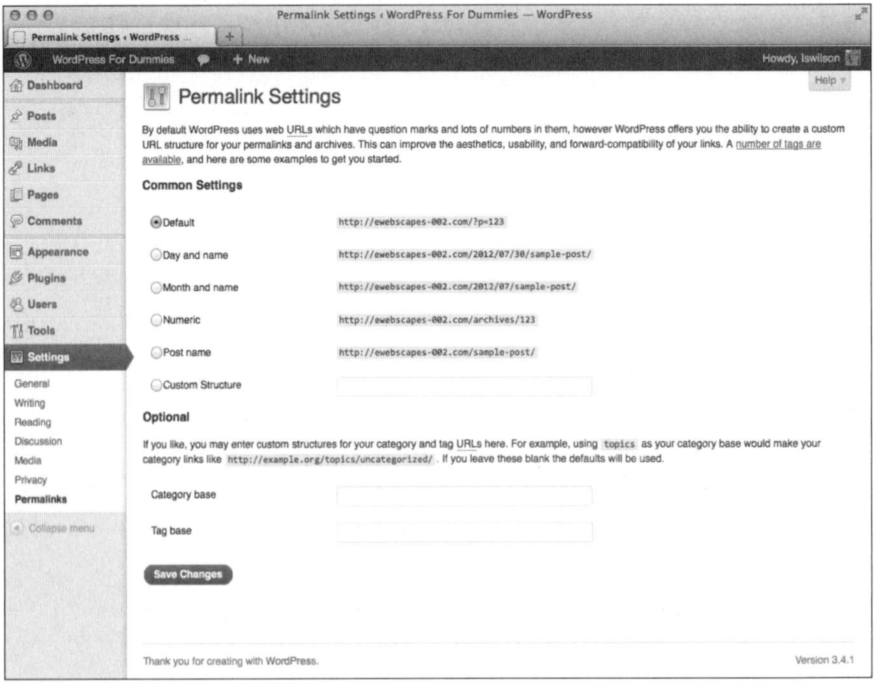

Figure 7-20:
The
Permalink
Settings
page.

Creating Your Personal Profile

The next place to visit to really personalize your blog is your profile page on your WordPress Dashboard.

To access your profile page, click the Your Profile link in the Users menu. You're taken to the Profile page. See Figure 7-21.

Here are the settings on this page:

✔ **Personal Options:** The Personal Options section is where you can set four preferences for your blog:

- *Visual Editor:* This selection enables you to use the Visual Editor when writing your posts. The Visual Editor gives you the formatting options you find in the Write Post page (discussed in detail in Chapter 8). By default, the Visual Editor is on. To turn it off, select the Disable the Visual Editor When Writing check box.

- *Admin Color Scheme:* These options set the colors on your Dashboard. The default is the Gray color scheme; you can also select a more colorful Blue color scheme for your Dashboard display.

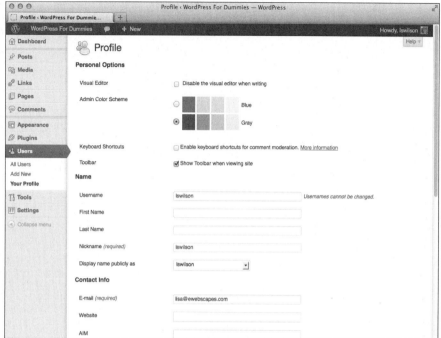

Figure 7-21:
Establish
your profile
details here.

- *Keyboard Shortcuts:* This enables you to use keyboard shortcuts for comment moderation. To learn more about keyboard short-cuts, click the More Information link; you're taken to the Keyboard Shortcuts page (`http://codex.wordpress.org/Keyboard_Shortcuts`) in the WordPress Codex.

- *Toolbar:* The Toolbar displays at the top of your WordPress web-site, but it displays only to the user who is logged in to the site; it cannot be seen by regular viewers of your website. The Toolbar contains helpful links that allow you to get to different sections of your Dashboard quickly and easily with a single click. You can choose to display the Toolbar while you are viewing your site or the Dashboard, or both.

✔ **Name:** This section is where you can input personal information such as your first name, last name, and nickname, and specify how you want your name to be displayed publicly. Fill in the text boxes with the requested information and choose your display name from the drop-down list.

✔ **Contact Info:** In this section, you provide your e-mail address and other contact information to tell your visitors who you are and where they may contact you. Aside from e-mail, you can provide your ID for various Internet chat programs such as Yahoo! IM, AIM (AOL Instant Messenger), and Jabber/Google Talk.

Note that your e-mail address is the only required entry here. This address is the one WordPress uses to notify you when you have new comments or new user registrations on your blog. Make sure to use a real e-mail address so that you get these notifications.

✔ **About Yourself:** This section is where you can provide a little bio about yourself and change the password for your blog.

When your profile is published to your website, it not only can be viewed by anyone, but also gets picked up by search engines such as Yahoo! and Google. Always be careful with the information in your profile. Think hard about the information you want to share with the rest of the world!

- *Biographical Info:* Type a short bio in the Biographical Info text box. This information can be shown publicly if you are using a theme that displays your bio, so be creative!

- *New Password:* When you want to change the password for your blog, type your new password in the first text box in the New Password section. To confirm your new password, type it again in the second text box.

Directly below the two text boxes is a little password helper. WordPress helps you create a secure password. It alerts you if the password you've chosen is too short or not secure enough by calling it *Very Weak, Weak,* or *Medium*. When creating a new password, use a combination of letters, numbers, and symbols to make it hard for anyone to guess (for example, `aty89!#4j`). When you create a password that WordPress thinks is a good one, it lets you know by calling it *Strong*.

Change your password frequently. I can't recommend this practice strongly enough. Some people on the Internet make it their business to attempt to hijack blogs for their own malicious purposes. If you change your password monthly, you lower your risk by keeping hackers guessing.

When you finish setting all the options on the Profile page, don't forget to click the Update Profile button to save your changes.

Setting Your Blog's Format

In addition to setting your personal settings on the Dashboard, you can manage the day-to-day maintenance of your blog. This next section takes you through the links to these sections in the navigation menu, directly underneath the Dashboard link.

Posts

Hover over the Posts menu and a submenu drops down with four links: All Posts, Add New, Categories, and Tags. Each link gives you the tools you need to publish content to your blog:

- ✔ **All Posts:** This link opens the Posts page where you see a listing of all the saved posts you've written on your blog. On this page, you can search for posts by date, category, or keyword. You can view all posts, only posts that have been published, or just posts that have been saved but not yet published (*drafts*). You can also edit and delete posts from this page. Check out Chapter 8 for more information on editing posts on your blog.

- ✔ **Add New:** This link opens the Add New Post page, which is where you compose your blog posts, set the options for each post (such as assigning a post to a category, or making it a private or public post), and publish the post to your blog. You can find more information on posts, post options, and publishing in Chapter 8.

  You can also get to the Add New Post page by clicking the Posts menu.

- ✔ **Categories:** This link opens the Categories page where you can view, edit, add, and delete categories on your blog. Find more information on categories in Chapter 8.

- ✔ **Tags:** This link opens the Tags page on your WordPress Dashboard where you can view, add, edit, and delete tags on your blog. Chapter 8 provides you with more information about what tags are and why you use them on your blog.

Media

Click the Media menu to expand the submenu of links for this section:

- ✔ **Library:** This link opens the Media Library page. On this page, you view, search, and manage all the media files you've ever uploaded to your WordPress blog.

- ✔ **Add New:** This link opens the Upload New Media page where you can use the built-in uploader to transfer media files from your computer to the media directory in WordPress. Chapter 9 takes you through the details of how to upload images, videos, audio, and other media files (such as Microsoft Word or PowerPoint documents) using the WordPress upload feature.

  You can also get to the Upload New Media page by clicking the Media menu.

Links

The next menu header in the navigation menu is Links. Expand the Links sub-menu by hovering over the Links menu:

- ✔ **All Links:** This link opens the Links page, where you can view, search, edit, and delete existing links in your WordPress blog. Chapter 8 gives you detailed information about links, link lists, and blogrolls.

- ✔ **Add New:** This link opens the Add New Link page where you can add new links to your link lists. (You can find more information about creating and managing link lists in Chapter 8.)

  You can also get to the Add New Link page by clicking the Links menu.

- ✔ **Link Categories:** This link opens the Link Categories page where you can add new, view, edit, and delete existing link categories (see Chapter 8).

Pages

People use this feature to create pages on their sites such as an About Me or Contact Me page. Flip to Chapter 8 for more information on pages. Click the Pages menu to reveal the submenu links:

- ✔ **All Pages:** This link opens the Pages page where you have the ability to search, view, edit, and delete pages in your WordPress blog.

- ✔ **Add New:** This link opens the Add New Page page, where you can compose, save, and publish a new page on your blog. Table 7-2 describes the difference between a post and a page — it's subtle, but posts and pages are very different from one another!

  You can also get to the Add New Page page by clicking the Pages menu.

Table 7-2	The Differences between a Post and a Page	
WordPress Options	*Page*	*Post*
Appears in blog post listings	No	Yes
Appears as a static page	Yes	No
Appears in category archives	No	Yes
Appears in monthly archives	No	Yes
Appears in Recent Posts listings	No	Yes
Appears in site RSS feed	No	Yes
Appears in search results	Yes	Yes

Comments

The Comments menu doesn't have a submenu of links. You simply click the Comments menu title to open the Comments page, where WordPress gives you the options to view:

- ✔ **All:** Shows all comments that currently exist on your blog. This includes approved, pending, and spam comments.

- ✔ **Pending:** Shows comments that are not yet approved by you but are pending in the moderation queue.

- ✔ **Approved:** Shows all comments that have been previously approved by you.

- ✔ **Spam:** Shows all the comments that are marked as spam.

- ✔ **Trash:** Shows comments that you have marked as Trash, but have not yet been deleted permanently from your blog.

You can find information in Chapter 2 about the purpose of comments. In Chapter 8, I give you details on how to use the Manage Comments section of your WordPress Dashboard.

Appearance

When you click the Appearance menu in the navigation menu, a submenu drops down with the following links to click:

- ✔ **Themes:** This link opens the Manage Themes page, where you can manage the themes available on your blog. Check out Chapter 11 to learn about using themes on your WordPress blog and how to manage those themes on this page.

- ✔ **Widgets:** The Widgets page allows you to add, delete, edit, and manage the widgets you use on your blog.

- ✔ **Menus:** This link opens the Menus page, where you can build navigation menus to display on your site. Chapter 13 provides information on creating menus using this feature.

- ✔ **Theme Options:** Some themes have an Options page where you can configure different settings for the theme, such as the default Twenty Eleven theme. The Theme Options link appears under the Appearance menu only if the theme you're currently using has options available for configuration; if it doesn't, you won't see the Theme Options link here.

✔ **Header:** In the Your Header Image page you can upload an image to use in the header (or top) of your WordPress blog; however, this menu item and page exist only if you have the Twenty Eleven theme activated, or any other theme that supports the Custom Header feature (more about that in Chapter 13). The Twenty Eleven theme is activated by default on all new WordPress blogs, which is why I've included this menu item in this list. Not all WordPress themes use the Custom Header feature, so you don't see this menu item if your theme doesn't take advantage of that feature.

✔ **Background:** This link opens the Custom Background page, where you can upload an image to use as the background of your WordPress blog design; as with the Custom Header option above, the Custom Background option exists in the Appearance menu only if you have the default Twenty Eleven theme activated, or any other theme that supports the Custom Background feature (more about that in Chapter 13). Not all WordPress themes use the Custom Background feature.

✔ **Editor:** This link opens the Theme Editor page, where you can edit your theme templates. Chapters 11, 12, and 13 have extensive information on themes and templates.

Uploading header and background images helps you to individualize the visual design of your blog or website. You can find more information on tweaking and customizing your WordPress theme in Chapter 13. Chapter 11 gives you a great deal of information about how to use WordPress themes (including where to find, install, and activate them in your WordPress blog) as well as detailed information on using WordPress widgets to display the content you want.

Part V provides information about WordPress themes and templates. You can dig deep into WordPress template tags and tweak an existing WordPress theme by using Cascading Style Sheets (CSS) to customize your theme a bit more to your liking.

Plugins

The next menu in the navigation menu is Plugins. Click the Plugins menu to expand the submenu of links:

✔ **Installed Plugins:** This link opens the Plugins page where you can view all the plugins currently installed on your blog. On this page, you also have the ability to activate, deactivate, and delete plugins on your blog (see Chapter 10).

✔ **Add New:** This link opens the Install Plugins page, where you can search for plugins from the official WordPress Plugin Directory by keyword, author, or tag. You can also install plugins directly to your blog from the WordPress Plugin Directory — you find out all about this exciting feature in Chapter 10!

✔ **Editor:** The Edit Plugins page allows you to edit the plugin files in a text editor. I very strongly advise against editing plugin files unless you know exactly what you're doing. (***Read:*** You are familiar with PHP and WordPress functions.) Head over to Chapter 10 to read more information on editing plugin files.

Users

The Users menu has three links:

✔ **All Users:** Click this link to go to the Users page where you can view, edit, and delete users on your WordPress blog. Each user has a unique login name and password, as well as an e-mail address assigned to her account. You can view and edit a user's information on the Users page.

✔ **Add New:** This link opens the Add New User page where you can add new users to your WordPress blog. Simply type the user's username, first name, last name, e-mail (required), website, and a password into the fields provided and click the Add User button. You can also select whether you want WordPress to send login information to the new user by e-mail. If you like, you can also assign a new role for the new user. Turn to the earlier section, "General," for more info about user roles.

✔ **Your Profile:** Turn to the "Creating Your Personal Profile" section, earlier in this chapter, for more information about creating a profile page.

Tools

The last menu item in the navigation menu (and subsequently in this chapter!) is Tools. Click the Tools menu to drop down the submenu of links that includes:

✔ **Available Tools:** WordPress comes packaged with two extra features that you can use on your blog. They are Press This and Category/Tag Conversion.

✔ **Import:** WordPress gives you the ability to import from a different blog platform. This feature is covered in depth in the Appendix.

✔ **Export:** WordPress also allows you to export your content from WordPress so that you can import it into a different platform or another WordPress blog. This information is also covered in the Appendix.

Chapter 8

Establishing Your Blog Routine

WordPress is a powerful publishing tool, especially when you use the full range of options available. With the basic settings configured (which I show you how to do in Chapter 7), now is the time to go forth and blog! You can skip to the "Blog It!: Writing Your First Entry" section in this chapter and jump right in to creating new posts for your blog. Or you can stay right here and discover some of the options you can set to make your blog a bit more organized and logical from the get-go.

A blog can become unwieldy and disorganized, requiring you to revisit these next few features sometime in the near future so that you can get the beast under control. So why not do a little planning and get the work over with now? I promise it won't take that long, and you'll thank me for it later.

Staying on Topic with Categories

In WordPress, a *category* is what you determine to be the main topic of a blog post. Through the use of categories, you can file your blog posts into topics by subject. To improve your readers' experiences in navigating through your blog, WordPress organizes posts by the categories you assign to them. Visitors can click the categories they're interested in to see the blog posts you've written on those particular topics. You should know ahead of time that the list of categories you set up is displayed on your blog in a few different places, including the following:

✔ **Body of the post:** In most WordPress themes, you see the title followed by a statement such as Filed In: *Category 1, Category 2.* The reader can click the category name to go to a page that lists all the posts you've made in that particular category. You can assign a single post to more than one category.

✔ **Sidebar of your blog theme:** You can place a full list of category titles in the sidebar. A reader can click any category and arrive at a page on your site that lists the posts you've made within that particular category.

Subcategories (also known as *category children*) can further refine the main category topic by listing specific topics related to the main (parent) category. On your WordPress Dashboard, on the Manage Categories page, subcategories are listed directly below the main category. Here's an example:

Books I Enjoy (main category)

Fiction (subcategory)

Nonfiction (subcategory)

Trashy romance (subcategory)

Biographies (subcategory)

For Dummies (subcategory)

Changing the name of a category

Upon installation, WordPress gives you one default category to get you started called *Uncategorized.* (See the Categories page shown in Figure 8-1). That category name is pretty generic, so you'll definitely want to change it to one that's more specific to you. (On my blog, I changed it to Life in General. Although that name's still a bit on the generic side, it doesn't sound quite so . . . well, uncategorized.)

The default category also serves as a kind of fail-safe. If you publish a post to your blog and don't assign that post to a category, the post is automatically assigned to the default category, no matter what you name the category.

So how do you change the name of that default category? When you're logged in to your WordPress Dashboard, just follow these steps:

1. Click the Categories link in the Posts Dashboard menu.

The Categories page opens, containing all the tools you need to set up and edit category titles for your blog.

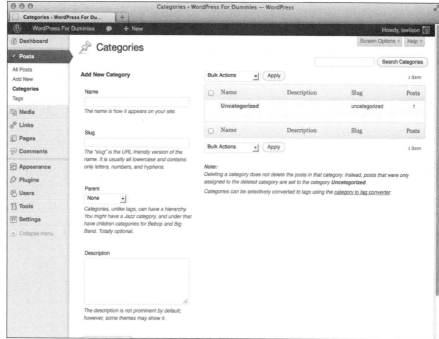

Figure 8-1:
The
Categories
page of a
brand-new
blog shows
the default
Uncategor-
ized
category.

2. **Click the title of the category you would like to edit.**

   To change the Uncategorized category, click the word Uncategorized, and you go to the Edit Category page. See Figure 8-2.

3. **Type the new name for the category in the Name text box.**

4. **Type the new slug in the Slug text box.**

   The term *slug* refers to the word(s) used in the web address for the specific category. For example, the Books category has a web address of `http://yourdomain.com/category/books`; if you change the Slug to *Books I Like,* the web address is `http://yourdomain.com/category/books-i-like`. (WordPress automatically inserts a dash between the slug words in the web address.)

5. **Choose a parent category from the Parent drop-down menu.**

   If you want this category to be a main category, not a subcategory, choose None.

6. **(Optional) Type a description of the category in the Description text box.**

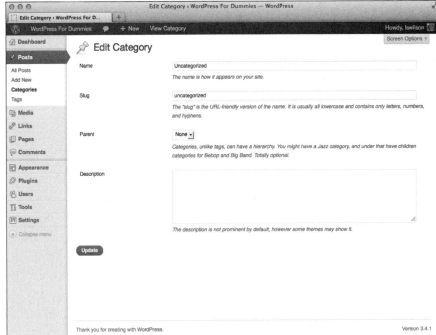

Figure 8-2:
Editing a
category in
WordPress
on the Edit
Category
page.

Use this description to remind yourself what your category is about. Some WordPress themes display the category description right on your site, too, which can be helpful for your visitors. (See Chapter 12 for more about themes.) You'll know if your theme is coded in this way if your site displays the category description on the category page(s).

7. Click the Update button.

The information you just edited is saved, and the Categories page reloads, showing your new category name.

If you want to edit a category's name only, you can click the Quick Edit link underneath the name on the Category page. Then you can do a quick name edit without having to load the Edit Category page.

Creating new categories and deleting others

Today, tomorrow, next month, next year — as your blog grows in size and age, you'll continue adding new categories to further define and archive the history of your blog posts. You aren't limited in the number of categories and subcategories you can create in your blog.

Creating a new category is as easy as following these steps:

1. **Click the Categories link in the Posts Dashboard menu.**

   The Categories page opens.

2. **The left side of the Categories page displays the Add New Category section.**

   See Figure 8-3.

3. **Type the name of your new category in the Name text box.**

   Suppose that you want to create a category in which you file all your posts about the books you read. In the Name text box, type something like **Books I Enjoy**.

4. **Type a name in the Slug text box.**

   The slug creates the link to the category page that lists all the posts you've made in this category. If you leave this field blank, WordPress automatically creates a slug based on the category name. If the category is Books I Enjoy, WordPress automatically creates a category slug like this: `http://yourdomain.com/category/books-i-enjoy`. If you want to shorten it, however, you can! Type **books** in the Category Slug text box, and the link to the category becomes this: `http://your domain.com/category/books`.

Add New Category

Name

_____

The name is how it appears on your site.

Slug

_____

The "slug" is the URL-friendly version of the name. It is usually all lowercase and contains only letters, numbers, and hyphens.

Parent

[None ▼]

Categories, unlike tags, can have a hierarchy. You might have a Jazz category, and under that have children categories for Bebop and Big Band. Totally optional.

Description

[   ]

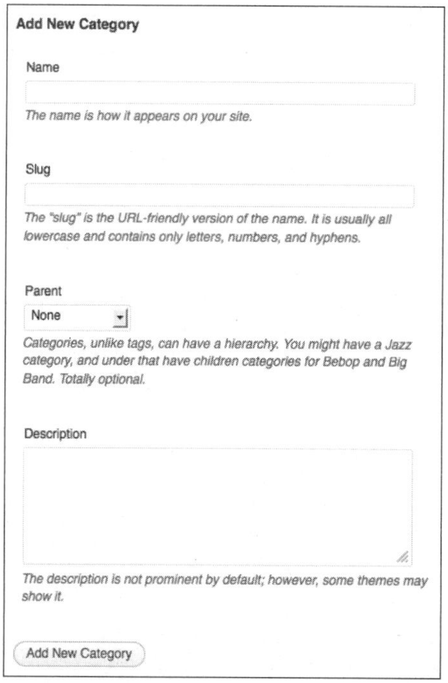

Figure 8-3: Create a new category on your blog.

The description is not prominent by default; however, some themes may show it.

(Add New Category)

5. **Choose the category's parent from the Parent drop-down menu.**

   Choose None if you want this new category to be a parent (or top-level) category. If you'd like this category to be a subcategory of another category, choose the category you want to be the parent of this one.

6. **(Optional) Type a description of the category in the Description text box.**

   Some WordPress templates are set up to display the category description directly beneath the category name (see Chapter 12). Providing a description helps you to further define the category intent for your readers. The description can be as short or as long as you like.

7. **Click the Add New Category button.**

   That's it! You've added a new category to your blog. Armed with this information, you can add an unlimited number of categories to your blog.

You can delete a category on your blog by hovering your mouse pointer over the title of the category you want to delete. Then click the Delete link that appears below the category title.

Deleting a category doesn't delete the posts and links in that category. Instead, posts in the deleted category are assigned to the Uncategorized category (or whatever you've named the default category).

If you have an established WordPress blog with categories already created, you can convert some or all of your categories to tags. To do so, look for the Category to Tag Converter link on the right side of the Categories page on your WordPress Dashboard. Click it to convert your categories to tags. (See the nearby sidebar "What are tags, and how/why do I use them?" for more information on tags.)

Link Lists: Sharing Your Favorite Sites

A *link list,* commonly referred to as a *blogroll,* is a list of links to other websites and blogs that you've collected and want to share with your readers. The link list is displayed in your blog, usually in the sidebar, through the use of widgets, or on a dedicated page of links, if your theme has a links page template (see Chapter 12 to find out how to create a template).

You can use a link list in various ways:

- ✔ Share links with other blogs that have linked to your blog
- ✔ Provide additional resources that you think your readers will find useful
- ✔ Provide links to other sites you own

What are tags, and how/why do I use them?

Tags are not to be confused with categories, but a lot of people do confuse them. *Tags* are clickable, comma-separated keywords that help you microcategorize a post by defining the topics in it. In contrast to WordPress categories, tags do not have a hierarchy; there are no parent tags and child tags. If you write a post about your dog, for example, you can put that post in the Pets category — but you can also add some specific tags that let you get a whole lot more specific, such as `poodle` or `small dogs`. If someone clicks your `poodle` tag, he finds all the posts you've ever made that contain the `poodle` tag.

Another reason to use tags: Search-engine spiders harvest tags when they crawl your site, so tags help other people find your site when they search for specific words.

You can manage your tags on the WordPress Dashboard by clicking the Tags link on the Posts menu. The Tags page opens where you can view, edit, delete, and add new tags.

Organizing your links

As with posts, you can create multiple categories for your links on the WordPress Dashboard if you want to have more than one link list. Sometimes, having a large list of links below the Blogroll heading is just too generic, and you may want to display groups of links with different headings that further define them.

By default, WordPress provides one link category called Blogroll. You can keep this name or change it in the same way that you change a post category name (see "Changing the name of a category," earlier in this chapter). Just click the name of the category and edit the details as you need to.

You can define your links by creating link categories on the Dashboard and then assigning links to the appropriate categories. To create link categories, follow these steps:

1. **Click the Link Categories link in the Links menu on the Dashboard.**

   The Link Categories page opens, as shown in Figure 8-4. The left side of the Link Categories page displays the Add New Link Category section.

2. **Type the name of the link category in the Name text box.**

3. **Type the slug of the link category in the Slug text box.**

   This entry is the same as the category slug described previously in the "Changing the name of a category" section in this chapter.

4. **(Optional) Type a description of the link category in the Description text box.**

Figure 8-4:
Add, edit, or
delete a link
category
on the Link
Categories
page.

Providing a description helps you further define the link category intent for your readers. The description can be as short or as long as you like. Some WordPress themes are set up to display the link category description directly beneath the link category name.

5. **Click the Add New Link Category button.**

The Link Categories page refreshes and displays your new link category.

Revisit the Link Categories page anytime you want to add, edit, or delete a link category. To edit or delete a link category, follow the same steps as in the previous section for post categories. You can create an unlimited number of link categories to sort your link lists by topics. (I know one blogger who has 50 categories for his links.)

In Chapter 5, I show you how to display your link lists by using WordPress widgets; and in Chapter 12, I provide information about different ways you can display your link lists by using template tags.

Adding new links

You've created your link categories; now you just need to add some new links! To add a new link, follow these steps:

1. **Click the Add New link in the Links Dashboard menu.**

   The Add New Link page opens, as shown in Figure 8-5.

2. **Type the name of the link in the Name text box.**

   This is the actual name of the site that you're adding to your link list.

3. **Type the URL of the link in the Web Address text box.**

   This is the destination you want your visitors to go to when they click the name of the site. Don't forget to include the `http://` part of the web address; for example, `http://lisasabin-wilson.com`.

4. **(Optional) Type a description of the site in the Description text box.**

   Providing a description helps further define the site for your readers. Some WordPress templates are coded to display the link description directly below the link name through the use of a specific WordPress template tag.

5. **(Optional) Select a category.**

   Assign your new link to a category by selecting the box to the left of the category you've chosen in the Categories module. If you don't select a category for your new link, it's automatically assigned to the default category. Figure 8-6 shows the list of link categories I have in my blog.

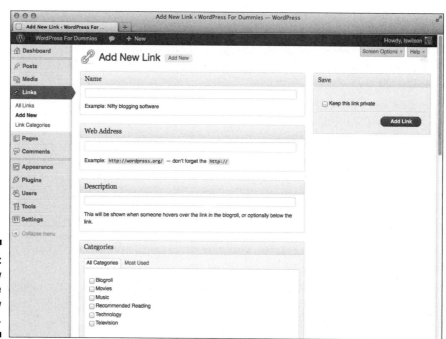

Figure 8-5:
Add a new link with the Add New Link page.

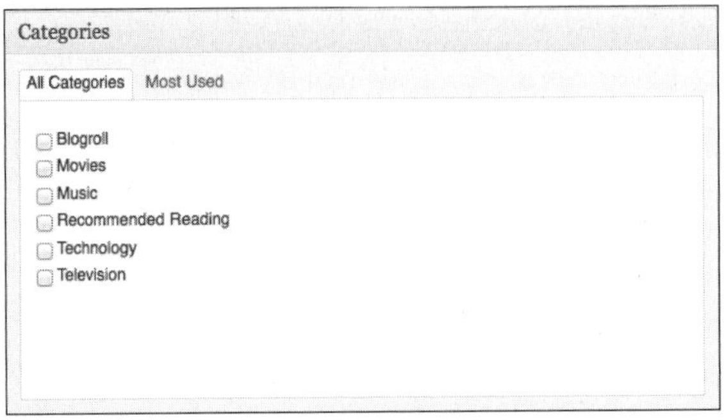

Figure 8-6:
You can
assign a
link to an
existing
category or
add a new
category
here.

Categories
All Categories   Most Used
☐ Blogroll
☐ Movies
☐ Music
☐ Recommended Reading
☐ Technology
☐ Television

If you find that the Link Category is not an option that you use regularly, you can collapse (close) this module by clicking anywhere in the Categories title bar. You can also move the Categories module on the Add New Link page by dragging and dropping it to a new location.

6. (Optional) Select a target for your new link.

Select one of the following radio buttons in the Target section:

- *_blank:* Loads the link in a new browser window
- *_top:* Loads the link in the top frame (if your site is designed with frames)
- *_none:* Loads the link in the same browser window

The third option — None — is my preference and recommendation. I like to let my visitors decide whether they want a bunch of new browser windows opening every time they click a link on my site.

You can reposition the Target module by dragging and dropping it to a new location on the Add New Link page. You can also collapse this module.

7. Set the Link Relationship (XFN) options (Optional).

XFN stands for XHTML Friends Network and allows you to indicate the relationship you have with the people you're linking to by defining how you know, or are associated with, them. Table 8-1 lists the different relationships you can assign to your links. Link Relationship (XFN) is kind of a silly bookmark-type assignment that indicates how well you know the person whose site or blog you're linking to by defining your relationship with her. You can find more information on XFN at `http://gmpg.org/xfn`.

You can reposition the Link Relationship module by dragging and dropping it to a new location on the Add New Link page. You can also collapse (close) this module.

Table 8-1	Link Relationships Defined
Link Relationship	**Description**
Identity	Select this box if the link is to a website you own.
Friendship	Select the option (Contact, Acquaintance, Friend, or None) that most closely identifies the friendship, if any.
Physical	Select this box if you've met the person you're linking to face to face. Sharing pictures over the Internet doesn't count; this selection identifies a person you've physically met.
Professional	Select one of these boxes if the person you're linking to is a co-worker or colleague.
Geographical	Select Co-Resident if the person you're linking to lives with you, or choose Neighbor or None, depending on which option applies to your relationship with the person you're linking to.
Family	If the blogger you're linking to is a family member, select the option that tells how the person is related to you.
Romantic	Select the option that applies to the type of romantic relationship, if any, you have with the person you're linking to. Do you have a crush on him? Is she your creative muse or someone you consider to be a sweetheart?

8. **Set the advanced options for your new link. See Figure 8-7.**

   You have four options in the Advanced module:

   - *Image Address:* Type the URL of the picture that you want to appear next to the link in your link list. This option associates an image with the link. To use it, you need to know the direct URL to the image source (such as `http://yourdomain.com/images/image.jpg`).

   To find the URL for an image displayed on a website, right-click the image and choose Properties from the shortcut menu. Copy and paste all the text from the Address (URL) field to the Image Address text box.

   - *RSS Address:* Add the site's RSS feed alongside the link that appears on your site. (Not all WordPress themes accommodate this feature.)

   To find the RSS URL of the site you're linking to, visit that site and locate the RSS link. (It's usually listed in the sidebar or footer of the site.) Right-click the link, and from the shortcut menu, choose Copy Shortcut (in Internet Explorer) or Copy Link Location (in Firefox). Then, in WordPress, paste the link in the RSS Address field.

- *Notes:* Type your notes in the Notes field. These notes aren't displayed on your site, so feel free to enter whatever notes you need to further define the details of this link. A month from now, you may not remember who this person is or why you linked to her, so here is where you can add notes to remind yourself.

- *Rating:* Use the Rating drop-down menu to rate the link from 0–10, 0 being the worst and 10 being the best. Some WordPress themes display your link list in the order in which you've rated your links, from best to worst.

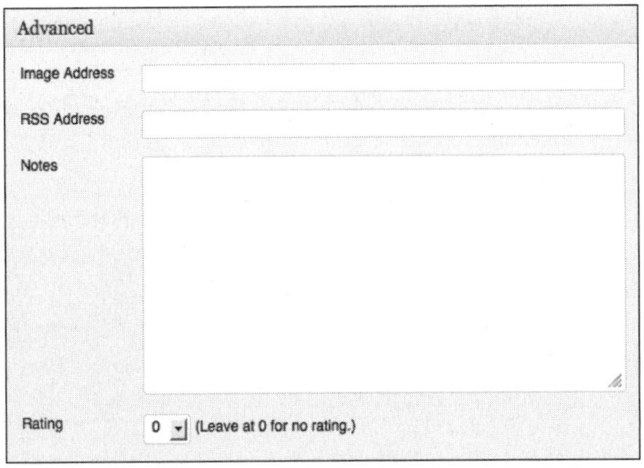

Figure 8-7:
Advanced
link options
help you
further
manage the
individual
links in your
blogroll.

You can reposition the Advanced module by dragging and dropping it to a new location on the Add New Link page. You can also collapse (close) this module.

9. **To save your changes, scroll up to the top of the Add New Links page and click the Add Link button. Choose whether to make the link public or private.**

   To keep the link private, select the Keep This Link Private check box and no one except you can see the link. If you want the link to be publicly displayed on your blog, leave that box deselected.

   You can reposition the Save module by dragging and dropping it to a new location on the Add New Link page. You can also collapse (close) this module.

   A blank Add New Links page opens, ready for you to add another new link!

Editing existing links

You can edit the links in your blog by clicking the All Links on the Links menu; the Links page opens and displays a list of all links on your Dashboard.

When you first view the Links page, some links are already assigned to your blog. By default, WordPress provides seven links in your link list. These links go to some helpful websites that contain information and resources for the WordPress software. You can delete these links, but I recommend saving them for future reference.

Here's what you can do with your links:

- ✔ **Edit an existing link:** Click the name of the link you'd like to edit. The Edit Link page opens. Edit the fields you need to change; click the Update Link button at the top right of the page.

- ✔ **Sort the links:** You can sort by Link ID, Name, Address, or Rating by using the Order by Name drop-down menu. Likewise you can sort your links by category by using the View All Categories drop-down menu and selecting the Link Category you'd like to filter your links by.

- ✔ **Search for specific links using keywords and phrases:** Enter your keyword in the text box at the top-right side of the Links page and click the Search Links button. If any links match the keywords and/or phrase you typed, they display on the page.

Examining a Blog Post's Address: Permalinks

Each WordPress blog post is assigned its own web page, and the address (or URL) of that page is called a *permalink*. Posts that you see in WordPress blogs usually put their permalinks in any of four areas:

- ✔ The title of the blog post
- ✔ The Comments link below the post
- ✔ A separate permalink that appears (in most themes) below the post
- ✔ The titles of posts appearing in a Recent Posts sidebar

Permalinks are meant to be permanent links to your blog posts (which is where the *perma* part of that word comes from, in case you're wondering). Other bloggers can use a post permalink to refer to that particular blog post. So ideally, the permalink of a post never changes. WordPress creates the permalink automatically when you publish a new post.

By default, a blog-post permalink in WordPress looks like this:

```
http://yourdomain.com/?p=100/
```

The p stands for *post,* and 100 is the ID assigned to the individual post. You can leave the permalinks in this format if you don't mind letting WordPress associate each post with an ID number.

WordPress, however, lets you take your permalinks to the beauty salon for a bit of a makeover. I'll bet you didn't know that permalinks could be pretty, did you? They certainly can. Allow me to explain.

Making your post links pretty

Pretty permalinks are links that are more pleasing to the eye than standard links and, ultimately, more pleasing to search-engine spiders. (See Bonus Chapter 1, on the companion website for this book, for an explanation of why search engines like pretty permalinks.) Pretty permalinks look something like this:

```
http://yourdomain.com/2013/10/31/pretty-permalinks/
```

Break down that URL and you see the date when the post was made, in year/month/day format. You also see the topic of the post.

To choose how your permalinks look, click Permalinks in the Settings menu. The Permalink Settings page opens. See Figure 8-8.

On this page, you find several options for creating permalinks:

- **Default** (ugly permalinks): WordPress assigns an ID number to each blog post and creates the URL in this format: http://yourdomain.com/?p=100.

- **Day and Name** (pretty permalinks): For each post, WordPress generates a permalink URL that includes the year, month, day, and post slug/title: http://yourdomain.com/2013/10/31/sample-post/.

- **Month and Name** (also pretty permalinks): For each post, WordPress generates a permalink URL that includes the year, month, and post slug/title: http://yourdomain.com/2013/10/sample-post/.

- **Numeric** (not so pretty): WordPress assigns a numerical value to the permalink. The URL is created in this format: http://yourdomain.com/archives/123.

✔ **Post Name (my preferred):** WordPress takes the title of your post or page and generates the permalink URL from those words. For example, the name of the page that contains my bibliography of books is called simply *Books;* therefore, with this permalink structure, WordPress creates the permalink URL: `http://lisasabin-wilson.com/books`. Likewise, a post titled *WordPress is Awesome* gets a permalink URL like this: `http://lisasabin-wilson.com/wordpress-is-awesome`.

✔ **Custom Structure:** WordPress creates permalinks in the format you choose. You can create a custom permalink structure by using tags or variables, as I discuss in the next section.

To create a pretty-permalink structure, select the Post Name radio button; then click the Save Changes button at the bottom of the page.

Customizing your permalinks

A *custom permalink structure* is one that lets you define which variables you want to see in your permalinks by using the tags in Table 8-2.

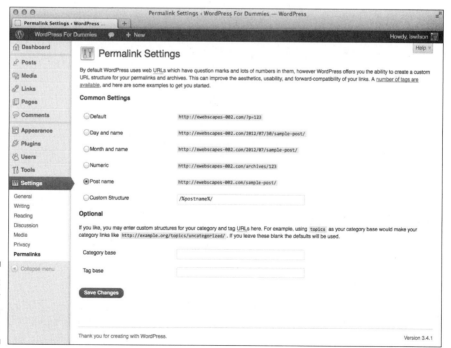

Figure 8-8:
Make your permalinks pretty.

Table 8-2	Custom Permalinks
Permalink Tag	*Results*
`%year%`	4-digit year (such as `2013`)
`%monthnum%`	2-digit month (such as `02` for February)
`%day%`	2-digit day (such as `30`)
`%hour%`	2-digit hour of the day (such as `15` for 3:00 p.m.)
`%minute%`	2-digit minute (such as `45`)
`%second%`	2-digit second (such as `10`)
`%postname%`	Text — usually, the post name — separated by hyphens (such as `making-pretty-permalinks`)
`%post_id%`	The unique numerical ID of the post (such as `344`)
`%category%`	The text of the category name that you filed the post in (such as `books-i-read`)
`%author%`	The text of the post author's name (such as `lisa-sabin-wilson`)

If you want your permalink to show the year, month, day, category, and post name, select the Custom Structure radio button in the Permalink Settings page and type the following tags in the Custom Structure text box:

```
/%year%/%monthnum%/%day%/%category%/%postname%/
```

Under this permalink format, the link for a post made on October 31, 2013, called WordPress For Dummies and filed in the Books I Read category, would look like this:

```
http://yourdomain.com/2013/10/31/books-i-read/wordpress-for-dummies/
```

Be sure to include the slashes (/) before tags, between tags, and at the very end of the string of tags. This format ensures that WordPress creates correct, working permalinks by using the correct `rewrite` rules located in the `.htaccess` file for your site. (See the following section for more information on `rewrite` rules and `.htaccess` files.)

Changing the structure of your permalinks in the future affects the permalinks for all the posts on your blog — new and old. Keep this fact in mind if you ever decide to change the permalink structure. An especially important reason: Search engines (such as Google and Yahoo!) index the posts on your site by their permalinks, so changing the permalink structure makes all those indexed links obsolete.

One nifty feature of WordPress is that it remembers when you change your permalink structure and automatically writes an internal redirect from the old permalink structure to the new one.

Don't forget to click the Save Changes button at the bottom of the Permalink Settings page; otherwise your permalink changes aren't saved!

Making sure that your permalinks work with your server

After you set the format for the permalinks for your site by using any options other than the default, WordPress writes specific rules, or directives, to the .htaccess file on your web sever. The .htaccess file in turn communicates to your web server how it should serve up the permalinks, according to the permalink structure you've chosen to use. To use an .htaccess file, you need to know the answers to two questions:

- ✔ Does your web server configuration use and give you access to the .htaccess file?
- ✔ Does your web server run Apache with the mod_rewrite module?

If you don't know the answers, contact your hosting provider to find out.

If the answer to both questions is yes, follow the upcoming steps. If the answer is no, skip to the "Working with servers that don't use Apache mod_rewrite" sidebar, later in this chapter.

You and WordPress work together in glorious harmony to create the .htaccess file that lets you use a pretty-permalink structure in your blog. The file works like this:

1. **Locate the .htaccess file on your web server or create one and put it there.**

   If .htaccess already exists, you can find it in the root of your directory on your web server — that is, the same directory where you find your wp-config.php file. If you don't see it in the root directory, try changing the options of your FTP client to show hidden files. (Because the .htaccess file starts with a period [.], it may not be visible until you configure your FTP client to show hidden files.)

   If you need to create the file and put it on your web server, follow these steps:

   a. *Using a plain-text editor (such as Notepad for Windows or TextEdit for a Mac), create a blank file and name it* htaccess.txt.

> *b. Upload* `htaccess.txt` *to your web server via FTP. (See Chapter 6 for more information about FTP.)*
>
> *c. Rename the file* `.htaccess` *(notice the period at the beginning), and make sure that it is writable by the server by changing permissions to either 755 or 777. (See Chapter 6 for information on changing permissions on server files.)*

2. **Create the permalink structure in the Permalink Settings page on your WordPress Dashboard.**

3. **Click the Save Changes button at the bottom of the Permalink Settings page.**

   WordPress inserts into the `.htaccess` file the specific rules necessary for making the permalink structure functional in your blog.

If you followed these steps correctly, you have an `.htaccess` file on your web server that has the correct permissions set so that WordPress can write the correct rules to it. Your pretty-permalink structure works flawlessly. Kudos!

If you open the `.htaccess` file and look at it now, you'll see that it's no longer blank. It should have a set of code in it called *rewrite rules,* which looks something like this:

```
# BEGIN WordPress
<IfModule mod_rewrite.c>
RewriteEngine On
RewriteBase /
RewriteCond %{REQUEST_FILENAME} !-f
RewriteCond %{REQUEST_FILENAME} !-d
RewriteRule . /index.php [L]
</IfModule>

# END WordPress
```

I could delve deeply into `.htaccess` and all the things you can do with this file, but I'm restricting this section to how it applies to WordPress permalink structures. If you'd like to unlock more mysteries about `.htaccess`, check out "Comprehensive Guide to .htaccess" at `http://javascriptkit.com/howto/htaccess.shtml`.

Through my experiences over the years, I have discovered that Yahoo! Hosting doesn't allow users access to the `.htaccess` file on its server, and it doesn't use `mod_rewrite`. So if you're hosting your domain on Yahoo!, use the custom permalink technique that I describe in the sidebar "Working with servers that don't use Apache mod_rewrite."

Discovering the Many WordPress RSS Options

In Chapter 2, you can read about RSS feed technology and why it's an important part of publishing your blog. Allow me to quote myself from that chapter: For your blog readers to stay updated with the latest and greatest content you post to your site, they need to subscribe to your RSS feed.

RSS feeds come in different flavors, including RSS 0.92, RDF/RSS 1.0, RSS 2.0, and Atom. The differences among them lie within the base code that makes up the functionality of the syndication feed. What's important is that WordPress supports all versions of RSS — which means that anyone can subscribe to your RSS feed with any type of feed reader available.

I mention many times throughout this book that WordPress is very intuitive, and this section on RSS feeds is a shining example of a feature that WordPress automates. WordPress has a built-in feed generator that works behind the scenes to create feeds for you. This feed generator creates feeds from your posts, comments, and even categories.

The RSS feed for your blog posts is *autodiscoverable,* which means that almost all RSS feed readers and most browsers (Firefox, Chrome, Internet Explorer 7-9, and Safari, for example) automatically detect the RSS feed URL for a WordPress blog. Table 8-3 gives you some good guidelines on how to find the RSS feed URLs for the different sections of your blog.

Table 8-3	URLs for Built-In WordPress Feeds
Feed Type	**Example Feed URL**
RSS 0.92	`http://yourdomain.com/wp-rss.php` or `http://yourdomain.com/?feed=rss`
RDF/RSS 1.0	`http://yourdomain.com/wp-rss2.php` or `http://yourdomain.com/?feed=rdf`
RSS 2.0	`http://yourdomain.com/wp-rss2.php` or `http://yourdomain.com/?feed=rss2`
Atom	`http://yourdomain.com/wp-atom.php` or `http://yourdomain.com/?feed=atom`
Comments RSS	`http://yourdomain.com/?feed=rss&p=50` p stands for *post,* and 50 is the post ID. You can find the post ID on the Dashboard by clicking the Posts link. Locate a post and hover the mouse pointer over the title to find the ID in the URL that displays in your browser status bar.

Category RSS	`http://yourdomain.com/wp-rss2.`
	`php?cat=50`
	
	cat stands for *category,* and 50 is the category ID. You can find the category ID on the Dashboard by clicking the Categories link. Locate a category and hover the mouse pointer over the title to find the ID in the URL that displays in your browser status bar.

If you're using custom permalinks (see "Making your post links pretty," earlier in this chapter), you can simply add `/feed` to the end of any URL on your blog to find the RSS feed. Some of your links will look similar to these:

- `http://yourdomain.com/feed` — your main RSS feed

- `http://yourdomain.com/comments/feed` — your comments RSS feed

- `http://yourdomain.com/category/cat-name/feed` — RSS feed for a category

Try it with any URL on your site. Add `/feed` at the end and you'll have the RSS feed for that page.

RSS feeds are important parts of delivering content from your blog to your readers. RSS feeds are expected these days, so the fact that WordPress has taken care of everything for you — WordPress provides the feeds for you, is compliant with all RSS formats, and offers so many internal feeds — gives the software a huge advantage over any of the other blog-software platforms.

If you intend to use the Atom publishing protocol, you need to enable it manually because it's disabled by default. Click the Writing link on the Settings menu and then select the two boxes in the Remote Publishing section to enable Atom publishing in WordPress.

Blog It!: Writing Your First Entry

It's finally time to write your first post in your new WordPress blog! The topic you choose to write about and the writing techniques you use to get your message across are all on you; I have my hands full writing this book! I *can* tell you, however, how to write the wonderful passages that can bring you blog fame. Ready?

Composing your blog post

Composing a blog post is a lot like typing an e-mail: You give it a title, you write the message, and you click a button to send your words into the world.

You can collapse or reposition all the modules on the Add New Post page to suit your needs. The only section on the Add New Post page that cannot be collapsed and repositioned is the section with the actual title and post box (where you write your blog post).

Follow these steps to write a basic blog post:

1. **Click the Add New link on the Posts Dashboard menu.**

   The Add New Post page opens, as shown in Figure 8-9.

2. **Type the title of your post in the Enter Title Here text field at the top of the Add New Post page.**

3. **Type the content of your post in the text box.**

   You can use the Visual Text Editor to format the text in your post. I explain the Visual Text Editor and the buttons and options after these steps.

4. **Click the Save Draft button in the Publish module, located at the top-right side of the Add New Post page.**

   The page refreshes with your post title and content saved but not yet published to your blog.

By default, the area in which you write your post is in Visual Editing mode, as indicated by the Visual tab that appears above the text. Visual Editing mode is how WordPress provides WYSIWYG (What You See Is What You Get) options for formatting. Rather than have to embed HTML code in your post, you can simply type your post, highlight the text you want to format, and click the buttons (shown in Figure 8-9) that appear above the Post text box.

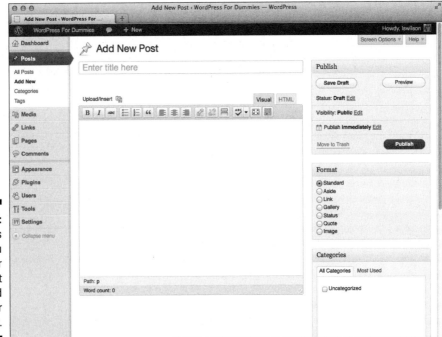

Figure 8-9:
This page is where you give your blog post a title and write your post body.

If you've ever used a word processing program, such as Microsoft Word, you'll recognize many of these buttons:

- ✔ **Bold:** Embeds the `<strong> </strong>` HTML tag to emphasize the text in bold. Example: **Bold Text.**

- ✔ **Italic:** Embeds the `<em> </em>` HTML tag to emphasize the text in italics. Example: *Italic Text.*

- ✔ **Strikethrough:** Embeds the `<strike> </strike>` HTML tag that puts a line through your text. Example: `Strikethrough Text.`

✔ **Unordered List:** Embeds the `<ul><li>` `</li></ul>` HTML tags that create an unordered, or bulleted, list.

✔ **Ordered List:** Embeds the `<ol><li>` `</li></ol>` HTML tags that create an ordered, or numbered, list.

✔ **Blockquote:** Inserts the `<blockquote>` `</blockquote>` HTML tag that indents the paragraph or section of text you've selected.

✔ **Align Left:** Inserts the `<p align="left">` `</p>` HTML tag that lines up the selected text against the left margin.

✔ **Align Center:** Inserts the `<p align="center">` `</p>` HTML tag that positions the selected text in the center of the page.

✔ **Align Right:** Inserts the `<p align="right">` `</p>` HTML tag that lines up the selected text against the right margin.

✔ **Insert/Edit Link:** Inserts the `<a href=" ">` `</a>` HTML tag around the text you've selected to create a hyperlink.

✔ **Unlink:** Removes the hyperlink from the selected text, if it was previously linked.

✔ **Insert More Tag:** Inserts the `<!--more-->` tag, which lets you split the display on your blog page. It publishes the text written above this tag with a Read More link, which takes the user to a page with the full post. This feature is good for really long posts.

✔ **Toggle Spellchecker:** Perfect for typo enthusiasts! Checking your spelling before you post is always a good idea.

✔ **Toggle Full Screen Mode:** Lets you focus purely on writing, without the distraction of all the other options on the page. Click this button, and the Post text box expands to fill the full height and width of your browser screen and displays only the barest essentials for writing your post. To bring the Post text box back to its normal state, click the Exit Full Screen link. Voilà — it's back to normal!

✔ **Show/Hide Kitchen Sink:** I saw this button and thought, "Wow! WordPress does my dishes, too!" Unfortunately, the button's name is a metaphor that describes the advanced formatting options available with the Visual Text Editor. Click this button to make a new drop-down list that gives you options for underlining, font color, custom characters, undo and redo, and so on — a veritable kitchen sink full of text formatting options, such as

- *Paragraph:* Inserts the `<p>` `</p>` HTML tags around the text to indicate paragraph breaks.

- *Address:* Inserts the `<address>` `</address>` HTML tags around the text to indicate the author or owner of a document.

- *Preformatted:* Inserts the `<pre>` `</pre>` HTML tags around the text to indicate preformatted text and preserves both spaces and line breaks.

- *Headings 1, 2, 3, 4, 5, 6:* Inserts header HTML tags such as `<H1>` `</H1>` around text to indicate HTML headings (H1 defines the largest, H6 defines the smallest; heading formats are usually defined in the CSS [see Chapter 13] with font size and/or colors).

- *Underline:* Inserts the `<u>` `</u>` HTML tags around the text to display it as underlined.

- *Text Color:* Displays the text in the color chosen.

- *Paste as Plain Text:* Useful if you copy text from another source, this option removes all formatting and special/hidden characters from the text and adds it to your post as unformatted text.

- *Paste from Word:* Useful if you're copying text from a Microsoft Word document because Word inserts a lot of hidden HTML and characters that could make your post text look funny on your website. Use the Paste from Word feature to transfer posts from Word to WordPress to preserve formatting without the hidden mess.

- *Remove Formatting:* Removes all formatting inside the post.

- *Insert Custom Character:* If you click this option, a pop-up window appears, offering different characters such as $, %, &, and ©. In the pop-up window, click the symbol that you want to add to your post.

- *Outdent:* Moves text to the left one preset level with each click.

- *Indent:* Moves text to the right one preset level with each click.

- *Undo:* Click to undo your last formatting action.

- *Redo:* Click to redo your last formatting action.

- *Help:* Pops open a window with helpful information about using the text editor, including time-saving keyboard shortcuts.

You can turn off the Visual Text Editor by clicking the Your Profile link on the Users menu. Deselect the Use the Visual Editor When Writing box to turn off this editor if you'd rather insert the HTML code yourself in your posts.

If you'd rather embed your own HTML code and skip the Visual Text Editor, click the HTML tab that appears to the right of the Visual tab. If you're planning to type HTML code in your post — for a table or video files, for example — you have to click the HTML tab before you insert that code. If you don't, the Visual Text Editor formats your code, and it most likely will look nothing like you intended it to.

At this point, you can skip to the "Publishing your post" section of this chapter for information on publishing your post to your blog, or continue with the following sections to discover how to refine the options for your post.

WordPress has a nifty, built-in autosave feature that saves your work while you're typing and editing a new post. If your browser crashes or you accidentally close your browser window before you've saved your post, it will be there for you when you get back. Those WordPress folks are so thoughtful!

Dressing up your posts with images, video, and audio

Directly above and to the left of the Visual Text Editor row of buttons is an Add Media area with a row of four icons. These icons let you insert images/photos, photo galleries, videos, and audio files into your posts. WordPress has an entire Media Library capability, which I describe in great detail in Chapter 9.

Refining your post options

After you write the post, you can choose a few extra options before you publish it for the entire world to see. These settings apply to the post you're currently working on — not to any future or past posts. You can find these options below and to the right of the Post text box. See Figure 8-10. Click the title of each option, and the settings for that specific option expand.

If you do not see these options on the Add New Post page on your Dashboard, that most likely means you have not enabled them in the Screen Options (discussed in Chapter 7). Click the Screen Options tab at the top of the Add New Post page and enable the modules on this page that you would like to use.

You can reposition the different post option modules on the Add New Post page to fit the way you use this page.

Here are the options found underneath the Post text box:

- **Excerpt:** Excerpts are short summaries of your posts. Many bloggers use snippets to show teasers of their blog posts, thereby encouraging the reader to click the Read More links to read the posts in their entirety. Type your short summary in the Excerpt box. Excerpts can be any length, in terms of words; however, the point is to keep it short and sweet and tease your readers into clicking the Read More link.

- **Send Trackbacks:** I discuss trackbacks in detail in Chapter 2. If you want to send a trackback to another blog, enter the blog's trackback URL in the Send Trackbacks To box. You can send trackbacks to more than one blog; just be sure to separate trackback URLs with spaces.

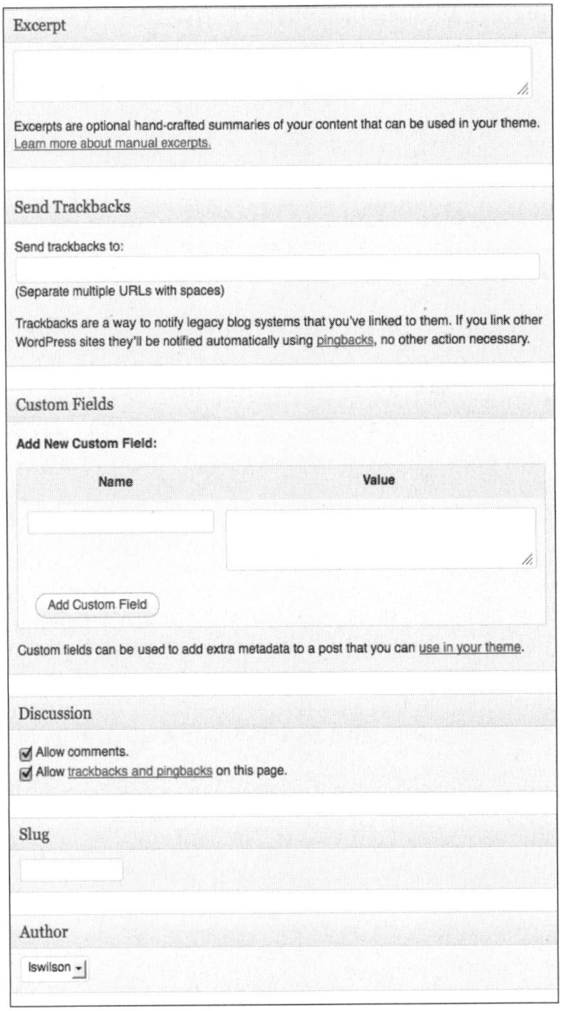

Excerpt

Excerpts are optional hand-crafted summaries of your content that can be used in your theme.
Learn more about manual excerpts.

Send Trackbacks

Send trackbacks to:

(Separate multiple URLs with spaces)

Trackbacks are a way to notify legacy blog systems that you've linked to them. If you link other WordPress sites they'll be notified automatically using pingbacks, no other action necessary.

Custom Fields

Add New Custom Field:

Name	Value

Add Custom Field

Custom fields can be used to add extra metadata to a post that you can use in your theme.

Discussion

☑ Allow comments.
☑ Allow trackbacks and pingbacks on this page.

Slug

Author

lswilson

Figure 8-10:
Several options are available for your blog post.

✔ **Custom Fields:** Custom fields add extra data to your posts and are fully configurable.

✔ **Discussion:** Decide whether to let readers submit comments through the comment system by selecting the Allow Comments box. By default, the box is selected; deselect it to disallow comments on this post.

Here are the options found to the right of the Post text box:

- ✔ **Publish:** These are the publishing and privacy options for your post, which I cover in the upcoming "Publishing your post" section.

- ✔ **Format:** This module appears only when the theme that you're using on your site supports a WordPress feature called Post Formats (which I cover in detail in Bonus Chapter 1 on the companion website for this book). In the Format module, you can select the type of format you want to use for the post you're publishing.

- ✔ **Categories:** You can file your posts in different categories to organize them by subject. (See more about organizing your posts by category in "Staying on Topic with Categories," at the start of this chapter.) Select the box to the left of the category you want to use. You can toggle between listing all categories and seeing just the categories you use the most by clicking the All Categories or Most Used links, respectively. Don't see the category you need listed here? Click the + Add New Category link, and you can add a category right there on the Add New Post page!

- ✔ **Post Tags:** Type your desired tags in the text box. Be sure to separate each tag with a comma so that WordPress knows where each tag begins and ends. `Cats`, `Kittens`, `Feline` represent three different tags, for example, but without the commas, WordPress would consider those three words to be one tag. Click the Add button to add the tags to your post. See the sidebar "What are tags, and how/why do I use them?" earlier in this chapter for more information on tags.

- ✔ **Featured Image:** Some WordPress themes are configured to use an image (photo) to represent each post that you have on your blog. The image can display on the home/front page, blog page, archives, or anywhere within the content display on your website. If you're using a theme that has this option, you can easily define the post thumbnail by clicking the Set Featured Image link under the Featured Image module on the Add New Post page. Then you can assign an image that you've uploaded to your site as the featured image for a particular post.

When you finish setting the options for your post, don't navigate away from this page; your options have not yet been fully saved. The next section covers all the options you need for saving your post settings!

Publishing your post

You have given your new post a title and have written the content of your new blog post. Maybe you've even added an image or other type of media file to your blog post (see Chapter 9) and have configured the tags, categories, and other options. Now the question is, Publish? Or not to publish (yet)?

WordPress gives you three options for saving or publishing your post when you're done writing it. The Publish module is located on the right side of the Add New (or Edit) Post page. Just click the title of the Publish module to expand the settings you need. Figure 8-11 shows the available options in the Publish module.

Figure 8-11:
The publish status for your blog posts.

The Publish module has several options:

✔ **Save Draft:** Choose this option to save your post as a draft. The Edit Post page reloads with all your post contents and options saved; you can continue editing it now, tomorrow, or the next day. To access your draft posts, click the Edit link on the Posts menu.

✔ **Preview:** Click the Preview button to view your post in a new window, as it would appear on your live blog if you had published it. Previewing the post doesn't publish it to your site yet. It gives you the opportunity to view it on your site and check it for any formatting or content changes you'd like to make.

✔ **Status:** Click the Edit link to open the settings for this option. A drop-down menu appears, and you can select Draft or Pending Review:

  • Select *Draft* to save the post but not publish it to your blog.

  • Select *Pending Review,* and the post shows up in your list of drafts next to a Pending Review header. This option lets the administrator of the blog know that contributors have entered posts that are waiting for administrator review and approval (helpful for blogs with multiple authors).

Click the OK button to save your settings.

✔ **Stick This Post to the Front Page:** Select this box to have WordPress publish the post to your blog and keep it at the very top of all blog posts until you change this setting.

This is otherwise known as a *sticky post*. Typically posts are displayed in chronological order on your blog, displaying the most recent post on top. If you make a post sticky, it remains at the very top no matter how many other posts you make after it. When you want to unstick the post, deselect the Stick This Post to the Front Page box.

✔ **Password Protected:** By assigning a password to a post, you can publish a post to your blog that only you can see. You can also share the post password with a friend, who can see the content of the post after entering the password. But why would anyone want to do this? Imagine that you just ate dinner at your mother-in-law's house and she made the *worst* pot roast you've ever eaten. You can write all about it! Protect it with a password and give the password to your trusted friends so that they can read all about it without offending your mother-in-law.

✔ **Private:** Publish this post to your blog so that only you can see it — no one else will be able to see it, ever. You may want to do this for posts that are personal and private (if you're keeping a personal diary, for example).

✔ **Publish Immediately:** Click the Edit link and you can set the timestamp for your post. If you want the post to have the current time and date, ignore this setting altogether.

If you'd like to future-publish this post, you can set the time and date for any time in the future. This feature has come in handy for me many times. For example, when I have a vacation planned and I don't want my blog to go without updates while I'm gone, I'll sit down and write a few posts and set the date for a time in the future. They're published to my blog while I'm somewhere tropical, diving with the fishes.

✔ **Move to Trash:** Clicking this link sends the entire post into the Trash bin. Your post isn't deleted permanently, which is a relief if you happen to click that link by accident; instead, it's saved in the Trash where you can retrieve it later, if you want to. You can find the items in Trash by clicking the All Posts link under the Posts menu on the Dashboard; then click the Trash link.

✔ **Publish:** This button wastes no time! It bypasses all the previous draft, pending review, and sticky settings and publishes the post directly to your blog immediately.

After you choose an option from the drop-down menu, click the Save button. The Add New Post page saves your publishing-status option.

If you want to publish your post right away, skip all the other options in the Publish module and just click the Publish button. This method eliminates the fuss with the Publish Status options and sends your new post to your blog in all its glory.

If you click Publish and for some reason don't see the post you just published on the front page of your blog, you probably left the Publish Status drop-down menu set to Unpublished. Your new post is in the draft posts, which you'll find by clicking the All Posts on the Posts menu.

You are your own editor

While I write this book, I have editors looking over my shoulder, making recommendations, correcting my typos and grammatical errors, and helping me by telling me when I get too long-winded. You, on the other hand, are not so lucky! You are your own editor and have full control of what you write, when you write it, and how you write it. You can always go back and edit previous posts to correct typos, grammatical errors, and other mistakes by following these steps:

1. **Find the post that you want to edit by clicking the All Posts link in the Posts menu.**

    The Posts page opens and lists the 20 most recent posts you've made to your blog.

    You can filter that listing of posts by date from the Show All Dates drop-down menu at the top of the Posts page. For example, if you choose December 2012, the Posts page reloads, displaying only those posts that were published in the month of December 2012.

    You can also filter the post listing by category. Select your desired category from the View All Categories drop-down menu.

2. **When you find the post you need, click its title.**

    The Edit Post window opens. In this window, you can edit the post and/or any of its options.

    You can also click the Edit link that appears beneath the post title on the Posts page.

    If you need to edit only the post options, click the Quick Edit link. The post options open, and you can configure post options such as the title, status, password, categories, tags, comments, and timestamp. Click the Save button to save your changes without ever leaving the Post page on your Dashboard.

3. **Edit your post; then click the Update button.**

    The Edit Post window refreshes with all your changes saved.

Look Who's Talking on Your Blog

The feature that really catapulted blogging into the limelight is the comments feature, which lets visitors interact with the authors of blogs. I cover the concept of blog comments and trackbacks in Chapter 2. They provide a great way for readers to interact with site owners, and vice versa.

Managing comments and trackbacks

To find your comments, click the Comments link on the Dashboard navigation menu; the Comments page opens. See Figure 8-12.

When you hover over your comments with your mouse, several links appear that give you the opportunity to manage those comments:

- **Unapprove:** This link appears only if you have comment moderation turned on and with only approved comments. The comment is placed in the moderation queue, which you get to by clicking the Awaiting Moderation link that appears below the Manage Comments header. The moderation queue is kind of a holding area for comments that haven't yet been published to your blog. (See the following section for more on the moderation queue.)

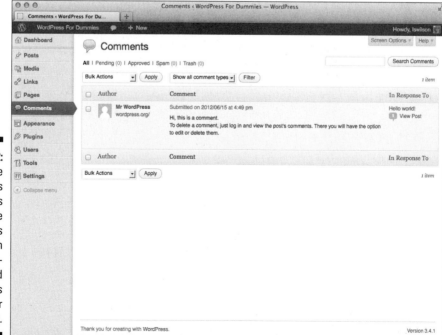

Figure 8-12: Clicking the Comments menu shows you the Comments page, with all the comments and trackbacks on your blog.

✓ **Reply:** Click this link and a text box drops down, into which you can type and submit your reply to the person who commented. This feature eliminates the need to have to load your live site to reply to a comment.

✓ **Quick Edit:** Click this link and, without ever leaving the Comments page, the comment options open, and you can configure the post options such as name, e-mail, URL, and comment content. Click the Save button to save your changes.

✓ **Edit:** Click this link to open the Edit Comment page, where you can edit the different fields such as name, e-mail, URL, and comment content. See Figure 8-13.

✓ **Spam:** Click this link to mark the comment as spam and toss it into the spam bin, where it will never be heard from again!

✓ **Trash:** This link does exactly what it says; it sends the comment to the trash can and deletes it from your blog.

If you have a lot of comments listed in the Comments page and want to bulk-edit them, select the boxes to the left of all the comments you want to manage; then select one of the following from the Actions drop-down menu at the top left of the Comments page: Approve, Mark As Spam, Unapprove, or Delete.

Figure 8-13:
Edit a user's
comment
in the Edit
Comment
page.

Moderating comments and trackbacks

If you have your options set so that comments aren't published to your blog until you approve them, you can approve comments from the Comments page as well. Just click the Pending link on the Comments page and you go to the Edit Comments page. If you have comments and/or trackbacks awaiting moderation, you see them on this page and you can approve them, mark them as spam, or delete them.

A nice feature of WordPress is that it immediately notifies you of any comments sitting in the moderation queue, awaiting your action. This notification appears as a small circle to the right of the Comments menu in the left navigation menu on every single page. Figure 8-14 shows my Dashboard page with an indicator in the Comments menu that I have 5 comments awaiting moderation. I'd better get busy and deal with those comments!

Tackling spam with Akismet

I touch on Akismet a few times throughout this book because it's my humble opinion that Akismet is the mother of all plugins and that no WordPress blog is complete without a fully activated version of Akismet running in it.

Apparently WordPress agrees because the plugin is packaged in every WordPress software release beginning with version 2.0. Akismet was created by the folks at Automattic — the same folks who brought you the WordPress.com-hosted version (discussed in Part II of this book). Automattic also works with some of the original developers of the WordPress software platform.

Akismet is the answer to combatting comment and trackback spam. Matt Mullenweg of Automattic says that Akismet is a "collaborative effort to make comment and trackback spam a non-issue and restore innocence to blogging, so you never have to worry about spam again" (from the Akismet website at http://akismet.com).

I've been blogging since 2002. I started blogging with the Movable Type blogging platform and moved to WordPress in 2003. As blogging became more and more popular, comment and trackback spam became more and more of a nuisance. One morning in 2004, I found that 2,300 pieces of disgusting comment spam had been published to my blog. Something had to be done! The folks at Automattic did a fine thing with Akismet. Since the emergence of Akismet, I've barely had to think about comment or trackback spam except for the few times a month I check my Akismet spam queue.

Five comments are waiting.

Figure 8-14:
A small
circle with
a number
telling me
that I have
comments
awaiting
moderation.

I talk in greater detail about plugin use in WordPress in Chapter 10, where you find out how to activate Akismet and make sure that it's protecting your blog from trackback and comment spam.

Part IV
Flexing and Extending WordPress

The 5th Wave   By Rich Tennant

"He should be alright now. I made him spend two and a half hours reading prisoner blogs on the state penitentiary Web site."

In this part . . .

Ready? Set? Action! This part of the book starts by showing you how to add media files — images, video, and audio — to your site to create a fun, interactive experience for your readers. This part also covers using WordPress plugins to extend the capabilities of your blog, and finding and using free WordPress themes to change the look of your blog.

Chapter 9

Media Management: Images, Audio, and Video

In This Chapter

▶ Adding images, photo galleries, and videos to your blog posts

▶ Uploading audio files

▶ Exploring the WordPress Media Library

Adding images and photos to your posts can really dress up the content. By using images and photos, you give your content a dimension that you can't express in plain text. Through visual imagery, you can call attention to your post and add depth to it.

The same goes for adding video and audio files to your posts and blog. Video lets you provide entertainment through moving, talking (or singing!), streaming video. Audio files let you talk to your visitors and add a personal touch. Many bloggers use video and audio to report news and to broadcast Internet radio and television shows. The possibilities are endless!

In this chapter, you discover how to enhance your blog posts by adding images, video, and audio. And you even find out how to run a full-fledged photo gallery on your site, all through the `WordPress.org` software and its integrated Media Library.

This chapter is pertinent to the WordPress.org platform only. If you're using the hosted `WordPress.com` version, check out Chapter 4 for information on adding images, video, and audio to your blog.

You add these extras to your blog posts in the Upload/Insert area of the Add New Post page. You can add them as you're writing your post or come back and add them later. The choice is yours!

Inserting Images into Your Blog Posts

Adding images to a post is pretty easy with the WordPress image uploader. Jump right in and give it a go by clicking the Add Media icon on the Add New Post page. The Add Media window lets you choose images from your hard drive or from a location on the web. See Figure 9-1.

WordPress uses an Adobe Flash–based interface for file uploads. Flash is a specific set of multimedia technologies programmed to handle media files on the web. Some browsers and operating systems are not configured to handle Flash-based applications. If you experience difficulties with the image uploader, WordPress gives you an easy alternative. Click the Browser Uploader link on the Add Media page, and you can use a non-Flash-based uploader to transfer your files.

Figure 9-1:
Insert
images into
your posts
with the
WordPress
Add Media
window.

To add an image from the web after you click the Add Media icon, follow these steps:

1. **Click the From URL tab in the Add Media window.**

   The Insert Media from Another Website window opens.

2. **Select Image as the file type you want to add.**

   The other option is Audio, Video or Other File — I cover those file types later in this chapter.

3. **Type the URL (Internet address) of the image in the URL text box.**

   Type the full URL, including the http and www portion of the address. You can easily find the URL of any image on the web by right-clicking (PC) or Control-clicking (Mac) and selecting Properties from the menu.

4. **Type a title for the image in the Title text box.**

5. **Type a description of the image in the Alternate Text text box.**

   The *alternate text* is what shows in a browser for visually impaired people who use text readers, or it appears when the image does not load properly for some reason. Although alternate text gives the visitors to your site a description of what the image is, adding it is also good for SEO (search engine optimization). Search engines read the alternate text (also called ALT tags) and give search engines additional descriptive text to further categorize and define your site in listings and directories.

6. **(Optional) Type the caption of the image in the Image Caption text box.**

   The words you type here display underneath the image on your blog as a caption — if your current theme supports image captions.

7. **Choose an alignment option by selecting the None, Left, Center, or Right radio buttons.**

8. **Type the URL you want the image linked to.**

   Whatever option you choose determines where your readers go when they click the image you've uploaded; you can type in a specific URL or you can select one of the two available presets:

   - *None:* You don't want the image to be clickable.
   - *Link to Image:* Readers can click through to the direct image itself.

9. **Click the Insert into Post button.**

To add an image from your own computer's hard drive after you click the Add Media icon, follow these steps:

1. **Click the From Computer tab and then click the Select Files button.**

   A dialog box opens from which you can select an image (or multiple images) from your hard drive.

   Earlier, I told you about the Flash uploader technology used for the Add Media feature and how you can use the Browser Uploader if Flash doesn't work on your individual system. If you're using the Browser Uploader, you may select only one image at a time to upload, whereas with the Flash uploader, you can select multiple images at a time.

2. **Select your image(s); then click Open.**

   The image is uploaded from your computer to your web server. WordPress displays a progress bar on the upload and displays an image options box when the upload is finished.

3. **Edit the details for the image(s) by clicking the Show link that appears to the right of the image thumbnail.**

   Clicking Show drops down a box (see Figure 9-2) that contains several image options:

   - *Title:* Type a title for the image.

   - *Alternate Text:* Type the alternate text (see previous section) for the image.

   - *Caption:* Type a caption for the image (such as, **This is a flower from my garden**).

   - *Description:* Type a description of the image.

   - *Link URL:* Type the URL you want the image linked to. Whatever option you choose determines where your readers go when they click the image you've uploaded. Type in your own URL or select one of three available presets:

     None: You don't want the image to be clickable.

     File URL: Readers can click through to the direct image itself.

     Attachment Post URL: Readers can click through to the post that the image appears in. You can type your own URL in the Link URL text box.

   - *Alignment:* Choose None, Left, Center, or Right. (See Table 9-1, in the following section, for styling information regarding image alignment.)

   - *Size:* Choose Thumbnail, Medium, Large, or Full Size.

WordPress automatically creates small and medium-size versions of the images you upload through the built-in image uploader. A *thumbnail* is a smaller version of the original file. You can edit the size of the thumbnail by clicking the Settings link and then clicking Miscellaneous. In the Image Sizes section, designate your desired height and width of the small and medium thumbnail images generated by WordPress.

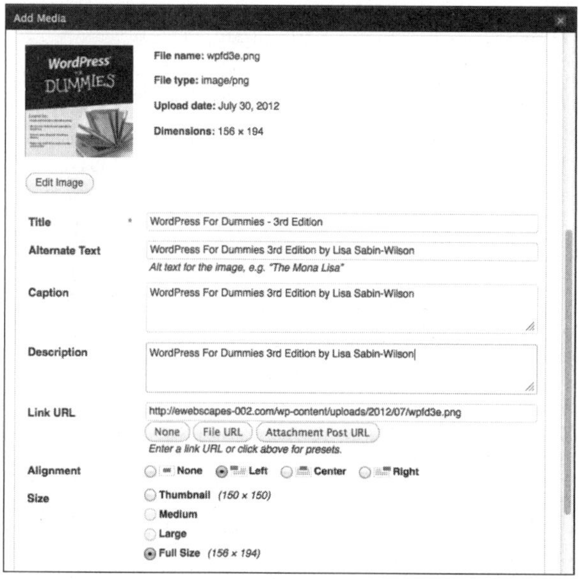

Figure 9-2:
You can
set several
options for
your images
after you
upload
them.

If you're uploading more than one image, skip to the "Inserting a photo gallery" section, later in this chapter.

4. **Click the Edit Image button (refer to Figure 9-2) to edit the appearance of the image. Be sure to click Save after you've edited the image.**

   The image editor (shown in Figure 9-3) options include the following tools:

   - *Crop:* Click this button to cut the image down to a smaller size.

   - *Rotate counterclockwise:* Click this button to rotate the image to the left.

   - *Rotate clockwise:* Click this button to rotate the image to the right.

   - *Flip vertically:* Click this button to flip the image upside down and back again.

   - *Flip horizontally:* Click this button to flip the image from right to left and back again.

   - *Undo:* Click this button to undo any changes you've made.

- *Redo:* Click this button to redo image edits that you've undone.

- *Scale Image:* Click this link to drop down the option menu that you use to set a specific width and height for the image.

Rotate counterclockwise

Rotate clockwise

Crop   Flip vertically   Flip horizontally   Undo   Redo

Figure 9-3:
The
WordPress
Image Editor
options.

5. **Click the Insert into Post button.**

You can find the Insert into Post button at the bottom of the Add Media window. The image uploader window closes, and you return to the Add New Post page (or the Add New Page page, if you're writing a page). WordPress has inserted the HTML to display the image in your post, as shown in Figure 9-4; you can continue editing your post, save it, or publish it.

To see the actual image and not the code, click the Visual tab that's just above the Post text box.

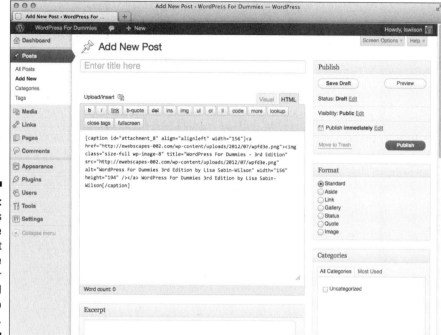

Figure 9-4:
WordPress
inserts the
correct
HTML code
for your
uploaded
image into
your post.

Aligning your images

When you upload your image, you can set the alignment for your image as
None, Left, Center, or Right. The WordPress theme you're using, however,
may not have these alignment styles in its stylesheet. If you set the alignment
to Left, for example, but the image on your blog doesn't appear to be aligned
at all, you may need to add a few styles to your theme's stylesheet.

I discuss themes and templates in great detail in Part V, but for the purpose
of making sure that you have the correct image alignment for your newly
uploaded images, here is a quick-and-dirty method:

1. **Click the Editor link in the Appearance menu.**

   The Edit Themes page opens. All the template files for your active theme
   are listed on the right side of the page.

2. **Click the Stylesheet template.**

   The Stylesheet (`style.css`) template opens in the text box on the left
   side of the page.

3. **Add your desired styles to the stylesheet.**

Table 9-1 shows the styles you can add to your stylesheet to make sure that image-alignment styling is in your theme.

Table 9-1	Styling Techniques for Image Alignment
Image Alignment	*Add This to Your Stylesheet (style.css)*
None	`img.alignnone {margin: 5px 0 5px 0;}`
Left	`img.alignleft {float:left; margin: 5px 10px 5px 0px;}`
Center	`img.aligncenter {display:block margin: 5px auto;}`
Right	`img.alignright {float:right; margin: 5px 0 5px 10px;}`

These styles are just examples of what you can do. Get creative with your own styling. You find more information about using CSS (Cascading Style Sheets) to add style to your theme(s) in Chapter 13.

Inserting a photo gallery

You can also use the WordPress image uploader to insert a full photo gallery into your posts. Upload your images; then, instead of clicking the Insert into Post button, click the Gallery tab at the top of the image uploader window, as shown in Figure 9-5. This tab displays thumbnails of all the images you have uploaded for your post.

Follow these steps to insert a photo gallery into a blog post:

1. **(Optional) On the Gallery tab, under the Actions column, type the order that you want the images to appear in the gallery.**

   Type the number in the text box of the sequence in which you want each image displayed. (If you want an image displayed first, for example, type **1** in the corresponding Actions column.)

2. **Set different options for your gallery:**

   - *Link Thumbnails To:* Select Image File or Attachment Page.
   - *Order Images By:* Select Menu Order, Title, Date/Time, or Random.
   - *Order:* Select Ascending or Descending.
   - *Gallery Columns:* Select how many columns of images you'd like to display in your gallery.

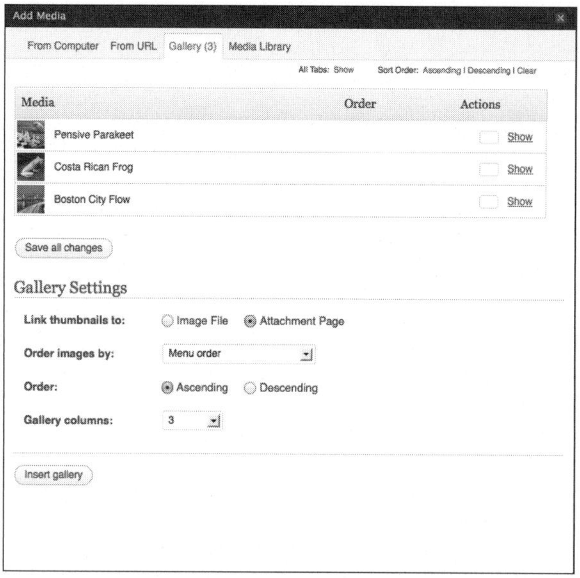

Figure 9-5:
Insert a
photo
gallery into
a post by
using the
Gallery tab
of the image
uploader.

3. **Click the Save All Changes button.**

   All the changes you made to each individual image listed in the gallery are saved.

4. **Click the Insert Gallery button.**

   WordPress inserts into your post a piece of shortcode that looks like this: [gallery].

   Table 9-2 shows some gallery shortcodes that you can use to manually set the display settings for your photo gallery.

5. **(Optional) Change the order of appearance of the images in the gallery, as well as the markup (HTML tags or CSS selectors):**

   • captiontag: Change the markup that surrounds the image caption by altering the gallery shortcode. For example: [gallery captiontag="div"] places <div></div> tags around the image caption (the <div> tag is considered a block-level element and creates a separate container for the content); to have the gallery appear on a line of its own, the [gallery captiontag="p"] code places <p class="gallery-caption"></p> tags around the image caption. The default markup for the captiontag option is dd.

   • icontag: Defines the HTML markup around each individual thumbnail image in your gallery. Change the markup around the icontag (thumbnail icon) of the image by altering the gallery shortcode to something like [gallery icontag="p"], which places `<p class="gallery-icon"></p>` tags around each thumbnail icon. The default markup for `icontag` is `dt`.

- `itemtag`: Defines the HTML markup around each item in your gallery. Change the markup around the `itemtag` (each item) in the gallery by altering the gallery shortcode to something like `[gallery itemtag="span"]`, which places `<span class="gallery-item"></span>` tags around each item in the gallery. The default markup for the `itemtag` is `dl`.

- `orderby`: Defines the order that the images are displayed within your gallery. Change the order used to display the thumbnails in the gallery by altering the gallery shortcode to something like `[gallery orderby="menu_order ASC"]`, which displays the thumbnails in ascending menu order. Another parameter you can use is `ID_order ASC`, which displays the thumbnails in ascending order according to their IDs.

Table 9-2	Gallery Shortcode Examples
Gallery Shortcode	*Output*
`[gallery columns="4" size="medium"]`	A four-column gallery containing medium-size images
`[gallery columns="10" id="215" size="thumbnail"]`	A ten-column gallery containing thumbnail images pulled from the blog post with the ID 215
`[gallery captiontag="p" icontag="span"]`	A three-column (default) gallery in which each image is surrounded by `<span></span>` tags and the image caption is surrounded by `<p></p>` tags

6. **Define the style of the** `<span>` **tags in your CSS stylesheet.**

   The `<span>` tags create an inline element; an element contained within a `<span>` tag stays on the same line as the element before it; there is no line break. You need a little knowledge of CSS to alter the `<span>` tags. Click the Editor link in the Appearance menu on your WordPress Dashboard to edit the stylesheet for your theme. Here's an example of what you can add to the stylesheet (`style.css`) for your current theme:

```
span.gallery-icon img {
        padding: 3px;
        background: white;
        border: 1px solid black;
        margin: 0 5px;
}
```

Placing this bit of CSS in the stylesheet (style.css) of your active theme automatically places a 1-pixel black border around each thumbnail, with 3 pixels of padding and a white background. The left and right margins are 5 pixels wide, creating nice spacing between images in the gallery.

7. **Click the Update File button to save changes to your stylesheet (style.css) template.**

Figure 9-6 shows my post with my photo gallery displayed, using the default image and gallery styling in the default WordPress theme: Twenty Eleven. This code is the gallery shortcode that I used for the gallery shown in Figure 9-6: [gallery columns="3"].

Matt Mullenweg, co-founder of the WordPress platform, created a very extensive photo gallery by using the built-in gallery options in WordPress. Check out the fabulous photo gallery at http://ma.tt/category/gallery/.

Some great WordPress plugins work in tandem with the WordPress gallery feature. Check out Chapter 10 for information on how to install and use WordPress plugins in your blog.

Figure 9-6:
A photo gallery inserted into my post with gallery shortcodes and CSS examples.

WordPress gallery plugins

Here is a handful of great plugins:

- ✔ **NextGEN Gallery by Alex Rabe** (`http://wordpress.org/extend/plugins/nextgen-gallery`): Create sortable photo galleries and more.

- ✔ **Gallery by BestWebSoft** (`http://wordpress.org/extend/plugins/gallery-plugin`): Implement as many galleries as you want with multiple photos and a description for each gallery; show them all at once or as individual galleries.

- ✔ **Slideshow Gallery by Antonie Potgieter** (`http://wordpress.org/extend/plugins/slideshow-gallery`): Use this JavaScript-powered slideshow gallery to display multiple galleries inside a dynamic slideshow.

- ✔ **WP Easy Gallery by Tyson Hahn** (`http://wordpress.org/extend/plugins/wp-easy-gallery`): Create and manage multiple galleries using WordPress shortcodes for easy integration.

Inserting Video Files into Your Blog Posts

Whether you're producing your own videos for publication or want to embed other people's videos that you find interesting, placing a video file in a blog post has never been easier with WordPress.

Check out a good example of a video blog at `www.thedogfiles.com`. The Dog Files is a website about dogs and the people who love them; the site serves up videos for information and entertainment.

Several video galleries on the web today allow you to add videos to blog posts; Google's YouTube service (`http://youtube.com`) is a good example of a third-party video service that allows you to share videos. To add a video from the web, click the Add Media icon and then click the From URL tab and follow these steps:

1. **Select the Audio, Video or Other File option.**

2. **Type the URL (Internet address) of the video in the URL text box.**

   Type the full URL, including the `http` and `www` portion of the address. Video providers, such as YouTube, usually list the direct link for the video file on their sites; you can copy and paste it into the URL text box.

3. **(Optional) Type the title of the video in the Title text box.**

   Giving a title to the video allows you to provide a bit of a description of the video. It's a good idea to provide a title if you can so that your readers know what the video is about.

4. **Click the Insert into Post button.**

   A link to the video is inserted into your post. WordPress doesn't embed the actual video in the post; it inserts only a link to the video. Your blog visitors click the link to load another page where the video can be played.

The previous steps give you the ability to insert a hyperlink that your readers can click and view the video on another website (such as YouTube.com). WordPress also has a nifty feature called Auto-Embed that automatically embeds videos within your posts and pages when you simply type the URL for the video into the body of your post, or page.

WordPress automatically detects that a URL you typed in your post is a video from YouTube (for example) and automatically wraps the correct HTML embed code around that URL to make sure that the video player displays in your post (in a standards- and XHTML-compliant way).

You do need to enable the Auto-Embed feature on the Media Settings page:

1. **Click the Media link under the Settings menu on your WordPress Dashboard.**

   The Media Settings page loads on the Dashboard.

2. **Select the Auto-Embeds check box.**

   This enables the automatic embedding of videos from a URL that WordPress detects as video, such as links from YouTube.

3. **Set the dimensions you want (the video) to display in the Maximum Embed Size box.**

   Enter your preferred size (width and height) that you want the videos to appear in your posts and pages.

4. **Be sure to click the Save Changes button!**

   You're ready to automatically embed links into your WordPress posts.

Currently, WordPress automatically embeds videos from YouTube, Vimeo, Dailymotion, blip.tv, Flickr, Hulu, Viddler, Qik, Revision3, Scribd, Photobucket, Polldaddy, Google Video, and VideoPress-type videos from WordPress.tv.

To upload and post to your blog a video from your computer, click the Add Media icon on the Edit Post or Add New Post page. Then follow these steps:

1. **Click the Select Files button.**

   An Open dialog box opens.

2. **Select the video file you want to upload and click Open (or double-click the file).**

   You return to the file uploader window in WordPress, which shows a progress bar while your video uploads. When the upload is complete, a box containing several options drops down.

3. **Type a title for the file in the Title text box.**

4. **Type a caption for the file in the Caption text box.**

5. **Type a description of the file in the Description text box.**

6. **Click the File URL button.**

   It provides a direct link in your post to the video file itself.

7. **Click Insert into Post.**

   WordPress doesn't embed a video player in the post; it inserts only a link to the video.

Inserting Audio Files into Your Blog Posts

Audio files can be music files or a recording of you speaking to your readers; audio adds a nice personal touch to your blog, and you can easily share audio files on your blog through the use of the Upload Audio feature in WordPress. After you've inserted an audio file in your blog posts, your readers can listen to it on their computers or download it onto an MP3 player and listen to it while they drive to work.

Click the Add Media icon on the Edit Post or Add New Post page and follow these steps to upload an audio file to your blog post:

1. **Click the Select Files button.**

   An Open dialog box opens.

2. **Choose the file you want to upload and click Open (or double-click the file).**

   You return to the file uploader window in WordPress, which shows a progress bar while your audio file uploads. When the upload is complete, a box containing several options drops down.

3. **Type a title for the file in the Title text box.**

4. **Type a caption for the file in the Caption text box.**

5. **Type a description of the file in the Description text box.**

6. **Click the File URL button.**

   You can provide a direct link in your post to the audio file itself.

7. **Click Insert into Post.**

   A link to the audio file is inserted into your post. WordPress doesn't embed an actual audio player in the post; it inserts only a link to the audio file. Visitors click the link to open another page where the audio file can be played.

Some great WordPress plugins for audio handling can enhance the functionality of the file uploader and help you manage audio files in your blog posts. Check out Chapter 10 for information on how to install and use WordPress plugins in your blog.

Keeping Media Files Organized

If you've been running your blog for any length of time, you can easily forget what files you've uploaded with the WordPress uploader. I used to have to log in to my web server via FTP and view the Uploads folder to see what I had in there.

Now, the WordPress Media Library makes it very convenient and easy to discover which files are in your Uploads folder.

To find an image, video, or audio file that you've already uploaded using the file uploader and use that file in a new post, follow these steps:

1. **Click the Upload/Insert Media icon to open the Add Media window.**

2. **Click the Media Library link at the top.**

   You see all the files you've ever uploaded to your blog with the file uploader feature; see Figure 9-7. Files you've uploaded through other methods, such as FTP, are not displayed in the Media Library.

3. **Select the file you want to reuse and click the Show link.**

4. **Set the options for that image: Title, Caption, Description, Link URL, Order, Alignment, and Size.**

5. **Click the Insert into Post button.**

   The correct HTML code is inserted into the Post text box.

Figure 9-7:
The Media
Library
shows all
the files
you've ever
uploaded to
your blog.

If you want to view only the files you've uploaded and don't need a particular image or file for a new post, click the Library link in the Media menu, which opens the Media Library page.

WordPress video and audio plugins

There are some great WordPress plugins for audio and video handling. Check out Chapter 10 for information on how to install and use WordPress plugins.

Here is a handful of great plugins for audio:

✔ **HTML5 jQuery Audio Player by EnigmaWeb** (http://wordpress.org/extend/plugins/html5-jquery-audio-player): Add a single audio file or a full audio playlist through the use of a simple WordPress shortcode.

✔ **oEmbed HTML5 audio by Honza Skypala** (http://wordpress.org/extend/plugins/oembed-html5-audio): This plugin autodetects MP3 files on your site and inserts a stylish player.

✔ **PowerPress by Angelo Mandato** (http://wordpress.org/extend/plugins/powerpress/): This plugin supports several media formats and automatically creates a podcast RSS feed and is up to date with the latest iTunes podcasting specifications.

Here is a handful of great plugins for video:

✔ **VideoPress by Automattic** (http://wordpress.org/extend/plugins/video): The VideoPress plugin allows blog administrators to upload new videos to their WordPress.com video account and manage existing videos from the convenience of their self-hosted WordPress.org blog's administrative interface. A VideoPress account is required: http://videopress.com.

✔ **Smart YouTube PRO by Vladimir Prelovac** (http://wordpress.org/extend/plugins/smart-youtube): With this plugin, insert videos into blog posts, comments, and RSS feeds, and it currently supports videos from YouTube, Vimeo, Metacafe, LiveLeak and Facebook.

The Media Library page lists all the files you've ever uploaded to your WordPress blog. By default, the page displays all types of files, but you can click the Images, Audio, or Video links to specify which file type you want to see; see Figure 9-8.

You can do the following tasks on the Media Library page:

- ✔ **Filter media files by date.** If you want to view all media files that were uploaded in December 2012, choose that date from the drop-down menu and click the Filter button; the page reloads and displays only the media files uploaded in the month of December 2012.

- ✔ **Search media files using a specific keyword.** If you want to search your Media Library for all files that reference kittens, type the word **kittens** in the Search box in the upper-right side of the Media Library page. Then click the Search Media button; the page reloads and displays only media files that contain the keyword or tag of `kittens`.

- ✔ **Delete media files.** Click the small white box that appears to the left of every thumbnail on the Media Library page; then select Delete in the Bulk Actions drop-down list that shows at the top left of the page. The page reloads, and the media file you've just deleted is now gone.

- ✔ **View media files.** On the Media Library page, click the thumbnail of the file you'd like to view. The actual file opens in your web browser. If necessary, you can copy the permalink of the file from your browser's address bar.

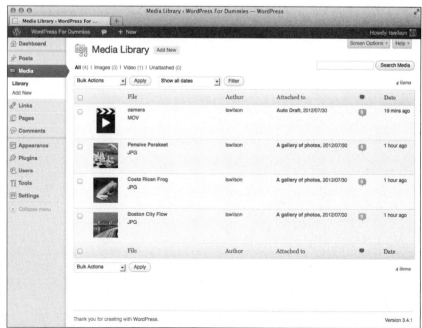

Figure 9-8:
Manage your media files with the WordPress Media Library page.

Chapter 10

Making the Most of WordPress Plugins

*H*alf the fun of running a WordPress-powered blog is playing with the hundreds of plugins that you can install to extend your blog's functions and options. WordPress plugins are like those really cool custom rims you put on your car: Although they don't come with the car, they're awesome accessories that make your car better than all the rest.

By itself, WordPress is a very powerful program for web publishing, but by customizing WordPress with *plugins* — add-on programs that give WordPress almost limitless ways to handle web content — you can make it even more powerful. You can choose any plugins you need to expand your online possibilities. Plugins can turn your WordPress installation into a full-featured gallery for posting images on the web, an online store to sell your products, a user forum, or a social networking site. WordPress plugins can be simple, adding (say) a few minor features to your blog, or they can be complex enough to change your entire WordPress site's functionality.

In this chapter, you find out what plugins are, how to find and install them, and how they enhance your blog to make it unique. Using plugins can also greatly improve your readers' experiences by providing them various tools to interact and participate — just the way you want them to!

Developing plugins — a community activity

Although plugins are written and developed by people who have the skills required to do so, the WordPress user community is also largely responsible for the ongoing development of plugins. Ultimately, the end users are the ones who put those plugins to the true test in their own blogs. Those same users are also the first to speak up and let the developers know when something isn't working right, helping the developers troubleshoot and fine-tune their plugins. The most popular plugins are created by developers who encourage open communication with the user base. Overall, WordPress is one of those great open source projects in which the relationship between developers and users fosters a creative environment that keeps the project fresh and exciting every step of the way.

In this chapter, I assume that you already have WordPress installed on your web server. Installing plugins pertains only to the WordPress.org software. If you're skipping around in the book and haven't yet installed WordPress on your web server, you can find instructions in Chapter 6.

WordPress.com users can't install or configure plugins on their hosted blogs. I don't make the rules, so please don't kill the messenger.

Finding Out What Plugins Are

A *plugin* is a small program that, when added to WordPress, interacts with the software to provide some extensibility to the software. Plugins aren't part of the core software, nor are they software programs themselves. They typically don't function as standalone software. They do require the host program (WordPress, in this case) to function.

Plugin developers are the people who write these gems and share them with the rest of us — usually for free. As is WordPress, most plugins are free to anyone who wants to further tailor and customize a site to meet specific needs.

Literally thousands of plugins are available for WordPress — certainly way too many for me to list in this chapter alone. I could, but then you'd need heavy machinery to lift this book off the shelf! So here are just a few examples of things that plugins let you add to your WordPress blog:

- ✔ **E-mail notification:** Your biggest fans can sign up to have an e-mail notification sent to them every time you update your blog.

- ✔ **Submit your blog to social networking services:** Allow your readers to submit your blog posts to some of the most popular social networking services such as Digg, Twitter, Facebook, and Reddit.

✔ **Stats program:** Keep track of where your traffic is coming from; which posts on your blog are the most popular; and how much traffic is coming through your blog on a daily, monthly, and yearly basis.

Chapter 14 gives you a peek at some of the most popular plugins on the scene today. In the meantime, this chapter takes you through the process of finding plugins, installing them in your WordPress blog, and managing and troubleshooting them.

Exploring the Plugins page

Before you start installing plugins for your blog, it's important for you to explore the Plugins page on your WordPress Dashboard and understand how to manage the plugins after you install them. Click the Installed Plugins link in the Plugins menu on your WordPress Dashboard to view the Plugins page shown in Figure 10-1.

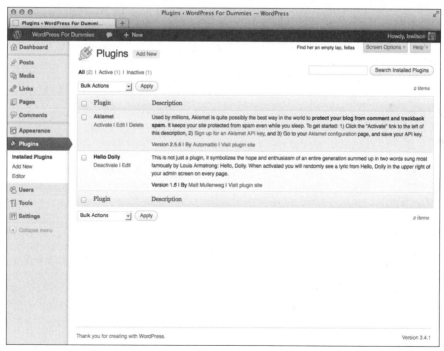

Figure 10-1:
Manage your plugins with the Plugins page on the WordPress Dashboard.

The Plugins page is where you manage all the plugins you install in your WordPress blog. By default, the Plugins page displays a full listing of all the WordPress plugins you currently have installed. You can filter the listing of plugins using the three links shown directly below the Plugins page title:

- ✔ **All:** This is the default view for the Plugins page and shows a listing of all plugins currently installed on your WordPress website, whether they are active or not.

- ✔ **Active:** Clicking this link shows a list of the plugins that are currently activated and in use on your WordPress website.

- ✔ **Inactive:** Clicking this link changes the display and shows the list of plugins that are installed but not currently active. (*Note:* This link displays on the Plugins page only if you have inactive plugins.)

- ✔ **Drop-Ins:** A very select few plugins actually have files that change the behavior of WordPress so substantially that it lets you know about it, just in case there's a question later. These plugins drop files into the `wp-content` directory that modify the core settings of WordPress (mostly having to do with caching or other server-specific settings). These files don't show up in the main plugin listing because they typically belong to other plugins. The Drop-Ins link appears only if you have drop-in plugins installed.

With a quick glance at the Plugins page, you can easily tell which plugins are active — and which aren't — by the background color of each plugin listed. A gray background means that the plugin is *not* active. A white background means that the plugin *is* active. In Figure 10-1, the background of the Akismet plugin is gray and the background of the Hello Dolly plugin is white. Akismet isn't active, but Hello Dolly is.

You can mass manage your plugins on the Plugins page. You can deactivate all your plugins simultaneously by selecting the box to the left of each plugin name and then selecting Deactivate in the Bulk Actions drop-down menu at the top or bottom of the page (as shown in Figure 10-1). Then click the Apply button. Likewise, you can activate, upgrade, or delete the plugins listed by selecting Activate, Update, or Delete in the Bulk Actions drop-down menu. To quickly select all your plugins with one click, select the box to the left of the Plugin heading on the Plugins page.

The Plugins page displays plugins in two columns, which give details for each plugin:

- ✔ **Plugin:** This column lists the plugin name so that you can find it easily when browsing the Plugins page. Directly beneath the plugin name, you see a few links for easy plugin management:

- *Activate:* This link appears below the title of only inactive plugins. Click the link to activate a plugin.

- *Deactivate:* This link appears below the title of only active plugins. Click the link to deactivate a plugin.

- *Delete:* This link appears below the title of only inactive plugins. Click the link to delete the plugin from your site. (See more about this topic in the "Uninstalling Plugins" section, later in this chapter.)

- *Edit:* This link appears below all listed plugins, whether they are active or not. Click the link to visit the Edit Plugins page. If you feel comfortable doing so, you can edit the individual plugin files.

✔ **Description:** This column lists a description for the plugin. Depending on the plugin, you may also see brief instructions on using the plugin. Directly below the description are the version number of the plugin, the plugin author's name, and a link to the website where you can read more information about the plugin.

Discovering the one-click plugin update

For a lot of reasons, mainly security reasons and feature updates, always use the most up-to-date versions of the plugins in your blog. With everything you have to do every day, how can you possibly keep up with knowing whether the plugins you're using have been updated?

You don't have to. WordPress does it for you.

Figure 10-2 shows an out-of-date version (2.5.5) of Akismet installed. WordPress notifies you when a new update is available for a plugin in three different ways, as shown in Figure 10-2:

✔ **Dashboard Updates link:** The Updates link below the Dashboard menu displays a circle with a white number. The number indicates how many plugins have updates available. In Figure 10-2, you see that there is one plugin with an update available on my site. Click the Update link to see which plugins have updates available.

✔ **Plugins menu title:** The Plugins menu title also displays a circle with a number. As with the Updates link, the number indicates how many plugins have updates available, as shown in Figure 10-2.

✔ **Plugins page:** Figure 10-2 shows the Plugins page. Below the Akismet plugin you see a message that says, `There is a new version of Akismet available. View version 2.5.6 details or update now.`

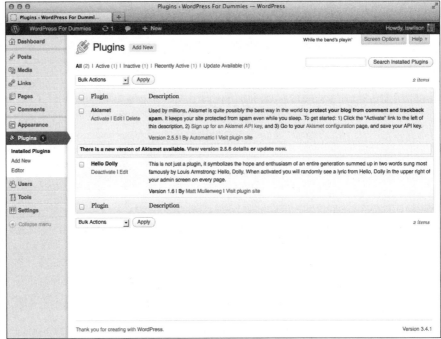

Figure 10-2:
WordPress
tells you
when a
new plugin
version is
available.

WordPress gives you not only a message that a new version of the plugin is available, but also a link to a page where you can download the new version, or a link that you can click to update the plugin right there and then — WordPress's one-click plugin update.

Click the Update Now link, and WordPress grabs the new files off the WordPress.org server, uploads them to your plugins directory, deletes the old plugin, and activates the new one. (If a plugin is deactivated at the time it's updated, WordPress gives you the option to activate the plugin after your update process is completed.) Figure 10-3 shows the Update Plugin page that you see while the plugin is being upgraded.

WordPress notifies you of an out-of-date plugin and provides you with the one-click upgrade function *only* for plugins that are in the official WordPress Plugin Directory (http://wordpress.org/extend/plugins). If a plugin you are using is not listed in the directory, the notification and one-click upgrade function won't be present for that plugin.

Another way that WordPress alerts you of out-of-date plugins is in the left navigation menu. When you have an out-of-date plugin, a number appears next to the Updates link on the Dashboard menu, indicating that you have a plugin, or plugins, that need to be upgraded. Figure 10-4 shows my Dashboard telling me that I have one plugin that needs to be upgraded. After you upgrade the plugin, the number disappears.

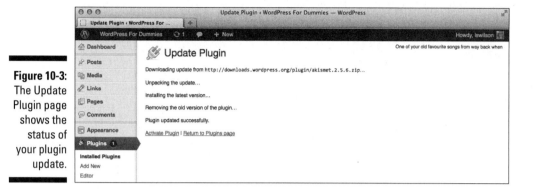

Figure 10-3:
The Update
Plugin page
shows the
status of
your plugin
update.

Whatever you do, do *not* ignore the plugin update messages that WordPress gives you. Plugin developers usually release new versions because of security problems or vulnerabilities that require an upgrade. If you notice that an upgrade is available for a plugin you're using, stop what you're doing and upgrade it — it takes only a few seconds.

Your out-of-date plugin alert

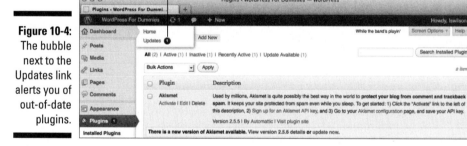

Figure 10-4:
The bubble
next to the
Updates link
alerts you of
out-of-date
plugins.

For the automatic plugin upgrade to work, your plugin directory (`/wp-content/plugins`) must be writable on your web server, which means that you should have set permissions of 755 or 777 (depending on your web server configuration). See Chapter 6 for information about changing file permissions on your web server, or contact your web-hosting provider for assistance.

Exploring the Plugins Included with WordPress

At this writing, WordPress packages two plugins with the installation files:

- **Akismet:** This plugin is essential.
- **Hello Dolly:** This plugin isn't necessary to make your blog run smoothly, but it adds some extra fun.

Incorporating Akismet

I touch on Akismet a few times throughout this book. It's my humble opinion that Akismet is the mother of all plugins and that no WordPress blog is complete without a fully activated version.

Apparently WordPress agrees, because the plugin has been packaged in every WordPress software release since version 2.0. Akismet was created by the folks at Automattic — the same folks who bring you the Sidebar Widgets plugin. Akismet is the answer to comment and trackback spam. Matt Mullenweg of Automattic says that Akismet is a "collaborative effort to make comment and trackback spam a non-issue and restore innocence to blogging, so you never have to worry about spam again" (from the Akismet website at `http://akismet.com`).

To use the plugin, follow these steps:

1. **On the Plugins page, click the Activate link under the Akismet plugin name.**

   A yellow box appears at the top of the page, saying: `Akismet is almost ready. You must enter your Akismet API key for it to work` (see Figure 10-5). An *API key* is a string of numbers and letters that function like a unique password given to you by WordPress.com; it's the key that allows your WordPress.org application to communicate with your WordPress.com account.

2. **Click the link in the yellow box to obtain your WordPress.com API key.**

   Clicking this link takes you to the Akismet Configuration page on your WordPress Dashboard, where you enter your API key in the Akismet API Key text field and then click the Update Options button to save your changes. You can stop here if you already have a key, but if you do not have an Akismet key, keep following the steps in this section.

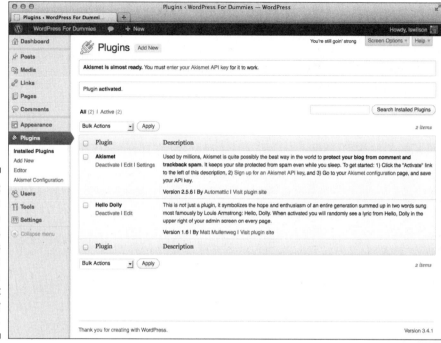

3. Click the Akismet.com link on the Akismet Configuration page.

This opens the Akismet website in your browser window at `http://akismet.com/get`.

4. Click the Get an Akismet API Key button.

This opens the signup page on the Akismet website, where you can choose from several different options for obtaining an Akismet key:

- *Enterprise:* $50/month for people who own multiple WordPress-powered websites and want to use Akismet on all of them.

- *Pro:* $5/month for people who own one small, nonpersonal (or business) WordPress-powered site.

- *Personal:* $0–$120/year for people who own one small, personal, WordPress-powered blog. You can choose to pay nothing ($0), or if you'd like to contribute a little cash toward the cause of combating spam, you can opt to spend up to $120 per year for your Akismet key subscription.

5. Select and pay for (if needed) your Akismet key.

After you've gone through the signup process, Akismet provides you with an API key. Copy that key by selecting it with your mouse pointer, right-clicking, and choosing Copy.

6. **When you have your API key, go to the Akismet Configuration page by clicking the Akismet Configuration link in the Plugins menu on your WordPress Dashboard.**

7. **Enter the API key in the Akismet API Key text box (see Figure 10-6) and click the Update Options button to fully activate the Akismet plugin.**

On the Akismet Configuration Page, after you've entered and saved your key, you also have two options that you can select to further manage your spam protection:

✓ **Auto-delete Spam Submitted on Posts More Than a Month Old:** Enable this option by selecting the check box next to it to tell Akismet to automatically delete spam comments on posts that are more than a month old.

✓ **Show The Number of Comments You've Approved Beside Each Comment Author:** Enable this option by selecting the check box next to it to tell Akismet to display the number of approved comments each comment author on your blog has.

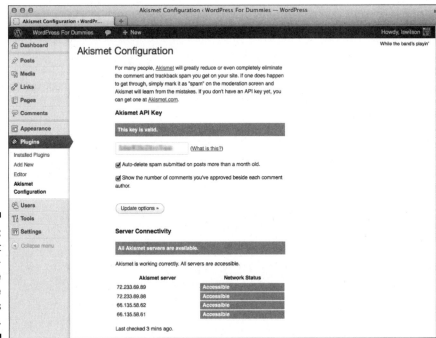

Figure 10-6:
Akismet
Configura-
tion Page
on the
WordPress
Dashboard.

Akismet catches spam and throws it into a queue, holding the spam for 15 days and then deleting it from your database. It's probably worth your while to check the Akismet Spam page once a week to make sure that the plugin hasn't captured any legitimate comments or trackbacks.

You can rescue those nonspam-captured comments and trackbacks by doing the following (after you've logged on to your WordPress Dashboard):

1. **Click the Comments menu.**

   The Comments page appears, displaying a list of the most recent comments on your blog.

2. **Click the Spam link.**

   The Comments page now displays all spam comments that the plugin caught.

3. **Browse through the list of spam comments, looking for any legitimate comments or trackbacks.**

4. **If you locate one that's legitimate, select the Approve link directly below the entry.**

   The comment is marked as legitimate. In other words, you don't consider this comment to be spam. The comment is then approved and published on your blog.

Check your spam filter often. I just found four legitimate comments caught in my spam filter and was able to de-spam them, releasing them from the binds of Akismet and unleashing them upon the world. Check out Chapter 8 for more information on managing comments in WordPress.

The folks at Automattic did a fine thing with Akismet. Since the emergence of Akismet, I've barely had to think about comment or trackback spam, except for the few times a month I check my Akismet spam queue.

Saying Hello Dolly

Matt Mullenweg, co-founder of WordPress, developed the Hello Dolly plugin. Anyone who follows the development of WordPress knows that Matt is a huge jazz fan. How do we know this? Every single release of WordPress is named after some jazz great. One of the most recent releases of the software, for example, is named Ella — after jazz great Ella Fitzgerald; another release was named Coltrane after the late American jazz saxophonist and composer John Coltrane.

So, knowing this, it isn't surprising that Mullenweg developed a plugin named Hello Dolly. Here's the description of it that you see in the Plugins page on your Dashboard:

> This is not just a plugin, it symbolizes the hope and enthusiasm of an entire generation summed up in two words sung most famously by Louis Armstrong: "Hello, Dolly." When activated, you will randomly see a lyric from "Hello, Dolly" in the upper right of your admin screen on every page.

Is it necessary? No. Is it fun? Sure!

Activate the Hello Dolly plugin on the Plugins page on your WordPress Dashboard. When you've activated it, your WordPress blog greets you with a different lyric from the song "Hello, Dolly!" each time.

If you want to change the lyrics in this plugin, you can edit them by clicking the Edit link to the right of the Hello Dolly plugin on the Plugins page. The Plugin Editor opens and lets you edit the file in a text editor. Make sure that each line of the lyric has its own line in the plugin file. This plugin may not seem very useful to you and, in fact, it may not be useful to the majority of WordPress users, but the real purpose behind the plugin is to provide WordPress plugin developers with a simple example of how to write a plugin. This book does not cover topics on how to create your own plugin, but if you are interested in that, you may want to check out my other book, *WordPress All-in-One For Dummies* (John Wiley & Sons, Inc.), which does cover that topic in detail.

Using Plugins: Just the Basics

In this section, I show you how to install a plugin in your WordPress blog using the built-in plugins feature. The auto-installation of plugins from within your WordPress Dashboard works only for plugins that are included in the official WordPress Plugin Directory (`http://wordpress.org/extend/plugins`). You can manually install plugins on your WordPress blog, a process that I cover in the next section.

WordPress makes it super easy to find, install, and then activate plugins for use on your blog. Just follow these simple steps:

1. **Click the Add New link in the Plugins menu.**

   The Install Plugins page opens, and you can browse the official WordPress Plugins Directory from your WordPress Dashboard.

2. **Search for a plugin to install on your blog:**

   • *Keyword:* If you want to search for plugins that allow you to add additional features for comments on your site, select Term in the drop-down menu and then enter the word **Comments** in the Search text box on the Install Plugins page. Click the Search Plugins button, and a list of plugins returns that deal specifically with comments.

   • *Author or Tag:* Select Author or Tag in the drop-down menu and then enter the author or tag name in the Search box; then click the Search Plugins button.

You can also search by tag by clicking any of the tag names that appear at the bottom of the Install Plugins page under the Popular heading.

I want to install a very popular plugin called Subscribe to Comments, by Mark Jaquith (see the next section in this chapter for a description of this plugin). To find it, enter the words **Subscribe to Comments** in the Search text box on the Install Plugins page. Then click Search Plugins.

Figure 10-7 shows the results page for the Subscribe to Comments search phrase, which is listed as the first plugin on the Search Results page.

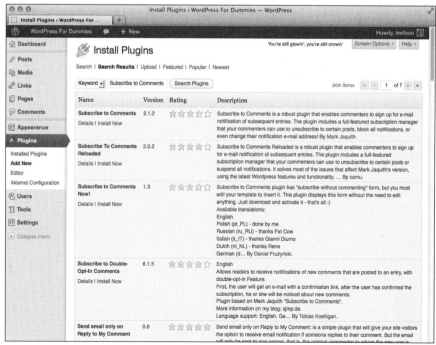

Figure 10-7: Finding a plugin to install using the built-in Plugin Directory search.

3. **Click the Details link below the plugin name.**

A Description window opens, giving you information about the Subscribe to Comments plugin, including a description of the plugin, version number, author name, and an Install Now button.

4. **Click the Install Now button.**

You go to the Installing Plugins page within your WordPress Dashboard, where you find a confirmation message that the plugin has been downloaded, unpacked, and successfully installed.

5. **Specify whether to activate the plugin or proceed to the Plugins page.**

Two links are shown below the confirmation message:

- *Activate Plugin:* Click this link to activate the plugin you just installed on your blog.

- *Return to Plugin Installer:* Click this link to go to the Install Plugins page without activating the plugin.

The auto-installation of plugins from your WordPress Dashboard works on most web-hosting configurations. However, some web-hosting services don't allow the kind of access that WordPress needs to complete the auto-installation. If you get any errors or find that you are unable to use the plugin auto-installation feature, get in touch with your web-hosting provider to find out whether it can assist you.

Installing Plugins Manually

In the following sections, I show you how to find, upload, and install the very popular Subscribe to Comments plugin, developed by Mark Jaquith. I'm using the Subscribe to Comments plugin as a real-world example to take you through the mechanics involved in downloading, unpacking, uploading, activating, and using a plugin in WordPress.

Subscribe to Comments gives your readers the opportunity to subscribe to individual comment threads on your site so that they receive a notification, via e-mail, when a new comment has been left on the comment thread (or blog post) that they have subscribed to. This plugin helps keep lively discussions active in your blog.

Installing the Subscribe to Comments plugin takes you through the process, but keep in mind that every plugin is different. Reading the description and installation instructions for each plugin you want to install is very important.

Finding and downloading the files

The first step in using plugins is locating the one you want to install. The absolute best place to find WordPress plugins is the official WordPress Plugins Directory found at `http://wordpress.org/extend/plugins` where, at the time of this writing, you will find over 21,000 plugins available for download.

To find Mark Jaquith's Subscribe to Comments plugin, follow these steps:

1. **Go to the official WordPress Plugin Directory, located at** `http:// wordpress.org/extend/plugins.`

2. **In the search box at the top of the Plugin Directory home page, enter the keywords** Subscribe to Comments **and then click the Search Plugins button.**

3. **Locate the Subscribe to Comments plugin on the search results page (see Figure 10-8) and click the plugin name.**

   The Subscribe to Comments page opens in the WordPress Plugin Directory, where you find a description of the plugin as well as other information about the plugin (see Figure 10-9). For example, in Figure 10-9, take note of the important information on the right side of the page:

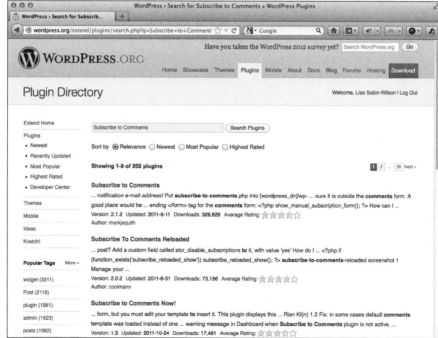

Figure 10-8:
Use the search feature of the WordPress Plugin Directory page to find the plugin you need.

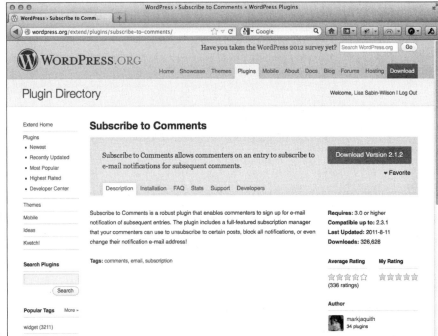

Figure 10-9:
The down-
load page
for the
Subscribe to
Comments
plugin.

- *Download Version:* This is the download link that you click to download the plugin, and the number shown in this area is the most recent version number of the plugin.

- *Requires:* This tells you what version of WordPress you need to successfully use this plugin. For example, Figure 10-9 shows that the Subscribe to Comments plugin requires WordPress version 3.0 or higher; this means that this plugin doesn't work with WordPress versions lower than 3.0. Helpful!

- *Compatible Up To:* This tells you what version of WordPress this plugin is compatible up to. For example, if this section tells you that the plugin is compatible up to version 2.3, this means that you usually can't use the plugin with versions higher than 2.3. I say *usually* because the plugin developer may not update the information in this section — especially if the plugin files themselves haven't changed. The best way to check is to download the plugin, install it, and see whether it works! (Figure 10-9 shows that Mark Jaquith's Subscribe to Comments plugin is compatible up to WordPress version 2.3.1 — however, I can verify that it does work in all versions up to the most recent, 3.4.1.)

- *Last Updated:* This displays the date that the plugin was last updated by the author.

- *Downloads:* This number tells you how many times this plugin has been downloaded by other WordPress users.

- *Ratings:* With a rating system of 1-5 stars (1 being the lowest, 5 being the highest), you can see how other WordPress users have rated this plugin.

4. **Click the Download button for the plugin version you want to download.**

   If you're using Internet Explorer, click the Download button, and a dialog box opens, asking whether you want to open or save the file. Click Save to save the zip file to your hard drive, and *remember where you saved it.*

   If you're using Mozilla Firefox, click the Download button, and a dialog box opens, asking what Firefox should do with the file. Select the Save File radio button and then click OK to save it to your hard drive. Again, *remember where you saved it.*

   For other browsers, follow the download instructions in the corresponding dialog box.

5. **Locate the file on your hard drive and open it with your favorite decompression program.**

   If you're unsure how to use your decompression program, refer to the documentation available with the program.

6. **Unpack (decompress) the plugin files you downloaded for the Subscribe to Comments plugin.**

Reading the instructions

Frequently, the plugin developer includes a `readme` file inside the zip file. Do what the title of the file says: Read it. Many times, it contains the exact documentation and instructions that you will find on the plugin developer's page.

Make sure that you read the instructions carefully and follow them correctly. Ninety-nine percent of WordPress plugins have great documentation and instructions from the plugin developer. If you don't follow the instructions correctly, the best scenario is that the plugin just doesn't work on your blog. At worst, the plugin creates all sorts of ugly errors, requiring you to start the plugin installation over from step one.

You can open `readme.txt` files in any text-editor program, such as Notepad or WordPad on a PC, or TextEdit on a Mac.

In the case of Mark Jaquith's Subscribe to Comments plugin, the `readme.txt` file contains instructions on how to upload and use the plugin, as well as some answers to frequently asked questions on troubleshooting the installation and use.

Every plugin is different in terms of where the plugin files are uploaded and what configurations and setup are necessary to make the plugin work on your site. Read the installation instructions very carefully and follow those instructions to the letter to install the plugin correctly on your site.

Uploading and Activating Plugins

Now you're ready to upload the plugin files to your web server. In earlier versions of WordPress, you needed to upload the unpacked plugin files to your web server via FTP (see Chapter 6). Now, all you need to do is upload the zip file you just downloaded from the WordPress Plugin Directory. Be sure you are logged on to your WordPress Dashboard.

Although, unpacking the zip file you've downloaded is helpful because it can contain files that give you insight into the use of the plugin itself. Locate the plugin files you just unpacked on your hard drive. In the event that the plugin developer didn't include a `readme.txt` file with instructions, check the plugin developer's page for specific instructions on how to install the plugin in your WordPress blog. Specifically, the documentation in the `readme.txt` file and/or on the plugin's website should address the following points:

- ✔ What directory on your web server you upload the plugin files to.
- ✔ What to do if you need to change permissions for any of the plugin files after you upload them to your web server. (See Chapter 6 if you need information on changing file permissions.)
- ✔ What to do if you need to set specific configurations in the plugin file to make it work.
- ✔ What to do if you need to modify your theme template files to include the plugin's functions in your blog.

Uploading a new plugin

To install the Subscribe to Comments plugin via the WordPress Dashboard, follow these easy steps:

1. **Click the Add New link in the Plugins menu.**

   This opens the Install Plugins page on your Dashboard.

2. **Click the Upload link at the top of the Install Plugins page.**

   The resulting page gives you an interface for uploading a plugin in zip format.

3. Click the Browse button.

In the resulting File Upload dialog box, you can locate the zip file for the plugin you'd like to install. In this case, the file is `subscribe-to-comments.zip` (see Figure 10-10). Click the file to select it and then click the Open button to return to the Install Plugins page.

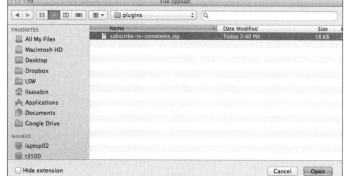

Figure 10-10: Uploading a plugin zip file via the Dashboard.

4. Click the Install Now button.

WordPress uploads the plugin's zip file into the `/wp-content/plugins/` folder on your web server, unpacks it, and installs it. Figure 10-11 shows the Installing Plugin page with messages for you during and after the (hopefully successful) installation.

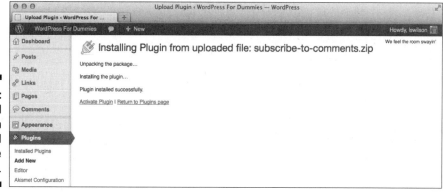

Figure 10-11: Successful plugin upload via the Dashboard.

Activating the plugin

All plugins listed on the Plugins page are either Active or Inactive (except the Drop-In plugins, which are active by default). When you want to activate an inactive plugin, follow these easy steps (in this case, you are activating the Subscribe to Comments plugin that you installed in the previous section):

1. **Click the Installed Plugins link on the Plugins menu.**

   The Plugins page opens, listing all the plugins installed in your WordPress blog.

2. **Locate the Subscribe to Comments plugin.**

   If you have a lot of plugins installed on your WordPress website, you can narrow your search by clicking the Inactive link, which lists the currently inactive plugins.

3. **Click the Activate link below the plugin name.**

   The Plugins page refreshes, and the Subscribe to Comments plugin now appears as an active plugin on the page.

If you've followed all these steps in your own blog, congratulations — you now have Subscribe to Comments installed. Great job!

Setting Plugin Options

Some, but not all, WordPress plugins provide an administration page where you can set options that are specific to that particular plugin. You may find the plugin administration page in any of these places:

- ✔ The Settings page (click the Settings menu)
- ✔ The Tools menu (located in the navigation menu)
- ✔ The Plugins menu (located in the navigation menu)
- ✔ A Dashboard menu (some plugins even create their own menus!)
- ✔ The Admin Toolbar (at the top of any Dashboard page)

You can find the Subscribe to Comments Options page by clicking the Subscribe to Comments link in the Settings menu. The Subscribe to Comments Options page opens (see Figure 10-12).

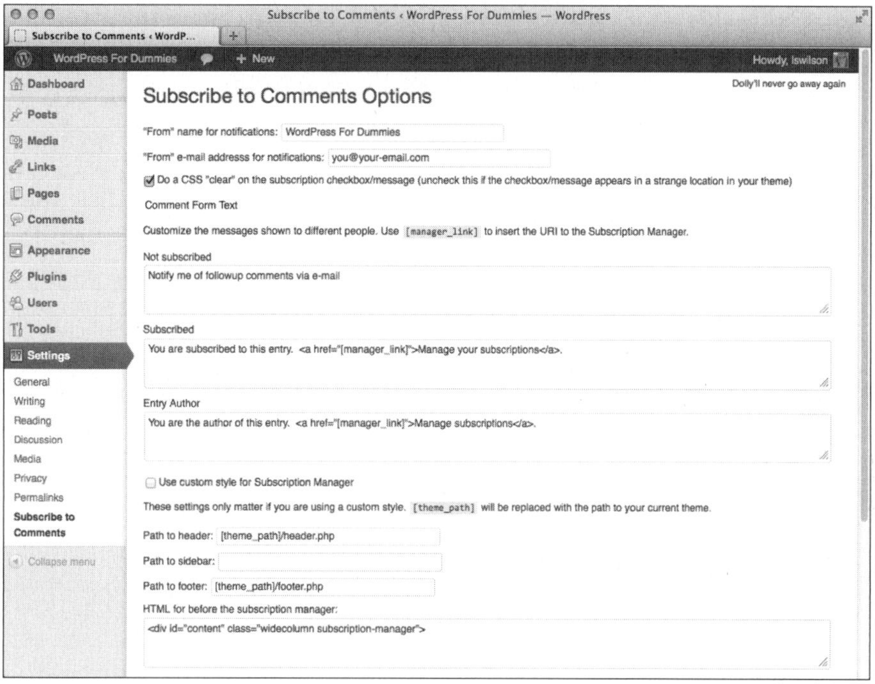

Subscribe to Comments ‹ WordPress For Dummies — WordPress

Figure 10-12:
The
Subscribe to
Comments
Options
administra-
tion page.

Uninstalling Plugins

After all this talk about installing and activating plugins, what happens if you install and activate a plugin and then at some point decide that it just isn't what you want? Don't worry — you aren't stuck forever with a plugin that you don't want. WordPress lets you be fickle and finicky in your plugin choices!

To uninstall a plugin from your WordPress blog

1. **Click the Installed Plugins link on the Plugins menu.**

   The Plugins page opens.

2. **Locate the plugin you want to uninstall.**

3. **Click the Deactivate link below the plugin title.**

   The Plugins page refreshes, and the plugin now appears as deactivated (or inactive).

4. **Click the Delete link that now appears below the plugin title.**

The Delete Plugin page opens, and a confirmation message displays asking you whether you're sure you want to delete this plugin. (See Figure 10-13.)

5. **Click the Yes, Delete These Files button.**

The Plugins page refreshes, and the plugin you just deleted is gone from the lists of plugins, with a message displayed at the top confirming the deletion of the plugin.

Figure 10-13:
Confirmation question on the Delete Plugin(s) page.

Bang! You're done. That's all it takes.

Don't forget to remove any bits of code that you may have added to your theme templates for that particular plugin; otherwise, it may cause ugly error messages to appear in your blog.

Understanding the Open Source Environment

The WordPress software was built on an existing platform called b2. Matt Mullenweg, co-founder of WordPress, was using b2 as a blogging platform at the time the developer of that program abandoned it. What did this mean for its users? It meant no more development unless someone somewhere picked up the ball and continued with the platform. Enter Mullenweg and WordPress.

Getting premium plugins

Not all plugins were created equally. In 2010, the WordPress community saw the emergence of premium, or paid, plugins. These plugins are slightly different from the plugins you find in the official WordPress Plugin Directory, mainly because they have a nominal fee associated with them. Most of the premium plugins also provide great value and support. Here are two examples of premium plugin directories available today:

✔ **Plugin Buddy** (`http://ewebscapes.com/pluginbuddy`): Run by WordPress experts and veterans from the team at iThemes (`http://ithemes.com`), Plugin Buddy is a repository of quality premium plugins like BackupBuddy and Billboard.

✔ **WPMU Premium Dev** (`http://ewebscapes.com/wpmu-premium`): Run by WordPress experts, Incsub, WPMU Premium Dev provide their members with hundreds of high-quality and useful plugins for WordPress, as well as themes and helpful support forums.

Apply this same concept to plugin development, and you'll understand that plugins sometimes fall by the wayside and drop off the face of the earth. Unless someone takes over when the original developer loses interest, future development of that plugin ceases. It's important to understand that most plugins are developed in an open source environment, which means a few things for you, the end user:

✔ **The developers who created your favorite plugin aren't obligated to continue development.** If they find a new hobby or simply tire of the work, they can give it up completely. If no one picks up where they left off, you can kiss that plugin goodbye if it doesn't work with the latest WordPress release.

✔ **Developers of popular plugins don't hold to a specific timetable.** Generally, developers are extremely good about updating their plugins when new versions of WordPress are released, or when a security bug or flaw is discovered. Keep in mind, however, that no timetable exists for these developers to follow. Many of these folks have day jobs, classes, or families that can keep them from devoting as much time to the project as you want them to.

✔ **In the world of plugin development, it's easy come, easy go.** Beware of the pitfalls of falling in love with any particular WordPress plugin. For example, don't let your website become dependent on a plugin, and don't be surprised if a plugin you love doesn't exist tomorrow. You can use the plugin for as long as it continues to work for you, but when it stops working (such as with a new WordPress release or a security exploit that makes it unusable), you have a tough decision to make. You can

- Stop using the plugin and try to find a suitable alternative.

- Hope that another developer takes over the project when the original developer discontinues his involvement.

- Try to find someone to provide a fix for you (in which case, you'll more than likely have to pay that someone for her time).

I don't want to make the world of WordPress plugins sound like gloom and doom, but I do think it's very important for you to understand the dynamics in play. Consider this section to be food for thought.

Chapter 11

Finding and Installing WordPress Themes

*I*n previous chapters, I cover how to use the WordPress platform to publish your posts and pages. In those chapters, you discover how to categorize your posts, build your link lists, and set the publishing and profile options on the WordPress Dashboard. In this chapter, I focus on the visual look and format of your blog — in other words, how other people see your blog after you start publishing your content.

In Chapter 10, I introduce WordPress plugins and discuss some of the thousands of free plugins you can use to add functionality to your blog. Similarly, thousands of free themes are available for you to download and use. This chapter shows you where to find them and takes you through the processes of downloading, installing, and using them.

As a bonus, in this chapter, you find out how to access and download five free WordPress themes that I've created exclusively for readers of this book.

Getting Started with Free Themes

WordPress comes packaged with one very useful default theme called Twenty Eleven (named after the year it was released in version 3.2 of WordPress). Most bloggers who use WordPress usually don't waste any time at all in finding a theme that they like better than the default theme. The Twenty Eleven theme is meant to get you started. Although you're not limited to the default theme, it's a very functional theme for a basic blog. Feel free to use it to get you started on your way.

Free WordPress themes, such as those I discuss in Chapter 15, are popular because of their appealing designs and their ease of installation and use. They're great tools to use when you launch your new blog, and if you dabble a bit in graphic design and CSS (Cascading Style Sheets), you can customize one of the free WordPress themes to fit your own needs. (See Chapter 13 for some resources and tools for templates and template tags, as well as a few great CSS references.) Also see the nearby sidebar "Are all WordPress themes free?" for information about free versus premium themes.

By using free themes, you can have your blog up and running with a new design — without the help of a professional — pretty fast. And with thousands of themes available, you can change your theme as often as you want.

Finding free themes

Finding the theme that fits you best may take some time, but with thousands available, you'll eventually find one that suits you. Trying out several free themes is like trying on different "outfits" for your blog. You can change outfits as needed until you find just the right theme.

In July 2008, WordPress launched the official WordPress Free Themes Directory at `http://wordpress.org/extend/themes` (see Figure 11-1).

The WordPress Free Themes Directory isn't the only place on the web to find free WordPress themes, but it's the place to find the most functional and *safe* themes available. Safe themes contain clean code and basic, fundamental WordPress functions to ensure that your WordPress blog functions with the minimum requirements. The WordPress.org website lists the basic requirements that theme designers have to meet before their theme is accepted into the themes directory; you can find that listing of requirements at `http://wordpress.org/extend/themes/about`.

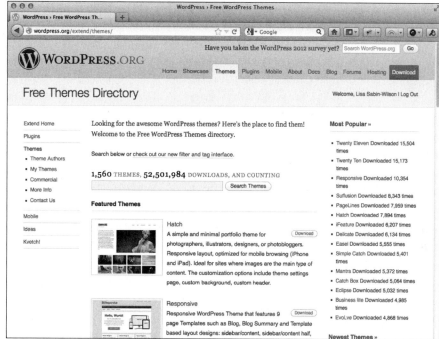

Figure 11-1:
Find the
right theme
for your
blog in the
WordPress
Free
Themes
Directory.

Are all WordPress themes free?

Not all WordPress themes are created equal, and it's important for you, the user, to know the difference between free and commercial themes:

- ✔ **Free:** These themes are free, period. You can download and use them on your website at absolutely no cost. It's a courtesy to include a link to the designer in the footer of your blog — but you can even remove that link if you want.

- ✔ **Commercial:** These themes cost money. You usually find commercial themes available

for download only after you've paid anywhere from $10 to $500. The designer feels that these themes are a cut above the rest and, therefore, are worth the money you spend for them. Generally, you're not allowed to remove any designer-credit links that appear in these themes and you're not allowed to redistribute the themes. (*Note:* You *won't* find commercial themes in the official WordPress Free Themes Directory.) I provide information on where to find commercial themes at the end of this chapter.

Avoiding unsafe themes

Unsafe themes, on the other hand, are developed by people who are looking to take advantage of the blog owners who use them. These particular themes are not allowed in the official WordPress Free Themes Directory. They contain elements such as the following:

- ✔ **Spam links:** These links usually appear in the footer of the theme and can link to some pretty unsavory places. The designers of these themes hope to benefit from traffic from your site. They count on the idea that most blog owners won't notice the links or know how to remove them.

- ✔ **Malicious code:** Unscrupulous theme designers can, and do, place code in theme files that inserts hidden malware and/or virus links and spam. Sometimes you see a line or two of encrypted code that looks as though it's just part of the theme code, and unless you have a great deal of knowledge of PHP, you may not know that the theme is infected with dangerous code.

The results of these unsafe theme elements can range from simply annoy-ing to downright dangerous, affecting the integrity and security of your computer, hosting account, or both. For this reason, the official WordPress Themes Directory is intended and set up to be a safe place from which to download free themes. WordPress designers develop these themes and upload them to the theme directory, and each theme gets vetted by the folks behind the WordPress platform. In the official directory, themes that contain unsafe elements are simply not allowed to play.

If you suspect or worry that you have malicious code on your site — either through a theme you're using or a plugin you've activated — the absolute best place to get your site checked is the Sucuri website (`http://sitecheck.sucuri.net/scanner`), which offers a free website malware scanner. Sucuri provides expertise in the field of web security, for WordPress users in par-ticular, and even has a free plugin you can install to periodically check your WordPress site for malware and/or malicious code: `http://wordpress.org/extend/plugins/sucuri-scanner/`.

My strong recommendation for finding free themes is to stick with the official WordPress Free Themes Directory. That way, you know you're getting a clean, quality theme for your blog. You can rest assured that themes from the official directory are safe and free of spam and malicious code.

Previewing themes

While you're visiting the WordPress Free Themes Directory, you can easily browse the various themes by using the following features:

✔ **Search:** Type a keyword in the Search box in the center of the page (refer to Figure 11-1) and then click the Search Themes button. A new page opens, displaying themes related to the keyword you searched for.

✔ **Featured Themes:** These themes are listed in the center of the themes directory, randomly. WordPress changes the featured themes listing regularly.

✔ **Most Popular:** These themes have been downloaded most often.

✔ **Newest Themes:** These themes are the latest to be added to the directory.

✔ **Recently Updated:** These themes have been updated most recently by their designers.

When you find a theme in the directory that you want to take a closer look at, click its name to open a page that describes that theme (see Figure 11-2):

✔ **Download:** Click this button to download the theme to your computer.

✔ **Preview:** Click this button to open a new window that shows what the theme looks like in a live blog.

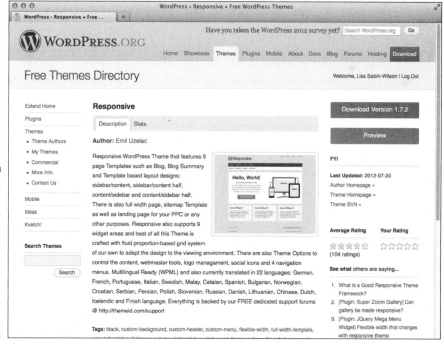

Figure 11-2: Download or preview a particular theme from the WordPress Free Themes Directory.

Downloading themes

To download the theme you want, follow these steps:

1. **Click the Download button on the theme page (refer to Figure 11-2).**

   The theme files show up on your computer as a compressed `.zip` file.

2. **Use your favorite decompression program to unpack the files to your own computer.**

3. **Connect to your web server via FTP and upload the entire theme folder to the /wp-content/themes/ directory of your web server. (You can also upload the theme zip file on the Dashboard via Themes⇨ Install Themes⇨Upload.)**

   You find the `/wp-content/themes/` folder in the WordPress installation directory on your web server.

Activating a New Theme

When you have uploaded the theme to your web server, you can activate it by logging on to your WordPress Dashboard and following these simple steps:

1. **Click the Themes link in the Appearance menu.**

   The Manage Themes page opens, listing all the themes currently installed in your `/themes` directory. The active theme is shown in the Current Theme section at the top of the page. All available themes you may have uploaded to your web server are shown in the Available Themes section (see Figure 11-3).

   Available themes appear on the Manage Themes page in alphabetical order. If you have a lot of themes in your `/themes` directory, you'll see ten to a page, with Next and Previous links to help you navigate all the themes available for your blog.

2. **Click the name or thumbnail image of the theme you want to use.**

   A preview window opens, showing you what your blog will look like with this new theme applied (see Figure 11-4). The preview window also has basic theme configuration settings so you can customize your theme before you activate it. You can customize items such as site title and tagline, theme colors, header and background images, and the static front page so that your theme is ready to go when you activate it. If you skip the customization step, you can return to the Manage Themes page and click the Customize link in the theme description to revisit the customization page.

Figure 11-3:
Themes displayed on the Manage Themes page on the WordPress Dashboard.

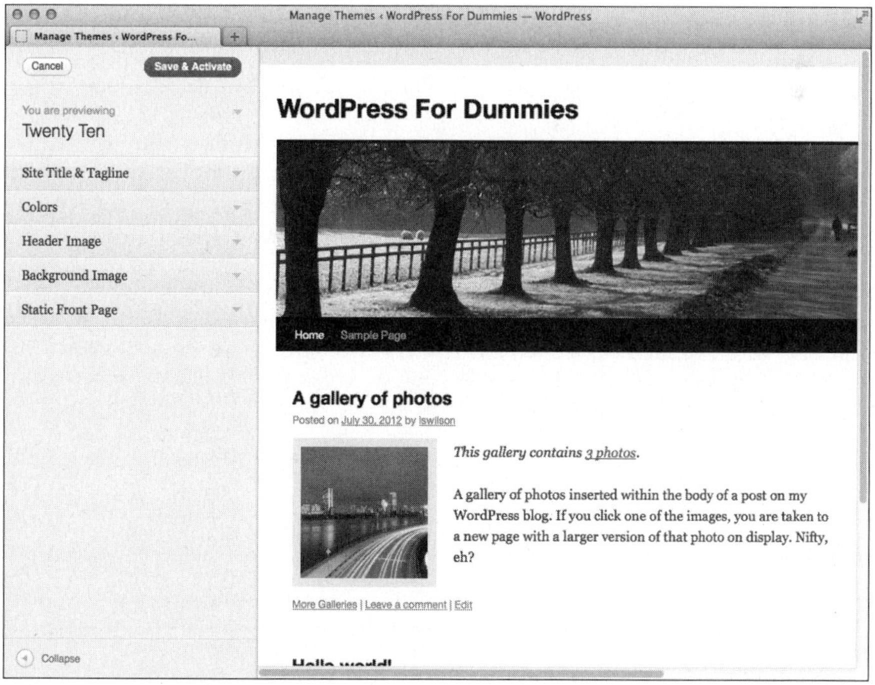

Figure 11-4:
Theme preview window on the WordPress Dashboard.

> Click the Cancel button in the top-left corner of the preview window to close the theme without customizing or activating it.

3. **Click the Save & Activate button.**

   This button resides in the top-left corner of the preview window.

   WordPress applies the theme you chose to your blog.

Browsing and Installing Themes from the Dashboard

Earlier in this chapter, I cover how to find and install a new theme on your WordPress blog by downloading it from the WordPress Free Themes Directory, uploading it to your web server via FTP, and activating the theme within your WordPress Dashboard. The WordPress platform does give you a much easier way to browse the Free Themes Directory to find, preview, and install themes on your site without ever leaving the comfort of the WordPress Dashboard. The following steps show you how to do it:

1. **Click the Themes link in the Appearance menu of your WordPress Dashboard.**

   The Manage Themes page opens.

2. **Click the Install Themes tab at the top of the Manage Themes page.**

   This opens the Install Themes page.

Using sidebar widgets

Most free WordPress themes come with built-in code that lets you take advantage of sidebar widgets for your blog. WordPress widgets are wonderful! (Say *that* ten times fast, why don't you?) Widgets are so wonderful because they let you arrange the content in your blog sidebar, such as your blogroll(s), recent posts, and monthly and category archive listings. With widgets, you can accomplish this arranging without needing to know a single bit of code.

In Chapter 5, I cover how to use sidebar widgets. Although that chapter pertains to the hosted WordPress.com platform, WordPress.org users can follow the same steps. One difference for WordPress.org users is the use of plugins (see Chapter 10). Some plugins have a built-in feature that enables you to include that plugin's functions in your sidebar through the use of a widget. (WordPress.com doesn't have this feature because it doesn't allow uploading and activating various plugins.)

3. Search for a new theme.

On the Install Themes page, you can search for a new theme by keyword, author, or tag. You can also further filter the results by using the Feature Filter check boxes that allow you to filter theme results by color, columns, width, features, and subjects. The Install Themes page is shown in Figure 11-5.

4. Preview a new theme.

After you search for a new theme, the search results page displays a list of themes for you to choose from. Click the Preview link underneath the theme of your choice to view a sample of how the theme looks. Figure 11-6 shows a preview of a theme called Pink Touch 2, which I found by searching for the keyword *Pink* on the Install Themes page.

5. Install a new theme on your blog.

After you find a theme you like, click the Install Now link next to the theme name to install the theme on your blog. This installs the theme and loads the Installing Theme page on your Dashboard with a message telling you that the theme installation was successful.

6. Activate the new theme.

Click the Activate link shown on the Installing Theme page to activate, display, and use the new theme on your site.

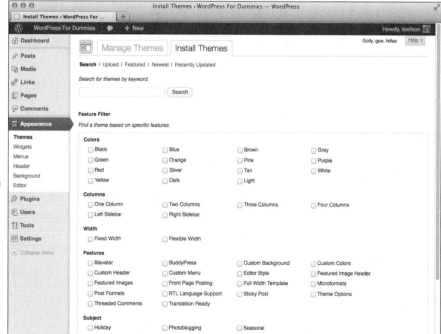

Figure 11-5: Find new themes on the Install Themes page on your WordPress Dashboard.

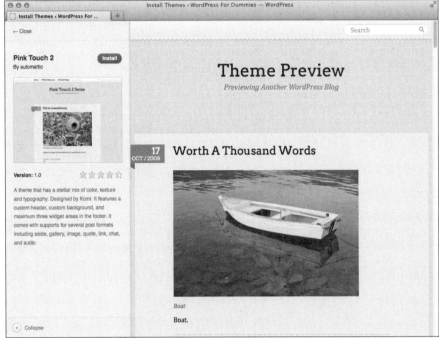

Figure 11-6:
A preview of the Pink Touch 2 theme on the Install Themes page.

At the beginning of this chapter, I mention that the only themes found in the official WordPress Free Themes Directory are free and vetted by the WordPress folks; you can trust that these themes are not only free of charge, but also free of any virus or malicious code. The same holds true for the themes you find by using the Add New Themes feature on your WordPress Dashboard. This feature hooks into the official WordPress Free Themes Directory, so you are sure to find only those themes that are free and safe.

Five free themes for you

At the beginning of this chapter, I tell you about a bonus provided exclusively to readers of this book. That bonus includes five free WordPress themes that I created during the writing of this book. The themes are made available exclusively for you! Without further ado, go ahead and download your themes from `www.dummies.com/go/wordpressfd5e`. Use the username DUMMIES2013 and password WPFDTHEMES to access them. I hope you enjoy the themes, and thank you for reading!

Deciding to Use Commercial Themes

As WordPress becomes more and more popular, I keep seeing many different business models crop up around the web that focus on providing WordPress users with commercial services and support, such as custom design, consulting, and development, for example.

Commercial WordPress themes have become a very popular way for talented designers to provide a service they are very passionate about (designing themes) while making a little money for their efforts at the same time. Commercial themes are also known as premium themes. There are many schools of thought as to what makes a theme *premium* as opposed to free. Actually, the topic of what is considered premium and what is not, with regard to WordPress themes, is guaranteed to spark passionate debate among designers and theme users alike. However, almost everyone agrees there are indicators of premium themes, for example:

✔ **High quality:** Very high-quality graphic design and CSS development.

✔ **Flexibility and ease of use:** A theme structure with functions that make it very easy for users to customize and adjust the theme to suit their own needs. This includes, but is not limited to, altering the header graphic/logo and color scheme and changing images and icons.

✔ **Comprehensive documentation:** Provides the user with extensive instructions on how to use the theme, especially if the theme has multiple features and customization options.

✔ **Supported:** Premium themes are fully supported by the designer who created them. Typically, when you buy a premium theme, you should expect full support on the use of that theme for as long as you're using it.

✔ **Expensive:** Premium themes are not free. I've seen pricing on premium themes in the range of $10 to $500.

This is not to say that some free themes don't have some, or all, of the features I just listed — it's just that, for the most part, they don't. Keep in mind that just because a designer calls a theme *premium* doesn't mean that the theme has passed through any kind of official quality review. One designer's view of what constitutes a premium theme can, and will, differ from the next.

Fully investigate any theme before you put money down on it. Some things to check out before you pay:

✔ E-mail the designer who is selling the premium theme and ask about a support policy.

✔ Find people who have purchased the theme and contact them to find out their experiences with the theme and the designer.

✔ Carefully read any terms that the designer has published on his site to find out any restrictions that exist with licensing.

✔ If the premium theme designer has a support forum, ask whether you can browse through the forum to find out how actively the designer answers questions and provides support. Are users waiting weeks to get their questions answered? Or does the designer seem to be on top of support requests?

✔ Do a search in Google for the theme and the designer. Often, users of premium themes post about their experiences with the theme and the designer. You can find out a lot of positive and, potentially, negative information about the theme and the designer before you buy it.

Although premium themes are cropping up all over the web, a handful really stand out with quality products and services. The following three commercial theme providers are tried and true, with a very stable and successful following of clients who use them.

✔ **iThemes:** Cory Miller and his team of designers and code wranglers provide a total of 30 premium themes available for purchase, with prices ranging from $79.95 to $199.95 each. You can also purchase an all-in-one package that includes all themes for $499.95. All theme purchases at iThemes include full support on the use of the theme(s) for the lifetime of your membership at iThemes. The iThemes premium themes can be found at `http://ithemes.com`.

✔ **StudioPress:** Created by long-time WordPress user, expert, and veteran Brian Gardner, StudioPress offers a variety of high-quality premium WordPress themes that you can purchase with a starting price of $59.95. You may also purchase an all-inclusive themes package starting at $249.95. Theme purchases at StudioPress include a complete support package with access to a support forum staffed by people who are ready to assist you with your most burning questions. You can find StudioPress and browse through its premium theme offerings at `http://studiopress.com`.

✔ **Press75:** Jason Schuller is the creative genius behind Press75, which is a nice option for those looking for quality, premium WordPress themes. You can purchase a subscription starting at $175.00 for access to all the themes in Press75's portfolio for one year, and $375.00 gets you access to the themes for a lifetime — including any new theme releases Jason puts out during that time. Jason's themes are of superb quality and you're sure to find something for everyone on the Press75 website at `http://press75.com`.

You can't find, preview, or install commercial themes using the Add New Themes feature on your WordPress Dashboard (covered in the previous section of this chapter). You can find, purchase, and download premium themes only at an official third-party website. After you find a premium theme you like, you need to install it via the FTP method that I cover in the "Downloading themes" section in this chapter. You can find a very nice selection of premium themes on the WordPress website: `http://wordpress.org/extend/themes/commercial`.

Part V
Customizing WordPress

The 5th Wave   By Rich Tennant

"I know it's a short About Me page, but I thought 'King of the Jungle' sort of said it all."

In this part . . .

This part of the book is about digging into WordPress themes and templates to discover how to tweak template code so that you can change the appearance of your blog. A walk-through on essential WordPress template tags and functions, basic HTML, and CSS helps you put together a nice-looking theme to suit your individual style and flair.

Chapter 12

Understanding Themes and Templates

*T*here are those who like to get their hands dirty (present company included!). If you're one of them, you need to read this chapter. WordPress users who create their own themes do so in the interest of

✔ **Individuality:** You can have a theme that no one else has. (If you use one of the free themes, you can pretty much count on the fact that at *least* a dozen other WordPress blogs will have the same look as yours.)

✔ **Creativity:** You can display your own personal flair and style.

✔ **Control:** You can have full control of how the blog looks, acts, and delivers your content.

Many of you aren't at all interested in creating your own theme for your WordPress blog, however. Sometimes, it's just easier to leave matters to the professionals and hire an experienced WordPress theme developer to create a custom look for your WordPress website or to use one of the thousands of free themes provided by WordPress designers (see Chapter 11). Chapter 15 also tells you where you can get ten free WordPress themes.

Creating themes requires you to step into the code of the templates, which can be a scary place sometimes — especially if you don't really know what you're looking at. A good place to start is by understanding the structure of a WordPress blog. Separately, the parts won't do you any good. But when you put them together, the real magic begins! This chapter covers the basics of doing just that, and near the end of the chapter, you find specific steps to put your own theme together.

You don't need to know HTML to use WordPress. If you plan to create and design WordPress themes, however, you need some basic knowledge of HTML and Cascading Style Sheets (CSS). For assistance with HTML, check out *HTML 4 For Dummies,* 5th Edition, by Ed Tittel and Mary Burmeister, or *HTML, XHML, and CSS Bible,* 5th Edition, by Steven M. Schafer (both published by John Wiley & Sons, Inc.).

Using WordPress Themes: The Basics

A WordPress theme is a collection of WordPress templates made up of WordPress template tags. When I refer to a WordPress *theme,* I'm talking about the group of templates that makes up the theme. When I talk about a WordPress *template,* I'm referring to only one of the template files that contain WordPress template tags. WordPress template tags make all the templates work together as a theme (more about this topic later in the chapter).

Understanding theme structure

The rest of this chapter provides important information about the steps to building a WordPress theme, but here is a brief overview of the templates that make up a WordPress theme and where you find them, both on your server and within your WordPress Dashboard. Follow these steps:

1. **Connect to your web server via FTP and have a look at the existing WordPress themes on your server.**

   The correct location is `/wp-content/themes/` (see the right side of Figure 12-1). When you open this folder, you find the `/twentyeleven` theme folder.

   If a theme is uploaded to any folder other than `/wp-content/themes`, it won't work.

2. **Open the folder for the Twenty Eleven theme** (`/wp-content/themes/twentyeleven`) **and look at the template files inside.**

   When you open the Twenty Eleven theme folder, you see several files. At minimum, you find these five templates in the default theme:

   - *Stylesheet* (`style.css`)

   - *Header template* (`header.php`)

   - *Main Index* (`index.php`)

   - *Sidebar template* (`sidebar.php`)

   - *Footer template* (`footer.php`)

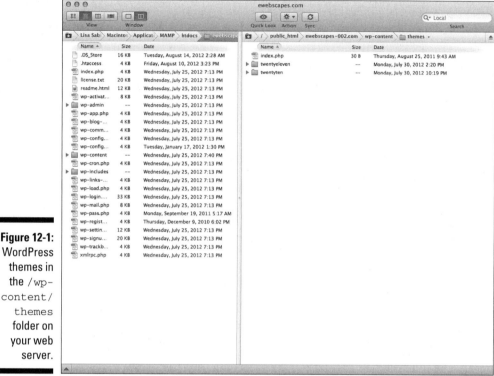

Figure 12-1:
WordPress
themes in
the /wp-
content/
themes
folder on
your web
server.

These files are the main WordPress template files, and I discuss them in more detail in this chapter. There are several template files, however, and you should try to explore all if you can. Take a peek inside and see the different template functions they contain. These filenames are the same in every WordPress theme. See the "Contemplating the Structure of a WordPress Blog" section, later in this chapter, for more information about these template files.

3. **Click the Editor link on the Appearance menu to look at the template files within a theme.**

This Edit Themes page lists the various templates available within the active theme. (Figure 12-2 shows the templates in the default Twenty Eleven theme.) A text box on the left side of the screen displays the contents of each template, and this box is also where you can edit the template file(s). To view and edit a template file, click the template name in the list on the right side of the page.

Figure 12-2:
A list of
templates
available in
the default
Twenty
Eleven
WordPress
theme.

The Edit Themes page also shows the HTML markup (Chapter 13) and template tags within the template file. These tags make all the magic happen in your blog; they connect all the templates to form a theme. The next section of this chapter discusses these template tags in detail, showing you what they mean and how they function. A later section provides steps for putting them all together to create your own theme (or edit an existing theme).

Below the text box on the Edit Themes page is a drop-down menu labeled Documentation. Click the arrow on the right side of the menu, and a list drops down that contains all of the template tags used in the template you're currently viewing. This list is helpful when you edit templates and it gives you some insight into some of the different template tags used to create functions and features within your WordPress theme. (**Note:** The Documentation menu does not appear when you view the Stylesheet because no template tags are used in the `style.css` template — only CSS, which I cover in Chapter 13.)

Connecting templates

The template files don't work alone; for the theme to function, the files need one another. To tie these files together as one working entity, you use template tags to pull the information from each template — Header, Sidebar, and Footer — into the Main Index. I refer to this procedure as *calling* one template into another. (You can find more information in the "Getting Familiar with the Four Main Templates," section, later in this chapter.)

Contemplating the Structure of a WordPress Blog

A WordPress blog, in its very basic form, has four main areas (labeled in Figure 12-3).

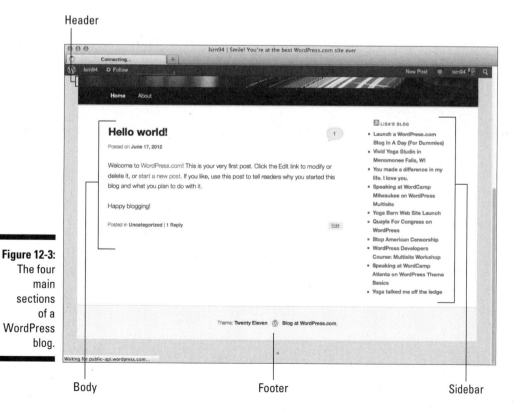

Figure 12-3: The four main sections of a WordPress blog.

Header

Body

Footer

Sidebar

These four main areas appear in the default theme that comes in every version of WordPress:

- ✔ **Header:** This area usually contains the name of the site along with the site tagline or slogan. Sometimes the header also contains a graphic or image.
- ✔ **Body:** This area is where your blog posts appear in chronological order.
- ✔ **Sidebar:** This area is where you find lists of blog-related elements, such as the blogroll, the archives, and a list of recent posts.
- ✔ **Footer:** This area, at the bottom of the page, often contains links to further information about the blog, such as who designed it, which company provides hosting for the blog, and copyright information.

These four areas are the absolute bare bones of a *basic* WordPress blog template. You can extend these areas and create new sections that carry more information, of course, but for the purpose of this chapter, I'm focusing on the basics.

The default WordPress theme is called Twenty Eleven, and in my opinion, it's a pretty doggone wonderful starting point for you, especially if you're just getting your feet wet in the blogosphere. I don't cover all the tags and templates that the Twenty Eleven theme includes; rather, I touch on the basics to get you on your way to understanding templates and template tags for WordPress.

Many themes developed for WordPress are free for public use, and I strongly recommend finding one that you like and downloading it. Use the free themes as a jumping-off place to get started in theme development. Really, why reinvent the wheel? With the free themes available today, most of the work has already been completed for you, and you may find it easier to use one of these themes than to start a theme from scratch.

Each free theme available for download is different, depending on what the developer included (such as CSS styling, display options, format, and layout). So experimenting with a few themes is a fun and great way to learn more about the development of WordPress themes. A great place to find free WordPress themes is the official WordPress Free Themes Directory at `http://wordpress.org/extend/themes`.

To build a *basic* WordPress theme that covers the four basic areas of a blog, you need these five templates:

- ✔ `header.php`
- ✔ `index.php`
- ✔ `sidebar.php`
- ✔ `footer.php`
- ✔ `style.css`

Each WordPress theme comes with a stylesheet (`style.css`), which drives the formatting and layout of your blog template in terms of where the elements are positioned on the page, what the font looks like, what colors your hyperlinks will be, and so on. As you may have already figured out, you don't use CSS to put content on your site; rather, you use CSS to style the content that's already there.

Chapter 13 provides information on tweaking the design of your theme by combining the template tags presented in this chapter with some CSS adjustments in your theme files.

Right now, I'm covering only the very basics; at the end of this chapter, however, I provide some ideas on how you can use various templates to further extend your blog functionality — using templates for categories, archives, static pages, multiple sidebars, and so on. After you build the basics, you can spread your wings and step into more advanced themes.

Examining the Anatomy of a Template Tag

Before starting to play around with template tags in your WordPress templates, it's important to understand what makes up a template tag, and why.

WordPress is based in PHP (a scripting language for creating web pages) and uses PHP commands to pull information from the MySQL database. Every tag begins with the function to start PHP and ends with the function to stop PHP. In the middle of those two commands lives the request to the database that tells WordPress to grab the data and display it.

A typical template tag looks like this:

```
<?php get_info(); ?>
```

This entire example tells WordPress to do three things:

- ✔ Start PHP (`<?php`).
- ✔ Use PHP to get information from the MySQL database and deliver it to your blog (`get_info();`).
- ✔ Stop PHP (`?>`).

In this case, `get_info` is the actual tag function, which grabs information from the database to deliver it to your blog. What information is retrieved depends on what tag function appears between the two PHP commands. As you may notice, a lot of starting and stopping of PHP happens throughout the WordPress templates. The process seems as though it would be resource intensive, if not exhaustive — but it really isn't.

For every PHP command you start, you need a stop command. Every time a command begins with `<?php`, somewhere later in the code is the closing `?>` command. PHP commands that aren't structured properly cause really ugly errors on your site, and they've been known to send programmers, developers, and hosting providers into loud screaming fits.

Getting Familiar with the Four Main Templates

In the following sections, I cover some of the template tags that pull in the information you want to include in your blog. To keep this chapter shorter than 1,000 pages, I focus on the four main templates that get you going with creating your own theme or with editing the template tags in the theme you're currently using. Here are those four main templates:

- Header
- Main Index
- Sidebar
- Footer

The difference between a template and a theme can cause confusion. *Templates* are individual files. Each template file provides the structure in which your content appears. A *theme* is a set of templates. The theme uses the templates to make the whole site.

The Header template

The Header template is the starting point for every WordPress theme because it tells web browsers the following:

- The title of your blog
- The location of the CSS
- The RSS feed URL
- The blog URL
- The tagline (or description) of the blog

Every page on the web has to start with a few pieces of code. In every `header.php` file in any WordPress theme, you find these bits of code at the top:

✔ The DOCTYPE (which stands for *document type declaration*) tells the browser which type of XHTML standards you're using. The Twenty Eleven theme uses `<!DOCTYPE html>`, which is a declaration for W3C standards compliance mode and covers all major browser systems.

✔ The `<html>` tag (*HTML* stands for *Hypertext Markup Language*) tells the browser which language you're using to write your web pages.

✔ The `<head>` tag tells the browser that the information contained within the tag shouldn't be displayed on the site; rather, that information is *about* the document.

In the header template of the Twenty Eleven theme, these bits of code look like the following example, and you should leave them intact:

```
<!DOCTYPE html>
<html <?php language_attributes(); ?>>
<head>
```

On the Edit Themes page, click the Header template link to display the template code in the text box. Look closely and you see that the `<!DOCTYPE html>` declaration, `<html>` tag, and `<head>` tag show up in the template.

The `<head>` tag needs to be closed at the end of the Header template, and the closing tag looks like this: `</head>`. You also need to include a fourth tag, the `<body>` tag, which tells the browser where the information you want to display begins. Both the `<body>` and `<html>` tags need to be closed at the end of the template, like this: `</body></html>`.

Using bloginfo parameters

The Header template makes much use of one WordPress template tag in particular: `bloginfo();`.

A *parameter* differentiates the type of information that a tag pulls in. Parameters are placed inside the parentheses of the tag, enclosed in single quotes. For the most part, these parameters pull information from the settings on your WordPress Dashboard. The template tag to get your blog title, for example, looks like this:

```
<?php bloginfo('name'); ?>
```

Table 12-1 lists the various parameters you need for the `bloginfo();` tag and shows you what the template tag looks like. The parameters in Table 12-1 are listed in the order of their appearance in the Twenty Eleven `header.php` template file and pertain to the `bloginfo();` template tag only.

Table 12-1	Tag Values for bloginfo(); in the Default Twenty Eleven Template Header	
Parameter	*Information*	*Tag*
charset	Character settings set in Settings/ General	`<?php bloginfo('charset'); ?>`
name	Blog title, set in Settings/General	`<?php bloginfo('name'); ?>`
description	Tagline for your blog, set in Settings/General	`<?php bloginfo('description'); ?>`
url	Your blog's web address, set in Settings/General	`<?php bloginfo('url'); ?>`
stylesheet_ url	URL of primary CSS file	`<?php bloginfo('stylesheet url'); ?>`
pingback_url	Displays the trackback URL for your blog on single post pages	`<?php bloginfo('pingback_ url'); ?>`

Creating title tags

Here's a useful tip about your blog's `<title>` tag: Search engines pick up the words used in the `<title>` tag as keywords to categorize your site in their search engine directories.

The `<title></title>` tags are HTML tags that tell the browser to display the title of your website in the title bar of a visitor's browser. Figure 12-4 shows how the title of my personal blog sits in the title bar of the browser window. The *title bar* is the top bar in your browser. In Figure 12-4, it says Lisa Sabin-Wilson — Designer, Author: WordPress For Dummies.

Search engines love the title bar. The more you can tweak that title to provide detailed descriptions of your site (otherwise known as *search engine optimization*, or SEO), the more the search engines love your blog site. Browsers show that love by giving your site higher rankings in their results.

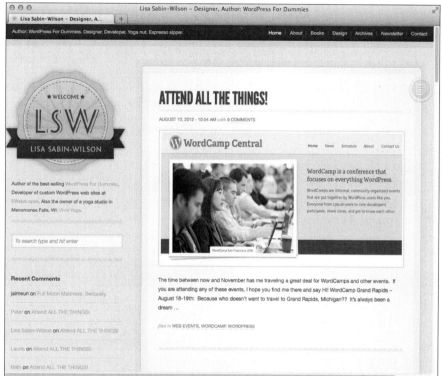

Figure 12-4:
The title
bar of a
browser.

The blog `<title>` tag is the code that lives in the Header template between these two tag markers: `<title></title>`. In the default Twenty Eleven theme, this bit of code looks like this (don't let this code scare you! I promise to break it down for you!):

```
<title>
<?php
/* * Print the <title> tag based on what is being viewed. */
    global $page, $paged;
    wp_title( '|', true, 'right' );
    // Add the blog name.
    bloginfo( 'name' );
    // Add the blog description for the home/front page.
    $site_description = get_bloginfo( 'description', 'display' );
    if ( $site_description && ( is_home() || is_front_page() ) )
    echo " | $site_description";

    // Add a page number if necessary:
    if ( $paged >= 2 || $page >= 2 )
    echo ' | ' . sprintf( __( 'Page %s', 'twentyeleven' ), max( $paged, $page )
            );
?>
</title>
```

It may help for me to put this example into plain English. The way the Twenty Eleven Header template displays the title is based on the type of page that's being displayed — and it shrewdly uses SEO to help you with the browser powers that be. Table 12-2 breaks down what's happening.

Table 12-2	Title Tags and What They Do	
Title Tags and Parameters	*Tags Used*	*What Is Displayed in the Title Bar*

`global $page, $paged;`
 	
`wp_title( '|', true, 'right' );`
 	
`bloginfo( 'name' );`
	`wp_title();`
	
	`bloginfo('name');`
		If the reader is viewing any page or post, the title and site name appear.

`$site_description = get_bloginfo( 'description', 'display' );`
 	
`if ( $site_description && ( is_home() || is_front_page() ) )`
 	
`echo "
	$site_description";`	`get_bloginfo ('description', 'display');`
		
		`is_home()`
		
		`is_front_page()`
			If the reader is viewing the home page or the front page, the site description appears along with the site name.

`if ( $paged >= 2 || $page >= 2 )` `echo '	' . sprintf(__('Page %s', 'twentyeleven'), max($paged, $page));`	`if( $paged >=2 | $page>=2)`	If the reader is viewing any other page within the site other than what has already been defined in the previous tags, the title of the page followed by the blog name appear, and these tags also display the page number.

The title bar of the browser window always displays your site name unless you're on a single post page. In that case, it shows your site title plus the title of the post on that page.

Displaying your site name and tagline

The default Twenty Eleven theme header shows your site name and tagline. My site name and tagline are

- ✔ **Site name:** Lisa Sabin-Wilson
- ✔ **Site tagline:** Designer, Author: WordPress For Dummies

Refer to Figure 12-4 to see these two elements in the header of the site.

You can use the `bloginfo();` tag plus a little HTML code to display your site name and tagline. Most sites have a clickable title, which is a site title that takes you back to the main page when clicked. No matter where your visitors are on your site, they can always go back home by clicking the title of your site in the header.

To create a clickable title, use the following HTML markup and WordPress template tags:

```
<a href="<?php bloginfo('url'); ?>"><?php
        bloginfo('name'); ?></a>
```

The `bloginfo('url');` tag is your main site Internet address, and the `bloginfo('name');` tag is the name of your site (refer to Table 12-1). So the code creates a link that looks something like this:

```
<a href="http://yourdomain.com">Your Site Name</a>
```

The tagline generally isn't linked back home. You can display it by using the following tag:

```
<?php bloginfo('description'); ?>
```

This tag pulls the tagline directly from the one that you've set up on the General Settings page on your WordPress Dashboard.

This example shows how WordPress is intuitive and user-friendly; you can do things such as change the blog name and tagline with a few keystrokes on the Dashboard. Changing your options on the Dashboard creates the change on every page of your site — no coding experience required. Beautiful, isn't it?

In the Twenty Eleven templates, these tags are surrounded by tags that look like these: `<h1></h1>` or `<h2></h2>`. These tags are `<header>` tags, which define the look and layout of the blog name and tagline in the CSS of your theme. I cover CSS further in Chapter 13.

The Main Index template

The Main Index template drags your blog posts out of the MySQL database and inserts them into your site. This template is to your blog what the dance floor is to a nightclub — where all the action happens.

The filename of the Main Index template is `index.php`. You can find it in the `/wp-content/themes/twentyeleven/` folder.

The first template tag in the Main Index template calls in the Header template, meaning that it pulls the information from the Header template into the Main Index template, as follows:

```
<?php get_header(); ?>
```

Your theme can work without calling in the Header template, but it'll be missing several essential pieces — the CSS and the blog name and tagline, for starters. Without the call to the Header template, your blog resembles the image shown in Figure 12-5.

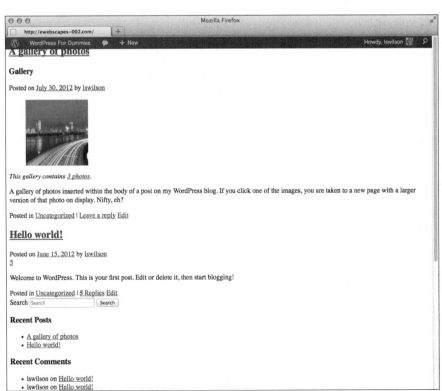

Figure 12-5:
A WordPress blog missing the call to the header. It's naked!

The Main Index template in the Twenty Eleven theme calls in three other files in a similar fashion:

- ✔ `get_template_part( 'content', 'get_post_format' );` — this function calls in the template file named `content.php` as well as prepares the theme to accept special templates for a feature called Post Formats, which I cover in Bonus Chapter 1 on the companion website for this book.

- ✔ `get_sidebar();` — this function calls in the template file named `sidebar.php`.

- ✔ `get_footer();` — this function calls in the template file named `footer.php`.

Each of these three functions and template files is covered in upcoming sections of this chapter.

Earlier in this chapter, in the "Connecting templates" section, I explain the concept of _calling in_ a template file using a function or template tag. That is exactly what the Main Index template does with the four functions for the header, loop, sidebar, and footer templates explained in this section.

The Loop

I'm not talking about America's second-largest downtown business district, originating at the corner of State and Madison streets in Chicago. I could write about some interesting experiences I've had there . . . but that would be a different book.

The Loop in this case is a function that WordPress uses to display content on your site such as blog posts and page content. The Loop has a starting point and an ending point; anything placed in between is used to display each post, including any HTML, PHP, or CSS tags and codes.

Quite a few variations of the WordPress Loop are available, but I cover the most common use in this section. When you understand the common use, you can begin to push the envelope a bit further and use variations to suit your needs. This common use displays your posts in chronological order, starting with your most recent post and followed by less recent posts, ordered by date.

The basic and most common use of The Loop in WordPress is to pull blog posts from the database and display them on your website. In the default Twenty Eleven theme, you find the loop in a template called: `loop.php`. The beginning, or first line, of The Loop looks like this:

```
<?php while ( have_posts() ) : the_post(); ?>
```

At the bottom of the template, The Loop ends with one line of code:

```
<?php endwhile; ?>
```

Here's a look at what the WordPress Codex calls "The World's Simplest Index."

```
<?php
get_header();
if (have_posts()) :
  while (have_posts()) :
    the_post();
    the_content();
  endwhile;
endif;
get_sidebar();
get_footer();
?>
```

First, the template starts by opening the php tag. Next, it includes the header, meaning that it retrieves anything contained in the header.php file and displays it. Now the good stuff starts happening. The Loop begins with the while (have_posts()) : bit. Anything between the while and the endwhile repeats for each post that displays. The number of posts displayed is determined in the settings section of the WordPress Dashboard.

Misplacement of the while or endwhile statements causes The Loop to break. If you're having trouble with The Loop in an existing template, check your version against the original and see whether the while statements are misplaced.

In your travels as a WordPress user, you may run across plugins or scripts with instructions that say something like this: "This must be placed within The Loop." That's The Loop that we discuss in this section, so pay particular attention. Understanding The Loop arms you with the knowledge you need for tackling and understanding your WordPress themes.

The Loop is no different from any other template tag; it must begin with a function to start PHP, and it must end with a function to stop PHP. The Loop begins with PHP and then makes a request: "While there are posts in my blog, display them on this page." This PHP function tells WordPress to grab the blog post information from the database and return it to the blog page. The end of The Loop is like a traffic cop with a big red stop sign telling WordPress to stop the function completely.

If, then, and else

We deal with if, then, else situations every day, as in these examples:

- **IF** I have a dollar, **THEN** I'll buy coffee, or **ELSE** I'll drink water.

- **IF** it's warm outside, **THEN** I'll take a walk, or **ELSE** I'll stay in.

- **IF** I understand this code, **THEN** I'll be happy, or **ELSE** I'll rip my hair out.

You can set the number of posts displayed per page in the Reading Settings page on the WordPress Dashboard. The Loop abides by this rule and displays only the number of posts per page that you've set.

The big if

PHP functions in a pretty simple, logical manner. It functions by doing what you and I do on a daily basis — making decisions based on questions and answers. PHP deals with three basic variables:

- if
- then
- else

The basic idea is this: IF this, THEN that, or ELSE this.

If your blog has posts (and most do, even when you first install it), WordPress proceeds with The Loop, starting with the piece of code that looks like this:

```php
<?php while (have_posts()) : the_post(); ?>
```

This code tells WordPress to grab the posts from the MySQL database and display them on your blog page.

Then The Loop closes with this tag:

```php
<?php endwhile; ?>
```

Near the beginning of The Loop template is a template tag that looks like this:

```php
<?php if ( ! have_posts() ) : ?>
```

The exclamation point (!) preceding the function: `have_posts()` means "does not." So a translation of that template tag into plain English reads: `If [this blog] does not have posts.`

If your blog meets that condition (that is, if it doesn't have any posts), WordPress skips The Loop and displays a message that no posts exist:

```
<div id="post-0" class="post error404 not-found">
<h1 class="entry-title"><?php _e( 'Not Found', 'mytheme' ); ?></h1>
<div class="entry-content">
<p><?php _e( 'Apologies, but no results were found for the requested
        Archive. Perhaps searching will help find a related post.',
        'mytheme' ); ?></p>
<?php get_search_form(); ?>
</div><!-- .entry-content -->
</div><!-- #post-0 -->
```

WordPress displays the title Not Found, followed by the statement Apologies, but no results were found for the requested Archive. Perhaps searching will help find a related post, which in turn is followed by the template tag to include a search box that lets users search your blog for more information.

Mixed within the template tags and functions explained in these sections of this chapter, you find basic HTML markup. For example

```
<div id="">
```

```
<h1>
```

and

```
<div class="">
```

HTML and CSS (Cascading Style Sheets) are explained in Chapter 13. HTML and CSS drive the formatting and style of your overall theme, from a visual standpoint (fonts, colors, images, and so on).

WordPress uses other template files besides the main index, such as the header, sidebar, and footer templates. The next section gives you a closer look at a few of them.

The Sidebar template

The filename of the default Sidebar template is sidebar.php. Typically, the sidebar is displayed on the right or left side of your WordPress template. In the default Twenty Eleven theme, the sidebar is displayed on the right side of the template, by default (refer to Figure 12-3).

Similarly to the Header template, the Sidebar template is called into the Main Index template with this function:

```
<?php get_sidebar(): ?>
```

This code calls the Sidebar template and all the information it contains into your blog page. Bonus Chapter 1 (on the companion website for this book — www.dummies.com/go/wordpressfd5e) addresses some additional ways you can call in the Sidebar template, including having multiple Sidebar templates and using an include statement to pull them into the Main Index template.

In the "Using Tags with Parameters for Sidebars" section, later in this chapter, you find information on template tags to use in the sidebar to display the usual sidebar elements, such as a list of the most recent posts or a list of categories.

The Footer template

The filename of the Footer template is footer.php. Usually, the footer sits at the bottom of the page (refer to Figure 12-3) and contains brief information about the site, such as copyright statements, credits to the theme designer or hosting company, or even a list of links to other pages within the site.

The default Twenty Eleven theme shows the site title and a statement that says "Proudly powered by WordPress." You can use the footer to include all sorts of information about your site, however; you don't have to restrict it to small bits of information. In this chapter, I cover the typical footer that you see in the default Twenty Eleven theme.

Similarly to the Header and Sidebar templates, the Footer template is called into the Main Index template through this bit of code:

```
<?php get_footer(); ?>
```

This code calls the Footer and all the information it contains into your blog page.

Other templates

Other templates are in the default Twenty Eleven theme, and I don't cover all of them in depth in this chapter, but having at least a basic understanding of them is a good idea. The ones I list in this section give you that good, solid kick in the pants you need to get started with understanding WordPress templates. When you have that task licked, you can move on to learning the rest.

These other (optional) templates include

- ✔ **Comments template (**`comments.php`**):** The Comments template is required if you plan to host comments on your blog; it provides all the template tags you need to display those comments. The template tag used to call the comments into the template is `<?php comments_template(); ?>`.

- ✔ **Single Post template (**`single.php`**):** When your visitors click the title or permalink of a post you've published to your blog, they're taken to that post's individual page. There, they can read the entire post, and if you have comments enabled, they see the comments form and can leave comments.

- ✔ **Page template (**`page.php`**):** You can use a Page template for static pages in your WordPress site.

- ✔ **Search Results (**`search.php`**):** You can use this template to create a custom display of search results on your site. When someone uses the search feature to search your site for specific keywords, this template formats the return of those results.

- ✔ **404 template (**`404.php`**):** Use this template to create a custom 404 page, which is the page visitors get when the browser can't find the page requested and returns that ugly 404 Page Cannot Be Found error.

The templates in the preceding list are optional. If these templates don't exist in your WordPress `themes` folder, nothing breaks. The Main Index template handles the default display of these items (the single post page, the search results page, and so on). The only exception is the Comments template. If you want to display comments on your site, you must have that template included in your theme.

Putting a Theme Together

In this section, you put together a basic theme by using the information on templates and tags I've provided so far in this chapter.

Template files can't do a whole lot by themselves. The real power comes when they're put together.

Connecting the templates

WordPress has built-in functions to include the main template files, such as `header.php`, `sidebar.php`, and `footer.php`, in other templates. An `include` function is a custom PHP function built in to WordPress, allowing you to retrieve the content of another template file and display it along with the content of another template file. Table 12-3 shows the templates and the functions to include them.

Table 12-3	Template Files and Include Functions
Template Name	`include` *Function*
`header.php`	`<?php get_header(); ?>`
`sidebar.php`	`<?php get_sidebar(); ?>`
`footer.php`	`<?php get_footer(); ?>`
`search.php`	`<?php get_search_form(); ?>`
`comments.php`	`<?php comments_template(); ?>`

If you want to include a file that doesn't have a built-in `include` function, you need a different piece of code. For instance, if you want to add a unique sidebar (different from the default `sidebar.php` file within your existing theme) to a certain page template, name the sidebar file `sidebar-page.php`. To include that in another template, use the following code:

```
<?php get_template_part('sidebar', 'page'); ?>
```

In this statement, the `get_template_part('sidebar', 'page');` function looks through the main theme folder for the `sidebar-page.php` file and displays the sidebar. The beautiful part about the `get_template_part()` template tag is that WordPress looks for the `sidebar-page.php` template first, but if it doesn't find it, it defaults to using the `sidebar.php` template.

In this section, you put together the guts of a basic Main Index template by using the information on templates and tags provided so far in this chapter. There seem to be endless lines of code when you view the `loop.php` template file in the Twenty Eleven theme, so I've simplified it for you with the following steps. These steps should give you a basic understanding of the WordPress Loop and common template tags and functions that you can use to create your own.

You create a new WordPress theme using some of the basic WordPress templates. The first steps in pulling everything together are as follows:

1. **Connect to your web server via FTP, click the `wp-content` folder, and then click the `themes` folder.**

   This folder contains the themes that are currently installed in your WordPress blog. (See Chapter 6 if you need more information on FTP.)

2. **Create a new folder and call it** `mytheme`.

   In most FTP programs, you can right-click and choose New Folder. (If you aren't sure how to create a folder, refer to your FTP program's help files.)

3. **In your favored text editor (such as Notepad for the PC or TextMate for the Mac), create and save the following files with the lines of code I've provided for each:**

   - **Header template:** Create the file with the following lines of code and then save with the filename `header.php`:

```
<!DOCTYPE html>
<html <?php language_attributes(); ?>>
<head>
<meta charset="<?php bloginfo( 'charset' ); ?>" />
<title><?php bloginfo( 'name' ); ?> <?php if ( is_single() ) { ?>
&raquo; Blog Archive <?php } ?> <?php wp_title(); ?></title>
<link rel="stylesheet" href="<?php bloginfo( 'stylesheet_url' );
?>" type="text/css" media="screen" />
<link rel="pingback" href="<?php bloginfo( 'pingback_url' ); ?>"
/>
<?php if ( is_singular() ) wp_enqueue_script( 'comment-reply' );
?>
<?php wp_head(); ?>
</head>
<body <?php body_class() ?>>
<div id="page">
<header class="masthead">
<hgroup>
 <h1><a href="<?php bloginfo('url'); ?>"><?php bloginfo('name');
?></a></h1>
<h2><?php bloginfo('description'); ?></h2>
</hgroup>
</header>
<div id="main">
```

   - **Theme Functions:** Create the file with the following lines of code and then save it using the filename `functions.php`:

```
<?php
if ( function_exists('register_sidebar') ) register_sidebar(arra
y('name'=>'Sidebar',
));
?>
```

   The Theme Functions file registers the widget area for your site so that you're able to add widgets to your sidebar using the WordPress widgets available on the Widget page on the Dashboard.

- **Sidebar template:** Create the file with the following lines of code and then save it using the filename `sidebar.php`:

```
<aside class="sidebar">
<ul>
<?php if ( !function_exists('dynamic_sidebar') || !dynamic_
sidebar('Sidebar') ) : ?>
<?php endif; ?>
</ul>
</aside>
```

The code here tells WordPress where you would like the WordPress widgets to display in your theme; in this case, widgets are displayed in the sidebar of your site.

- **Footer template:** Create the file with the following lines of code and then save with the filename `footer.php`:

```
</div>
<footer>
<p>&copy; Copyright <a href="<?php bloginfo('url'); ?>"><?php
bloginfo('name'); ?></a>. All Rights Reserved</p>
</footer>
<?php wp_footer(); ?>
</body>
</html>
```

- **Stylesheet:** Create the file with the following lines of code and then save it with the filename `style.css` (more CSS is covered in Chapter 13 of this book — this example gives you just some very basic styling to create your sample theme):

```
/*
Theme Name: My Theme
Description: Basic Theme from WordPress For Dummies example
Author: Lisa Sabin-Wilson
Author URI: http://lisasabin-wilson.com
*/


body {
font-family: verdana, arial, helvetica, sans-serif;
font-size:16px;
color: #555;
background: #ffffff;
}

#page {
width: 960px;
margin: 0 auto;
background: #ffffff;
border: 1px solid silver;
```

```
display:block
}

header.masthead {
width: 950px;
background: black;
color: white;
padding: 5px;
text-align:center;
}

header.masthead h1 a {
color: white;
font-size: 28px;
font-family: Georgia;
text-decoration: none;
}

header.masthead h2 {
font-size: 16px;
font-family: Georgia;
color: #eee;
}

header.masthead nav {
background: #ffffff;
text-align: left;
height: 25px;
padding: 4px;
}

header.masthead nav ul {
list-style:none;
margin:0;
}

#main {
width: 600px;
float:left;
padding: 20px ;
}

#main .hentry {
margin: 10px 0;
}

aside.sidebar {
width: 290px;
margin: 0 15px;
float:left;
}
```

```
aside.sidebar ul {
list-style:none;
}

footer {
clear:both;
width: 960px;
height: 50px;
background: black;
color: white;
margin: 0 auto;
}

footer p {
text-align:center;
padding: 15px 0;
}

footer a {
color:white;
}
```

Using the tags provided in Table 12-4, along with the information on The Loop and the calls to the Header, Sidebar, and Footer templates provided in earlier sections, you can follow the next steps for a bare-bones example of what the Main Index template looks like when you put the tags together.

When typing templates, use a text editor such as Notepad or TextMate. Using a word-processing program such as Microsoft Word opens a whole slew of problems in your code. Word-processing programs insert hidden characters and format quotation marks in a way that WordPress can't read.

Now that you have the basic theme foundation, the last template file you need to create is the Main Index template. To create a Main Index template to work with the other templates in your WordPress theme, open a new window in a text editor and then go through the following steps. (Type the text in each of these steps on its own line. Press the Enter key after typing each line so that each tag starts on a new line.)

1. **Type** `<?php get_header(); ?>`.

   This template tag pulls the information in the Header template of your WordPress theme.

2. **Type** `<section>`.

   This is HTML5 markup that tells the browser that this is a grouping of content (in this case, blog posts).

3. **Type** `<?php if (have_posts()) : ?>`.

   This template tag is an `if` statement that asks, "Does this blog have posts?" If the answer is yes, it grabs the post content information from your MySQL database and displays the posts in your blog.

4. **Type** `<?php while (have_posts()) : the_post(); ?>`.

   This template tag starts The Loop.

5. **Type** `<article <?php post_class() ?> id="post-<?php the_ID(); ?>">`.

   This is HTML5 markup that tells the browser that this is the start of a new, single article, along with the `post_class` CSS designation (covered in Bonus Chapter 1).

6. **Type** `<h1><a href="<?php the_permalink(); ?>"><?php the_title(); ?></a></h1>`.

   This tag tells your blog to display the title of a post that's clickable (linked) to the URL of the post, surrounded by HTML Header tags.

7. **Type** `Posted on <?php the_date(); ?> at <?php the_time(); ?>`.

   This template tag displays the date and time when the post was made. With these template tags, the date and time format are determined by the format you set on the Dashboard.

8. **Type** `Posted in <?php the_category(','); ?>`.

   This template tag displays a comma-separated list of the categories to which you've assigned the post — *Posted in: category 1, category 2,* for example.

9. **Type** `<?php the_content('Read More..'); ?>`.

   This template tag displays the actual content of the blog post. The `'Read More..'` portion of this tag tells WordPress to display the words *Read More,* which are clickable (hyperlinked) to the post's permalink, where the reader can read the rest of the post in its entirety. This tag applies when you're displaying a post excerpt, as determined by the actual post configuration on the Dashboard.

10. **Type** `Posted by: <?php the_author(); ?>`.

    This template tag displays the author of the post in this manner: *Posted by: Lisa Sabin-Wilson.*

11. **Type** `<?php comments_popup_link('No Comments', '1 Comment', '% Comments'); ?>`.

    This template tag displays the link to the comments for this post, along with the number of comments.

12. **Type** `</article>`.

    This is HTML5 markup that tells the browser that the article has ended.

13. **Type** `<?php endwhile; ?>`.

    This template tag ends The Loop and tells WordPress to stop display-ing blog posts here. WordPress knows exactly how many times The Loop needs to work, based on the setting on the WordPress Dashboard. That's exactly how many times WordPress will execute The Loop.

14. **Type** `<?php next_posts_link('&laquo; Previous Entries'); ?>`.

    This template tag displays a clickable link to the previous page of blog entries, if any.

15. **Type** `<?php previous posts link('&raquo; Next Entries'); ?>`.

    This template tag displays a clickable link to the next page of blog entries, if any.

16. **Type** `<?php else : ?>`.

    This template tag refers to the `if` question asked in Step 3. If the answer to that question is no, this step provides the `else` statement — IF this blog has posts, THEN list them here (Step 3 and Step 4), or ELSE display the following message.

17. **Type** `Not Found. Sorry, but you are looking for something that isn't here.`

    This is the message followed by the template tag displayed after the `else` statement from Step 16. You can reword this statement to have it say whatever you want.

18. **Type** `<?php endif; ?>`.

    This template tag ends the `if` statement from Step 3.

19. **Type** `</section>`.

    This is HTML5 markup that closes the `<section>` tag opened in Step 2, and tells the browser that this grouping of content has ended.

20. **Type** `</div>`.

    This is HTML markup closing the `<div id="main">` that was opened in the `header.php` file.

21. **Type** `<?php get_sidebar(); ?>`.

    This template tag calls in the Sidebar template and pulls that information into the Main Index template.

22. Type `<?php get_footer(); ?>`.

This template tag calls in the Footer template and pulls that information into the Main Index template. *Note:* The code in the `footer.php` template ends the `<body>` and `<html>` tags that were started in the Header template (`header.php`).

When you're done, the display of the Main Index template code looks like this:

```
<?php get_header(); ?>
<section>
<?php if (have_posts()) : ?>
 <?php while (have_posts()) : the_post(); ?>
 <article <?php post_class() ?> id="post-<?php the_ID(); ?>">
        <h1><a href="<?php the_permalink(); ?>"><?php the_title(); ?></
        a></h1>
        Posted on: <?php the_date(); ?> at <?php the_time(); ?>
        Posted in: <?php the_category(','); ?>

        <?php the_content('Read More..'); ?>
        Posted by: <?php the_author(); ?> | <?php comments_popup_
        link('No Comments', '1 Comment', '% Comments'); ?>
</article>

<?php endwhile; ?>
<?php next_posts_link('&laquo; Previous Entries') ?>
<?php previous_posts_link('Next Entries &raquo;') ?>
<?php else : ?>
Not Found
Sorry, but you are looking for something that isn't here.
<?php endif; ?>
</section>
</div>
<?php get_sidebar(); ?>
<?php get_footer(); ?>
```

23. Save this file as `index.php` **and upload it to the** `mythemes` **folder.**

In Notepad, you can save it by choosing File⇨Save As. Type the name of the file in the File Name text box and click Save.

24. Activate the theme on the WordPress Dashboard and view your blog to see your handiwork in action!

My Main Index template code has one template tag that I explain in Bonus Chapter 1 on the companion website for this book. That template tag is `<article <?php post_class() ?> id="post-<?php the_ID();` `?>">`. This tag helps you create some interesting styles in your template using CSS, so check out Bonus Chapter 1 to find out all about it!

This very simple and basic Main Index template that you just built does not have the standard HTML markup in it, so you will find that the visual display of your blog differs somewhat from the default Twenty Eleven theme. This example was used to give you the bare-bones basics of the Main Index template and The Loop in action. Chapter 13 goes into details about using HTML and CSS to create nice styling and formatting for your posts and pages.

If you're having a hard time typing out the code provided on this page, I have made this sample theme available for download on my website. The zip file contains the files discussed in this chapter so you can compare your efforts with mine, electronically. You can download the theme zip file here: `http://lisasabin-wilson.com/wp4d/my-theme.zip`.

Using additional stylesheets

Often a theme uses multiple stylesheets for browser compatibility or consistent organization. If you use multiple stylesheets, the process for including them in the template is the same as with any other stylesheet.

To add a new stylesheet, create a directory in the root theme folder called `css`. Next, create a new file called `mystyle.css` within the `css` folder. To include the file, you must edit the `header.php` file. The following example shows the code you need to include in the new CSS file:

```
<link rel="stylesheet" href="<?php bloginfo('stylesheet_directory');
?>/css/mystyle.css" type="text/css" media="screen" />
```

Additional stylesheets come in handy when working with a concept called Parent/Child themes, which is the practice of creating a child theme that depends upon a separate parent theme for features and functions. I write more about Parent/Child themes, as well as provide you with additional information on HTML and CSS, in Chapter 13.

Customizing Your Blog Posts with Template Tags

This section covers the template tags that you use to display the body of each blog post you publish. The body of a blog post includes information such as the post date and time, title, author name, category, and content. Table 12-4 lists the common template tags you can use for posts, available for you to use in any WordPress theme template. The tags in Table 12-4 work only if you place them within The Loop (covered earlier in this chapter and found in the `loop.php` template file).

Table 12-4	Template Tags for Blog Posts
Tag	**Function**
`get_the_date();`	Displays the date of the post.
`get_the_time();`	Displays the time of the post.
`the_title();`	Displays the title of the post.
`get_permalink();`	Displays the permalink (URL) of the post.
`get_the_author();`	Displays the post author's name.
`the_author_posts_url();`	Displays the URL of the post author's site.
`the_content('Read More...');`	Displays the content of the post. (If you use an excerpt [next item], the words *Read More* appear and are linked to the individual post page.)
`the_excerpt();`	Displays an excerpt (snippet) of the post.
`the_category();`	Displays the category (or categories) assigned to the post. If the post is assigned to multiple categories, they'll be separated by commas.
`comments_popup_link('No Comments', 'Comment (1)', 'Comments(%)');`	Displays a link to the comments, along with the comment count for the post in parentheses. (If no comments exist, it displays a *No Comments* message.)
`next_posts_link('&laquo; Previous Entries')`	Displays the words *Previous Entries* linked to the previous page of blog entries.*
`previous_posts_link('Next Entries &raquo;')`	Displays the words *Next Entries* linked to the next page of blog entries.*

* These two tags aren't like the others. You don't place these tags in The Loop; instead, you insert them after The Loop but before the `if` statement ends. Here's an example:

```
<?php endwhile; ?>
<?php next_posts_link('&laquo; Previous Entries') ?>
<?php previous_posts_link('Next Entries &raquo;') ?>
<?php endif; ?>
```

Using Tags with Parameters for Sidebars

If you've been following along in this chapter as I've covered the Header and Main Index templates and tags, you have a functional WordPress blog with blog posts and various metadata displayed in each post.

In this section, I give you the template tags for the items commonly placed in the sidebar of a blog. I say "commonly placed" because it's possible to get creative with these template tags and place them in other locations (the Footer template, for example). To keep this introduction to sidebar template tags simple, I stick with the most common use, leaving the creative and uncommon uses for you to try when you're comfortable with building the basics.

This section also introduces *tag parameters,* which are additional options you can include in the tag to control some of its display properties. Not all template tags have parameters. You place tag parameters inside the parentheses of the tag. Many of the parameters discussed in this section were obtained from the WordPress software documentation in the WordPress Codex at `http://codex.wordpress.org`.

Table 12-5 helps you understand the three variations of parameters used by WordPress.

Table 12-5	Three Variations of Template Parameters	
Variation	*Description*	*Example*
Tags without parameters	These tags have no additional options available. Tags without parameters have nothing within the parentheses.	`the_tag();`
Tags with PHP function-style parameters	These tags have a comma-separated list of values placed within the tag parentheses.	`the_tag('1,2,3');`
Tags with query-string parameters	These types of tags generally have several available parameters. This tag style enables you to change the value for each parameter without being required to provide values for all available parameters for the tag.	`the_ tag('parameter=true);`

Identifying some blog-post metadata

Metadata is simply data about data. In WordPress, *metadata* refers to the data about each blog post, including:

✔ The author name

✔ The category or categories to which the post is assigned

✔ The date and time of the post

✔ The comments link and number of comments

You need to know these three types of parameters:

✔ **String:** A line of text that can be anything from a single letter to a long list of words. A string is placed between single quotation marks and sets an option for the parameter or is displayed as text.

✔ **Integer:** A positive or negative number. Integers are placed within the parentheses and either inside or outside single quotation marks. Either way, they'll be processed correctly.

✔ **Boolean:** Sets the parameter options to `true` or `false`. This parameter can be numeric (0=false and 1=true) or textual. Boolean parameters aren't placed within quotation marks.

The WordPress Codex, located at `http://codex.wordpress.org`, has every conceivable template tag and possible parameter known to the WordPress software. The tags and parameters that I share with you in this chapter are the ones used most often.

The calendar

The `calendar` tag displays a calendar that highlights each day of the week on which you've posted a blog. Those days are also hyperlinked to the original blog post. Here's the tag to use to display the calendar:

```
<?php get_calendar(); ?>
```

The `calendar` tag has only one parameter, and it's Boolean. Set this parameter to `true` and it displays the day of the week with one letter (Friday = F, for example). Set this parameter to `false` and it displays the day of the week as a three-letter abbreviation (Friday = Fri., for example). Here are examples of the template tag used to display the calendar on your WordPress blog:

```
<?php get_calendar(true); ?>
<?php get_calendar(false); ?>
```

List pages

The `<?php wp_list_pages(); ?>` tag displays a list of the static pages you can create on your WordPress site (such as About Me or Contact pages). Displaying a link to the static pages makes them available so that readers can click the links and read the content you've provided.

WordPress has a very handy navigation menu–building tool that I cover in Chapter 13. It allows you to build different custom navigation menus. If you like the navigation tool, you may never need to use the `wp_list_pages();` template tag. Still, I'm including it here because you may want to use it if you want to have complete control over how the list of pages appears on your website.

The `<list>` tag parameters use the string style. (Table 12-6 lists the most common parameters used for the `wp_list_pages` template tag.)

An alternative to using the `wp_list_pages()` template tag to create a navigation system is to use the built-in feature in WordPress called Menus, which enables you to build custom menus that aren't completely dependent upon your WordPress pages but that can include links to posts, categories, and custom links that you define. Chapter 13 contains information about the Menus feature, along with the `wp_nav_menu()` template tag that you use to display menus.

Table 12-6	Most Common Parameters (Query-String) for wp_list_pages();	
Parameter	*Type*	*Description and Values*
`child_of`	integer	Displays only the subpages of the page; uses the numeric ID for a page as the value. Defaults to 0 (display all pages).
`sort_ column`	string	Sorts pages with one of the following options: `'post_title'` — Sorts alphabetically by page title (default). `'menu_order'` — Sorts by page order (the order in which they appear in the Manage tab and Pages subtab of the Dashboard). `'post_date'` — Sorts by the date on which pages were created. `'post_modified'` — Sorts by the time when the page was last modified. `'post_author'` — Sorts by author, according to the author ID #. `'post_name'` — Sorts alphabetically by the post slug.

(continued)

Table 12-6 *(continued)*

Parameter	Type	Description and Values
Exclude	string	Lists the numeric page ID numbers, separated by commas, that you want to exclude from the page list display (for example, `'exclude=10, 20, 30'`). There is no default value.
Depth	integer	Uses a numeric value for how many levels of pages are displayed in the list of pages. Possible options: `0` — Displays all pages, including main and sub-pages (default). `-1` — Shows subpages but doesn't indent them in the list display. `1` — Shows only main pages (no subpages).
show_date	string	Displays the date when the page was created or last modified. Possible options: `' '` — Displays no date (default). `'modified'` — Displays the date when the page was last modified. `'created'` — Displays the date when the page was created.
date_format	string	Sets the format of the date to be displayed. Defaults to the date format configured in the Options tab and General subtab of the Dashboard.
title_li	string	Types text for the heading of the page list. Defaults to display the text: `"Pages"`. If value is empty (''), no heading is displayed; for example, `'title_li=My Pages'` displays the heading `My Pages` above the page list.

Page lists are displayed in an *unordered list* (you may know it by the term *bulleted list*). Whichever term you use, it's a list with a bullet point in front of every page link.

The following tag and query string displays a list of pages without the text heading `"Pages"`. In other words, it displays no title at the top of the page's link list:

```php
<?php wp_list_pages('title_li='); ?>
```

The next tag and query string displays the list of pages sorted by the date when they were created; the date is also displayed along with the page name:

```php
<?php wp_list_pages('sort_column=post_date&show_date='created'); ?>
```

Take a look at the way query-string parameters are written:

```
'parameter1=value&parameter2=value&parameter3=value'
```

The entire string is surrounded by single quotation marks, and no white space is within the query string. Each parameter is joined to its value by the = character. When you use multiple parameters/values, you separate them with the & character. You can think of the string like this: parameter1=value **AND**parameter2=value**AND**parameter3=value. Keep this convention in mind for the remaining template tags and parameters in this chapter.

Bookmarks (blogroll)

On the WordPress Dashboard, you can manage your links from the Blogroll tab. Before I forge ahead and dig in to the template tag for the blogroll display, I want to clear up a little terminology.

A *blogroll* is a list of links that you add to the Blogroll area on the Dashboard. The specific template tag used to call those links into your template, however, refers to *bookmarks*. So this begs the question "Are they links, or are they bookmarks?" The answer is "Both." For simplicity, and to ensure that you and I are on the same wavelength, I refer to them the same way that half the planet does — as links.

Here is the tag used to display your blogroll:

```php
<?php wp_list_bookmarks(); ?>
```

In Chapter 8, I show you how to add links to your blogroll as well as discuss the options you can set for each link. The parameters for this tag give you control of how the links are displayed and put some of the options to work. Table 12-7 shows the most common parameters used for the wp_list_ bookmarks template tag.

In the Possible Values column of Table 12-7, values that appear in bold are the default values set by WordPress. Keep this convention in mind for all the parameter values in the rest of this chapter.

Table 12-7 **Most Common Parameters (Query-String)**
for wp_list_bookmarks();

Parameter and Type	Possible Values	Example
`categorize` (Boolean) Displays links within the assigned category.	**1 (True)** 0 (False)	`<?php wp_list_ bookmarks('categorize=0'); ?>` Returns the list of links not grouped into the categories.
`category` (string) Displays only the link categories specified; if none is specified, all link categories are shown.	Category ID numbers separated by commas	`<?php wp_list_ bookmarks('category=10, 20, 30'); ?>` Displays the list of links from the categories with ID numbers 10, 20, and 30.
`category_name` (string) Displays only the link categories specified by name; if none is specified, all link categories are shown.	Text of the category names separated by commas	`<?php wp_list_ bookmarks('category_ name=books'); >` Displays only the links from the Books category.
`category_ orderby` (string) Sorts the order in which links are displayed on your site.	**Name** id	`<?php wp_list_ bookmarks('category_ orderby=name'); ?>` Displays the link categories alphabetically by name.
`title_li` (string) Text title appears above the link list.	**bookmarks** If left blank, no title is displayed.	`<?php wp_list_ bookmarks('title_li=Links'); ?>` Displays the Links header. `<?php wp_list_ bookmarks('title_li='); ?>` Displays no heading.

Parameter and Type	Possible Values	Example
`title_before` (string) Formatting to appear before the category title — only if the `'categorize'` parameter is set to 1 (true).	**`<h2>`**	`<?php wp_list_ bookmarks('title_ before='<strong>'); ?>` Inserts the `<strong>` HTML tag in front of the link category title.
`title_after` (string) Formatting to appear after the category title — only if the `'categorize'` parameter is set to 1 (true).	**`</h2>`**	`<?php wp_list_ bookmarks('title_after='</ strong>'); ?>` Inserts the `</strong>` HTML tag after the link category title.
`include` (string) Lists link ID numbers, separated by commas, to include in the display.	If no ID numbers are listed, displays all links.	`<?php wp_list_ bookmarks('include="1,2,3'); ?>` Displays only links with the IDs of 1, 2, and 3.
`exclude` (string) List of link ID numbers, separated by commas, to exclude from the display.	If no ID numbers are listed, all links are displayed.	`<?php wp_list_ bookmarks('exclude='4,5,6'); ?>` Displays all links except for the links with IDs of 4, 5, and 6.
`orderby` (string) Tells WordPress how your link lists will be sorted.	**`name`** `id` `url` `target` `descrip- tions` `owner` `rating` `updated` `rel` (XFN) `notes` `length` `rand` (random)	`<?php wp_list_ bookmarks('orderby=rand'); >` Displays the links in random order. `<?php wp_list_ bookmarks('orderby='id'); ?>` Displays the links in order by ID number.

(continued)

Table 12-7 *(continued)*

Parameter and Type	Possible Values	Example
before (string) Formatting to appear before each link in the list.	`<li>`	`<?php wp_list_bookmarks ('before=<strong>'); ?>` Inserts the `<strong>` HTML tag before each link in the list.
after (string) Formatting to appear after each link in the list.	`</li>`	`<?php wp_list_ bookmarks('after=</ strong'); ?>` Inserts the `</strong>` HTML tag after each link in the list.

Here are a couple of examples of tags used to set a link list.

The following tag displays a list of links in the category ID of 2 and orders that list by the length of the link name (shortest to longest):

```
<?php wp_list_bookmarks('categorize=1&category=2&orderby=length'); ?>
```

This next tag displays only the list of links in a category (the Espresso category, in this example):

```
<?php wp_list_bookmarks('category_name=Espresso'); ?>
```

Post archives

The `<?php wp_get_archives(); ?>` template tag displays the blog post archives in a number of ways, using the parameters and values shown in Table 12-8. Again, values that appear in bold are the default values set by WordPress. Here are just a few examples of what you can produce with this template tag:

- ✔ Display the titles of the last 15 posts you've made to your blog.
- ✔ Display the titles of the posts you've made in the past ten days.
- ✔ Display a monthly list of archives.

Table 12-8	Most Common Parameters (Query-String) for wp_get_archives();	
Parameter and Type	*Possible Values*	*Example*
type (string) Determines the type of archive to display.	**monthly** daily weekly postbypost	`<?php wp_get_archives ('type=postbypost'); ?>` Displays the titles of the most recent blog posts.
format (string) Formats the display of the links in the archive list.	**html** — Surrounds the links with `<li> </li>` tags. option — Places archive list in drop-down menu format. link — Surrounds the links with `<link> </link>` tags. custom — Use your own HTML tags, using the before and after parameters.	`<?php wp_get_ archives('format=html'); ?>` Displays the list of archive links where each link is surrounded by the `<li> </li>` HTML tags.
limit (integer) Limits the number of archives to display.	If no value, all are displayed.	`<?php wp_get_ archives('limit=10'); ?>` Displays the last ten archives in a list.
before (string) Places text or formatting before the link in the archive list when using the custom parameter.	No default	`<?php wp_get_archives ('before=<strong>'); ?>` Inserts the `<strong>` HTML tag before each link in the archive link list.

(continued)

Table 12-8 *(continued)*

Parameter and Type	Possible Values	Example
`after` (string) Inserts text or formatting after the link in the archive list when using the custom parameter.	No default	`<?php wp_get_archives('after=</strong>'); ?>` Inserts the `</strong>` HTML tag after each link in the archive link list.
`show_post_count` (Boolean) This value displays the number of posts in the archive. You would use this if you use the `'type'` of `monthly`.	true or 1 **false or 0**	`<? wp_get_archives('show_post_count=1'); ?>` Displays the number of posts in each archive after each archive link.

Here are a couple of examples of tags used to display blog-post archives.

This tag displays a linked list of monthly archives (for example, November 2011, December 2011, and so on).

```
<?php wp_get_archives('type=monthly'); ?>
```

This next tag displays a linked list of the 15 most recent blog posts:

```
<?php wp_get_archives('type=postbypost&limit=15'); ?>
```

Categories

WordPress lets you create categories and assign posts to a specific category (or multiple categories). Categories provide an organized navigation system that helps you and your readers find posts you've made on certain topics.

The `<?php wp_list_categories(); ?>` template tag lets you display a list of your categories by using the available parameters and values. (Table 12-9 shows some of the most popular parameters.) Each category is linked to the appropriate category page that lists all the posts you've assigned to it. The values that appear in bold are the default values set by WordPress.

Table 12-9	Most Common Parameters (Query-String) for wp_list_categories();	
Parameter and Type	**Possible Values**	**Example**
orderby (string) Determines how the category list will be ordered.	**ID** name	`<?php wp_list_ categories('orderby=name'); ?>` Displays the list of categories by name, alphabetically, as they appear on the Dashboard.
style (string) Determines the format of the category list display.	**List** none	`<?php wp_list_categories ('style=list'); ?>` Displays the list of category links where each link is surrounded by the `<li>` `</li>` HTML tags. `<?php wp_list_ categories('style=none'); ?>` Displays the list of category links with a simple line break after each link.
show_count (Boolean) Determines whether to display the post count for each listed category.	true or 1 **false or 0**	`<?php wp_list_ categories('show_count=1'); ?>` Displays the post count, in parentheses, after each category list. Espresso (10), for example, means that there are ten posts in the Espresso category.
hide_empty (Boolean) Determines whether empty categories should be displayed in the list (meaning a category with zero posts assigned to it).	**true or 1** false or 0	`<?php wp_list_ categories('hide_empty=0'); ?>` Displays only those categories that currently have posts assigned to them.

(continued)

Table 12-9 *(continued)*

Parameter and Type	Possible Values	Example
`feed` (string) Determines whether the RSS feed should be displayed for each category in the list.	rss Default is no feeds displayed.	`<?php wp_list_ categories('feed=rss'); ?>` Displays category titles with an RSS link next to each one.
`feed_image` (string) Provides the path/filename for an image for the feed.	No default	`<?php wp_list_ categories('feed_image=/wp- content/images/feed.gif'); ?>` Displays the `feed.gif` image for each category title. This image is linked to the RSS feed for that category.
`hierarchical` (Boolean) Determines whether the child categories should be displayed after each parent category in the category link list.	**true or 1** false or 0	`<?php wp_list_categories ('hierarchical=0'); ?>` Doesn't display the child categories after each parent category in the category list.

Here are a couple of examples of tags used to display a list of your categories.

This example, with its parameters, displays a list of categories sorted by name without showing the number of posts made in each category; the example also displays the RSS feed for each category title:

```
<?php wp_list_categories('orderby=name&show_count=0&feed=RSS'); ?>
```

This example, with its parameters, displays a list of categories sorted by name with the post count showing and shows the subcategories of every parent category:

```
<?php wp_list_categories('orderby=name&show_count=1&hierarchical=1'); '>
```

Getting widgetized

About 99.99 percent of the WordPress themes available today are coded with *widgetized sidebars* — which means you can use the widgets within WordPress to populate your sidebar area with content, navigation menus, and lists. In Chapter 5, I go into detail about what widgets are and how you can use them to dress up your sidebar — so check out that chapter if you need more information about widgets.

With widgets in place, you generally have no reason to mess around with the code in the `sidebar.php` template file because most of the content you want to add into your sidebar can be added through the use of widgets.

In a WordPress theme, the Theme Functions template (`functions.php`) and the Sidebar template (`sidebar.php`) create the functionality and the possibility for widgets to exist within your theme. You're not limited to where you place and use widgets, by and large. I am using the Sidebar template (`sidebar.php`) in this example.

First, you have to define the widgets in your theme. This means that you need to alert WordPress to the fact that this theme can handle widgets — which is known as *registering* a widget with the WordPress software. To register a widget, add the `register_sidebar` function to the Theme Functions template (`functions.php`). In the `functions.php` file in the Twenty Eleven theme, the code for registering a widget looks like this:

```
register_sidebar( array(
    'name' => __( 'Main Sidebar', 'twentyeleven' ),
    'id' => 'sidebar-1',
    'before_widget' => '<aside id="%1$s" class="widget %2$s">',
    'after_widget' => "</aside>",
    'before_title' => '<h3 class="widget-title">',
    'after_title' => '</h3>',
) );
```

Within that code, you see seven different *arrays.* An array is a set of values that tells WordPress how you would like your widgets handled and displayed:

✔ name: This name is unique to the widget and appears on the Widgets page on the Dashboard. It is helpful if you register several different widgetized areas on your site.

✔ id: This is the unique ID given to the widget.

✔ description (optional): This is a text description of the widget. The text that gets placed here displays on the Widgets page on the Dashboard.

✔ `before_widget`: This is the HTML markup that gets inserted directly before the widget. It is helpful for CSS styling purposes.

✔ `after_widget`: This is the HTML markup that gets inserted directly after the widget.

✔ `before_title`: This is the HTML markup that gets inserted directly before the widget title.

✔ `after_title`: This is the HTML markup that gets inserted directly after the widget title.

With that code in your `functions.php` file, WordPress now recognizes that you've registered a widget called Primary Widget Area for your theme and makes the widget area available for you to drag and drop widgets onto the Widgets page on the Dashboard. All that's left to do now is to call that widget into your `sidebar.php` file. By doing so, you allow the widgets to display on your site. Follow these steps to call widgets to your site (these steps assume that the widget code isn't already in the Sidebar template):

1. **Click the Editor link below the Appearance menu.**

   The Edit Themes page opens.

2. **Click the Sidebar (`sidebar.php`) template.**

   The Sidebar template opens in the text box on the left side of the page.

3. **Type the following code in the Sidebar (`sidebar.php`) template:**

   ```
   <?php if ( ! dynamic_sidebar( 'Primary Widget Area' ) ) : ?>
   <?php endif; ?>
   ```

   The parameter within the `dynamic_sidebar` template tag corresponds to the name that you provided in the widget array called *'name'* earlier in this section. It must be the same; otherwise, it will not display on your website.

4. **Click the Update File button.**

   The changes you've made to the Sidebar (`sidebar.php`) template file are now saved.

You can register an unlimited number of widgets for your theme. This flexibility allows you to create several different widgetized areas and widget features in different areas of your site. Bonus Chapter 1 on the companion website for this book goes into more detail about using different sidebar templates to create different widgetized areas and features on your site.

Chapter 13

Tweaking WordPress Themes

· ·

In This Chapter

▶ Exploring basic CSS and defining CSS properties and values

▶ Setting a new background color, creating a header, and customizing navigation menus

▶ Changing fonts

▶ Knowing HTML essentials

▶ Working with parent/child themes

· ·

Chapter 11 shows how you can use free WordPress themes in your blog. Many people are quite happy to use these themes without making any adjustments to them at all. I can't tell you, however, how many times people have asked me whether they can customize a theme that they've found. The answer to their question is always, "Of course you can make changes on your own."

The practice of changing a few elements of an existing WordPress theme is known as *tweaking*. Thousands of WordPress blog owners tweak their existing themes on a regular basis. This chapter provides information on some of the most common tweaks you can make to your theme, such as changing the header image, changing the color of the background or the text links, and changing font styles — and these changes are pretty easy to make, too! You'll be tweaking your own theme in no time flat.

Using a theme exactly as a theme author released it is great. If a new version is released that fixes a browser compatibility issue or adds features offered by a new version of WordPress, a quick theme upgrade is very easy to do.

However, chances are good that you'll want to tinker with the design, add new features, or modify the theme structure. If you modify the theme, you won't be able to upgrade to a newly released version without modifying the theme again.

If only you could upgrade customized versions of themes with new features when they're released. . . . Fortunately, child themes give you this best-of-both-worlds theme solution. This chapter explores what child themes are, how to create a parent theme that's child-theme ready, and how to get the most out of using child themes.

Before you go too wild with tweaking templates, make a backup of your theme so that you have the original files from which to easily restore it if necessary. You can back up your theme files by connecting to your web server via FTP (see Chapter 6) and downloading your theme folder to your computer. When you have the original theme files safe and secure on your hard drive, feel free to tweak away, comfortable in the knowledge that you have a backup.

Styling with CSS: The Basics

A *Cascading Style Sheet (CSS)* is a cascading sheet of style markup that controls the appearance of content on a website. Every single WordPress theme you use in your blog uses CSS. The CSS provides style and design flair to the template tags in your templates. (See Chapter 12 for information about WordPress template tags.) The CSS for your WordPress theme is pulled in through the Header template (`header.php`) and is named `style.css`.

On your Dashboard, click the Editor link on the Appearance menu and look at the Header template for the Twenty Eleven WordPress theme by clicking the Header link on the Edit Themes page. You find the following line of code, which pulls the CSS (`style.css`) into the page to provide the formatting of the elements of your blog:

```
<link rel="stylesheet" type="text/css" media="all" href="<?php bloginfo(
          'stylesheet_url' ); ?>" />
```

Don't tweak the line of code that pulls in the `style.css` file; otherwise the CSS won't work for your blog.

Chapter 12 covers the commonly used parameters for the `bloginfo();` template tag used in WordPress themes.

CSS selectors

With CSS, you can provide style (such as size, color, and placement) to the display of elements on your blog (such as text links, header images, font size and colors, paragraph margins, and line spacing). *CSS selectors* contain names, properties, and values to define which HTML elements in the templates you will style with CSS. CSS selectors are used to declare (or select) which part of the markup the style applies to. Table 13-1 provides some examples of CSS selectors and their use.

Table 13-1		Basic CSS Selectors	
CSS Selector	**Description**	**HTML**	**CSS**
body	Sets the style for the overall body of the site, such as background color and default fonts	`<body>`	`body {back-ground-color: white}` The background color on all pages is white.
p	Defines how paragraphs are formatted	`<p>This is a paragraph</p>`	`p {color:black}` The color of the fonts used in all paragraphs is black.
h1, h2, h3, h4, h5, h6	Provides bold headers for different sections of your site	`<h1>This is a site title</h1>`	`h1 {font-weight: bold;}` A font surrounded by the `<h1>..</h1>` HTML tags is bold.
a	Defines how text links display in your site	`<a href="http:// wiley. com">Wiley Publishing</a>`	`a {color: red}` All text links appear in red.

Classes and IDs

You can find the stylesheet (`style.css`) for the default Twenty Eleven theme on the Edit Themes page on your Dashboard (see Figure 13-1). Everything in it may look foreign to you right now, but I want to bring your attention to two items you see when you scroll down that template:

✔ `#content`: One type of CSS selector. The hash mark (#) indicates that it's a CSS *ID*.

✔ `.singular`: Another type of CSS selector. The period (.) indicates that it's a CSS *class*.

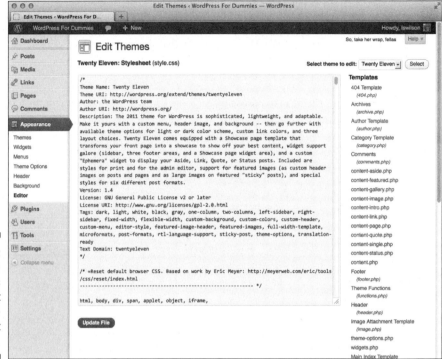

Figure 13-1:
The
WordPress
default
theme
stylesheet
(style.css).

IDs and classes define styling properties for different sections of your WordPress theme. Table 13-2 shows examples of IDs and classes from the `header.php` template in the Twenty Eleven WordPress theme. Armed with this information, you'll know where to look in the stylesheet when you want to change the styling for a particular area of your theme.

Table 13-2   Connecting HTML with CSS Selectors

HTML	CSS Selector	Description
`<div id="page">` In this case, the CSS selector name is `page`.	`#page`	Styles the elements for the `page` ID in your template(s).
`<header id="branding">`	`#banner`	Styles the elements for the `branding` ID in your template(s).
`<h1 id="site-title">`	`#site-title`	Styles the elements for your `site-title` ID in your template(s), but also follows rules for the `h1` values set in the CSS.

HTML	CSS Selector	Description
`<h2 id="site-description">`	`#site-description`	Styles the elements for your `site-description` ID in your template(s).
`<nav id="access">`	`#access`	Styles the elements for the `access` ID in your template(s).

If you find an element in the template code that says `id` (such as `div id=` or `p id=`), look for the hash symbol in the stylesheet. If you find an element in the template code that says `class` (such as `div class=` or `p class=`), look for the period in the stylesheet followed by the selector name.

CSS properties and values

CSS properties are assigned to the CSS selector name. You also need to provide values for the CSS properties to define the style elements for the particular CSS selector you're working with.

In the default Twenty Eleven WordPress theme, for example, the first piece of markup in the Header template (`header.php`) is `<div id="page">`. This ID, with the name `page`, provides styling for the site page.

In the default Twenty Eleven WordPress theme stylesheet, the CSS defined for the `page` ID is as follows:

```
#page {
    margin: 2em auto;
    max-width: 1000px;
}
```

Every CSS property needs to be followed by a colon (`:`), and each CSS value needs to be followed by a semicolon (`;`).

The CSS selector is `#page`, which has two properties:

✔ The first CSS property is `margin`, which has the value of `0 auto;`.

✔ The second CSS property is `max-width`, which has the value `1000px` (absolute, fixed pixel width).

Table 13-3 provides some examples of commonly used CSS properties and values.

Table 13-3	Common CSS Properties and Values	
CSS Property	*CSS Value*	*Examples*
`background-color`	Defines the color of the background (such as red, black, or white)	**Markup:** `<div id="page">` **CSS:** `#page {background-color: white}`
`background`	Defines a background image	**Markup:** `<header id="banner">` **CSS:** `header#banner {background: url(images/header.jpg) no-repeat;}`
`font-family`*	Defines the fonts used for the selector	**Markup:** `<body>` **CSS:** `body { font-family: 'Lucida Grande', Verdana, Arial, Sans-Serif;}`
`color`	Defines the color of the text	**Markup:** `<h1>Website Title</h1>` **CSS:** `h1 {color: blue}`
`font-size`**	Defines the size of the font used for the text	**Markup:** `<h1>Website Title</h1>` **CSS:** `h1 {font-size: 18px;}`
`text-align`	Defines the alignment of the text (left, center, right, or justified)	**Markup:** `<div id="wrapper">` **CSS:** `#wrapper {text-align: left;}`

* *W3Schools has a good resource on the* `font-family` *property here:*
`http://www.w3schools.com/cssref/pr_font_font-family.asp`
** *W3Schools has a good resource on the* `font-size` *property here:*
`http://www.w3schools.com/cssref/pr_font_font-size.asp`

Changing the Background Color

In Chapter 12, I discuss the Header template (`header.php`) in detail. In this section, I show you how to tweak the background color in the default Twenty Eleven theme. If you're not using the default Twenty Eleven theme, you can also use the `<body>` tag in a Header template to change the background color of your website.

Creating a custom background

The Twenty Eleven WordPress theme is packaged with the option to change the background to a different color or use an image for your background. To use the nifty, built-in custom background feature to change the Twenty Eleven background for your blog, follow these steps:

1. **Click the Background link under the Appearance menu.**

   The Custom Background page loads on the Dashboard.

2. **To change the background color, type the hexadecimal color code in the Color text box.**

   If you don't know what hex color code you want to use, click the Select a Color link and click a color within the provided color wheel (see Figure 13-2). The color selected in Figure 13-2 is #f1f1f1, which is gray.

   A hexadecimal (or *hex*) code represents a certain color. Hex codes always start with a hash symbol (#) and have six letters and/or numbers to represent a particular color; for example, the code #d5d6d7 represents the color gray in hexadecimal code. I talk more about hexadecimal values in the section "Changing the background using CSS," later in this chapter.

3. **To use an image file for the background, upload an image from your computer.**

   Click the Browse button under Choose an Image from Your Computer and select a file from your computer. Then click the Upload button.

4. **Change the display options for your new background image.**

   - *Position:* Select Left, Center, or Right to set the screen position of the background image on your website.

   - *Repeat:* Select No Repeat, Tile, Tile Horizontally, or Tile Vertically in the drop-down menu to set the image repeat behavior of the background image on your website.

   - *Attachment:* Select Scroll to set the background image to scroll down the page, or select Fixed to set the background image in a static position (so that it doesn't scroll down the page).

5. **Save your changes.**

   Be sure to click the Save Changes button before navigating away from the Custom Background page. Otherwise your new settings won't be saved.

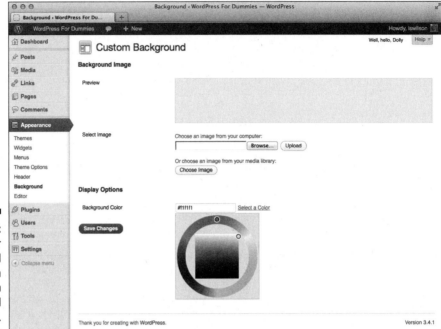

Figure 13-2:
The color
wheel
selector on
the Custom
Background
page.

You can add support for the Custom Background feature to any theme with just a few lines of code. Just follow these steps:

1. **Browse to the Edit Themes page and click the Theme Functions** (`functions.php`) **template.**

   The Theme Functions template opens in the text editor on the left side of the page.

2. **Add the following line of code to the Theme Functions template somewhere after the line that says `<?php`:**

   ```
   add_custom_background();
   ```

   This line of code tells WordPress that your theme has added the Custom Background feature.

3. **Click the Update File button.**

   The Theme Functions template is saved, along with your changes. The Background link now displays below the Appearance menu.

4. **View your website page to see your changes.**

Changing the background using CSS

The <body> tag is simple HTML markup. Every theme has this tag, which defines the overall default content for each page of your website — the site's *body*.

In the Twenty Eleven stylesheet (style.css), the background for the body is defined like this:

```
body {
  background: #ffffff;
}
```

The background for the <body> tag uses a hexadecimal color code of #ffffff that gives the background a white color. You can use a color or an image (or both) to style the background of your website:

- ✔ **Color:** The W3Schools website has a great resource on hex codes at http://w3schools.com/HTML/html_colornames.asp.

- ✔ **Image:** You can easily use an image as a background for your site by uploading the image to the images folder in your theme directory. That value looks like background: url(images/*yourimage*.jpg). (***Note:*** The url portion of this code automatically pulls in the URL of your blog, so you don't have to change the url part to your URL.)

You can also use a combination of colors and images in your backgrounds.

In the case of some basic colors, you don't have to use the hex code. For colors such as white, black, red, blue, and silver, you can just use their names — background-color: white, for example.

If you want to change the background color of your theme, follow these steps:

1. **On the WordPress Dashboard, click the Editor link on the Appearance menu.**

   The Edit Themes page opens.

2. **From the Select Theme to Edit drop-down menu, choose the theme you want to change.**

3. **Click the Stylesheet template link.**

   The style.css template opens in the text editor on the left side of the Edit Themes page (refer to Figure 13-1).

4. **Scroll down in the text editor until you find the CSS selector body.**

   If you're tweaking the default theme, this section is what you're looking for:

   ```
   body {
     background: #ffffff;
   }
   ```

   If you're tweaking a different template, the CSS selector body will look similar.

5. **Edit the `background` property's values.**

   For example, in the default template, if you want to change the background color to black, you can use one of the following:

   ```
   background: #000000;
   ```

   or

   ```
   background: black;
   ```

6. **Click the Update File button in the bottom-left corner of the page.**

   Your changes are saved and applied to your theme.

7. **Visit your site in your web browser.**

   The background color of your theme has changed.

Using Your Own Header Image

Most themes have a header image that appears at the top of the page. This image is generated by a graphic defined either in the CSS value for the property that represents the header area, or through the use of a feature in WordPress called a custom header. In the WordPress default Twenty Eleven theme, all the hard work's been done for you. Including a custom header image on a blog that uses the Twenty Eleven theme is pretty darn easy.

To use existing header images, follow these steps:

1. **Click the Header link in the Appearance menu on your Dashboard.**

   The Your Header Image page appears.

2. **Choose from one of eight header images.**

   Scroll down to the bottom of the page and select one of the cool header images that WordPress provides for you by clicking the circle to the left of your chosen image.

3. **Click the Save Changes button.**

   The header image you've chosen is now saved. When you view your website, you should see it displayed at the top.

To upload a new header image, follow these steps:

1. **Click the Browse button under the Upload Image title. Select the image from your computer and then click Open.**

2. **Click Upload.**

   Your image uploads to your web server. The Crop Header Image page appears, where you can crop the image and adjust which portion of the header image you would like displayed (see Figure 13-3).

3. **Click the Crop and Publish button.**

   The Header Image page appears, and your new header image is now displayed.

4. **View your website.**

   Your new header image appears at the top of your website.

In themes that do not have the custom header image feature, you can easily define a background image for the header image using CSS.

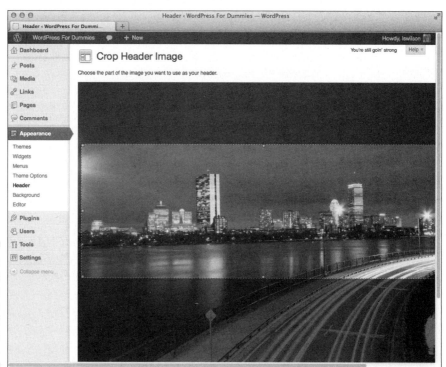

Figure 13-3:
Adjust the dotted lines to choose the area of the image to display.

For purposes of this example, the HTML markup for the header in the template is

```
<header id="branding"></div>
```

In the CSS (`style.css`) file, you can use a background image by defining it in the CSS properties for `#branding`. Use this code:

```
#branding {
background: url(/images/header-image.jpg) no-repeat;
width: 1000px;
height: 228px;
}
```

The background value indicates an image called `header-image.jpg`. For it to display on your site, you need to create the image and upload it to your web server under `/wp-content/theme-name/images/`.

Creating Custom Navigation Menus

A *navigation menu* is a listing of links displayed on your site. These links can be to pages, posts, or categories within your site, or they can be links to other sites. Either way, you can define navigation menus on your site through the built-in Custom Menus feature in WordPress.

It's to your advantage to provide at least one navigation menu on your site so that readers can see everything your site has to offer. Providing visitors with a link — or several — to click keeps the point-and-click spirit of the web.

Adding the Custom Menu feature to your theme

The Custom Menu feature is already built in to the default Twenty Eleven WordPress theme, so you don't have to worry about preparing your theme for it. However, if you're using a different theme, adding support for the Menu feature to your theme is easy:

1. **Click the Editor link under the Appearance menu. Then click the Theme Functions (`functions.php`) template.**

   The Theme Functions template opens in the text editor on the left side of the Edit Themes page.

2. **Type the following function on a new line in the Theme Functions template file somewhere underneath this line: `<?php`:**

```
add_theme_support( 'nav-menus' );
```

3. **Click the Update File button to save the changes to the template.**

   This template tag tells WordPress that your theme can use the Custom Menu feature, and a Menus link now appears under the Appearance menu on the Dashboard.

4. **Open the Header template (`header.php`).**

   Click the Header link on the Edit Themes page to open the Header template in the text editor on the left side of the Edit Themes page.

5. **Add the following template tag by typing it on a new line in the Header template (`header.php`):**

```
<?php wp_nav_menu(); ?>
```

   This template tag is needed so that the menu you build using the Custom Menu feature will display at the top of your website. Table 13-4 gives the details on the different parameters you can use with the `wp_nav_menu();` template tag to further customize the display to suit your needs.

6. **Save the changes you've made to the Header template.**

   Click the Update File button at the bottom of the page.

Table 13-4   Common Tag Parameters for wp_nav_menu();

Parameter	Information	Default	Tag
id	The unique ID of the menu (because you can create several menus, each has a unique ID number)	Blank	`wp_nav_menu( array( 'id' => '1' ) );`
slug	The menu name in slug form (for example, nav-menu)	Blank	`wp_nav_menu( array( 'slug' => 'nav-menu' ) );`

(continued)

Table 13-4 *(continued)*

Parameter	Information	Default	Tag
menu	The menu name	Blank	wp_nav_menu(array('menu' => 'Nav Menu'));
menu_ class	The CSS class used to style the menu list	Menu	wp_nav_menu(array('menu_class' => 'mymenu'));
format	The HTML markup used to style the list (either an unordered list (ul/li) or div class)	div	wp_nav_menu(array('format' => 'ul'));
fall- back_cb	The param- eter that creates a fallback if a custom menu doesn't exist	wp_ page_ menu (the default list of page links)	wp_nav_menu(array(' fallback_cb' => 'wp_ page_menu'));
before	The text that displays before the link text	None	wp_nav_menu(array('before' => 'Click Here'));
after	The text that displays after the link text	None	wp_nav_menu(array('after' => '»'));

Building custom navigation menus

After you add the menu feature to your theme (or if you're already using a theme that has the menu feature), building menus is super-easy — just follow these steps:

1. **Click the Menus link in the Appearance menu on your Dashboard.**

   The Menus page opens on your WordPress Dashboard.

2. **Type a name in the Menu Name box and click the Create Menu button.**

   The Menus page is reloaded with a message that tells you your new menu has been created.

3. **Add links to your newly created menu.**

   WordPress gives you three ways to add links to the new menu you just created (the items in this list are shown in Figure 13-4):

   • *Custom Links:* In the URL field, type the URL of the website that you want to add (http://www.google.com). Next, type the name of the link that you want displayed in your menu in the Label text field (Google). Then click the Add to Menu button.

   • *Pages:* Click the View All link to display a list of all the page(s) you have published on your site. Select the box next to the page names you want to add to your menu. Then click the Add to Menu button.

   • *Categories:* Click the View All link to display a list of all the categories you've created on your site. Select the box next to the category names you want to add to the menu. Then click the Add to Menu button.

4. **Review your menu choices on the right side of the page.**

   When you add new menu items, the column on the right side of the Menus page populates with your menu choices.

5. **Edit your menu choices, if needed.**

   Click the Edit link to the right of the menu link name () to edit the information of each individual link in your new menu.

6. **Save your menu before leaving the Menus page.**

   Be sure to click the Save Menu button under Menu Settings on the right side at the top of the Menus page. A message appears, confirming that the new menu has been saved.

TIP

You can create as many menus as you need to for your website. Just follow the parameters for the menu template tag to make sure you're pulling in the correct menu in the correct spot on your theme. Pay attention to either the menu ID or menu name in the template tag. Additionally, you find more options for your navigation menus by clicking the Screen Options tab at the top-right corner of your Dashboard. From there, you can add things like Posts and Custom Post Types to your menu options, as well as add descriptions for menu items.

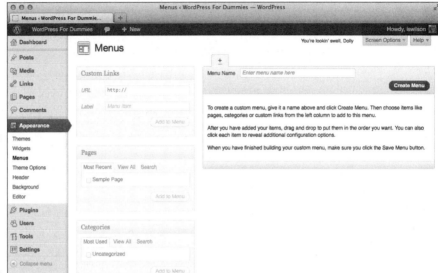

Figure 13-4:
The Build
Custom
Menus
options on
the Menus
page on the
Dashboard.

The HTML markup for the menu is generated as an unordered list, by default, and looks like this:

```
<ul id="menu-main" class="menu">
<li id="menu-item-1" class="menu-item menu-item-type-custom menu-item-object-
            custom menu-item-1"><a href="/">Home</a></li>
<li id="menu-item-2" class="menu-item menu-item-type-post_type menu-item-object-
            page menu-item-2"><a href="http://localhost/wpdemo/blog/">Blog</
            a></li>
<li id="menu-item-3" class="menu-item menu-item-type-post_type menu-item-object-
            page menu-item-3"><a href="http://localhost/wpdemo/about/">About</
            a></li>
</ul>
```

Notice, in the HTML markup, that the first line defines CSS ID and class: `<ul id="menu-main" class="menu">`.

The ID in that line reflects the name that you gave your menu. Because I gave my menu the name of "Main" when I created it on the Dashboard, the CSS ID is `menu-main`. If I had named it "Foo," the ID would instead be `menu-foo`. This assignment of menu names in the CSS and HTML markup is why WordPress allows you to use CSS to create different styles and formats for your different menus.

When developing themes for yourself or others to use, you want to make sure that the CSS you define for the menus can do things like account for sub-pages by creating drop-down menu effects. You can do this several different ways, and Listing 13-1 gives you just one example of a block of CSS that you can use to create a nice style for your menu (this CSS example assumes that you have a menu named "Main"; therefore, the HTML and CSS markup indicate 'menu-main').

Listing 13-1:   Sample CSS for Drop-down Menu Navigation

```
#menu-main {
            width: 960px;
            font-family: Georgia, Times New Roman, Trebuchet MS;
            font-size: 16px;
            color: #FFFFFF;
            margin: 0 auto 0;
            clear: both;
            overflow: hidden;
            }

#menu-main ul {
            width: 100%;
            float: left;
            list-style: none;
            margin: 0;
            padding: 0;
            }

#menu-main li {
            float: left;
            list-style: none;
            }

#menu-main li a {
            color: #FFFFFF;
            display: block;
            font-size: 16px;
            margin: 0;
            padding: 12px 15px 12px 15px;
            text-decoration: none;
            position: relative;
            }
#menu-main li a:hover, #menu-main li a:active, #menu-main .current_page_item a,
            #menu-main .current-cat a, #menu-main .current-menu-item {
            color: #CCCCCC;
            }

#menu-main li li a, #menu-main li li a:link, #menu-main li li a:visited {
            background: #555555;
            color: #FFFFFF;
            width: 138px;
            font-size: 12px;
            margin: 0;
            padding: 5px 10px 5px 10px;
```

(continued)

Listing 13-1 *(continued)*

```
                border-left: 1px solid #FFFFFF;
                border-right: 1px solid #FFFFFF;
                border-bottom: 1px solid #FFFFFF;
                position: relative;
                }

#menu-main li li a:hover, #menu-main li li a:active {
                background: #333333;
                color: #FFFFFF;
                }

#menu-main li ul {
                z-index: 9999;
                position: absolute;
                left: -999em;
                height: auto;
                width: 160px;
                }

#menu-main li ul a {
                width: 140px;
                }

#menu-main li ul ul {
                margin: -31px 0 0 159px;
                }

#menu-main li:hover ul ul, #menu-main li:hover ul ul {
                left: -999em;
                }

#menu-main li:hover ul, #menu-main li li:hover ul, #menu-main li li li:hover ul,
                {
                left: auto;
                }

#menu-main li:hover {
                position: static;
                }
```

The CSS you use to customize the display of your menus will differ; the example that I provide in the previous section is just that: an example. After you get the hang of using CSS, you can try different methods, colors, and styling to create a custom look of your own. (Find additional information about Basic CSS later in this chapter.)

Displaying Custom Menus using widgets

You don't have to use the `wp_nav_menu();` template tag to display the menus on your site because WordPress also provides you with Custom Menu widgets that you can add to your theme. You can therefore use widgets instead of template tags to display the navigation menus on your site. This feature is especially helpful if you have created multiple menus in and around your site in various different places. Have a look at Chapter 5 for more information on using WordPress widgets.

Your first step is to register a special widget area for your theme to handle the Custom Menu widget display. To register this widget, open your theme's `functions.php` file and add the following lines of code:

```
// ADD MENU WIDGET
if ( function_exists('register_sidebars') )
            register_sidebar(array('name'=>'Menu Widget',));
```

These few lines of code create a new widget area called Menu on the Widgets page on your Dashboard. At this point, you can drag the Custom Menu widget into the Menu widget to indicate that you want to display a Custom Menu in that area. The Available Widget area with the Custom Menu widget displayed is in Figure 13-5.

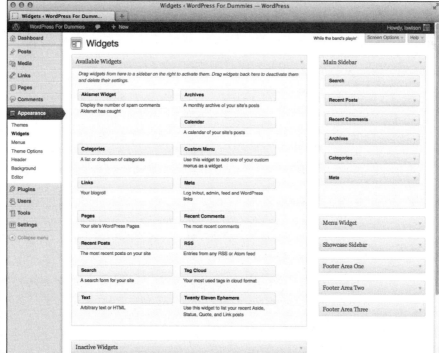

Figure 13-5: Widget page displaying the Custom Menu widget under Available Widgets.

To add the widget area to your theme, head over to the Theme Editor (Appearance⇨Editor) and open the `header.php` file; then add these lines of code in the area you want the Menu widget displayed:

```
<ul>
<?php if ( !function_exists('dynamic_sidebar') || !dynamic_sidebar('Menu
       Widget') ) : ?>
<?php endif; ?>
</ul>
```

These lines of code tell WordPress that you want information contained in the Menu widget area displayed on your site.

Changing Font Family, Color, and Size

You can change the fonts in your theme for style or readability. I've seen typographic (or font) design experts use simple font variations to achieve amazing design results. You can use fonts to separate headlines from body text (or widget headlines and text from the main content) to be less distracting. Table 13-5 lists some examples of often-used font properties.

Table 13-5	Fonts	
Font Properties	*Common Values*	*CSS Examples*
font-family	Georgia, Times, serif	body {font-family: Georgia; serif;}
font-size	px, %, em	body {font-size: 14px;}
font-style	Italic, underline	body {font-style: italic;}
font-weight	bold, bolder, normal	body {font-weight: normal}

The web is actually kind of picky about how it displays fonts, as well as what sort of fonts you can use in the `font-family` property. Not all fonts appear correctly on the web. To be safe, consider sticking to some commonly used font families that appear correctly in most browsers:

✔ **Serif fonts:** Times New Roman, Georgia, Garamond, Bookman Old Style

✔ **Sans-serif fonts:** Verdana, Arial, Tahoma, Trebuchet MS

Changing font color

With more than 16 million different HTML color combinations available, you can find just the right color value for your project. After some time, you'll memorize your favorite color codes. I find that knowing codes for different shades of gray helps me quickly add an extra design touch. For example, I often use the shades of gray listed in Table 13-6 for backgrounds, borders on design elements, and widget headers.

Table 13-6 lists some of the CSS colors that I use often.

Table 13-6	My Favorite CSS Colors
Color	*Value*
White	#FFFFFF
Black	#000000
Grays	#CCCCCC
	#DDDDDD
	#333333
	#E0E0E0

You can easily change the color of your font by changing the color property of the CSS selector you want to tweak. You can use hex codes to define the colors.

You can define the overall font color in your site by defining it in the body CSS selector like this:

```
body {
color: #333333;
}
```

Changing font size

To tweak the size of your font, change the font-size property of the CSS selector you want to change. Font sizes are generally determined by units of measurement, as in these examples:

- ✔ px: Pixel measurement. Increasing or decreasing the number of pixels increases or decreases the font size (12px is larger than 10px).

- ✔ pt: Point measurement. As with pixels, increasing or decreasing the number of points affects the font size accordingly (12pt is larger than 10pt).

✔ %: Percentage measurement. Increasing or decreasing the percentage number affects the font size accordingly (50% is the equivalent to 7 pixels; 100% is the equivalent to 17 pixels).

In the default template CSS, the font size is defined in the <body> tag in pixels, like this:

```
font-size: 12px;
```

When you put all three elements (font family, color, and font size) together in the <body> tag, they style the font for the overall body of your site. Here's how they work together in the <body> tag of the default template CSS:

```
body {
font-size: 12px;
font-family: Georgia, "Bitstream Charter", serif;
color: #666666;
}
```

Serif fonts have little tails, or curlicues, at the edges of letters. (This book's text is in a serif font.) *Sans-serif* fonts have straight edges and are devoid of any fancy styling. (The heading in Table 13-6 uses a sans-serif font. . . no tails!)

When you want to change a font family in your CSS, open the stylesheet (style.css), search for property: font-family, change the values for that property, and save your changes.

In the default template CSS, the font is defined in the <body> tag like this:

```
font-family: Georgia, "Bitstream Charter", serif;
```

Borders

Using CSS borders can add an interesting and unique flair to elements of your theme design. Table 13-7 illustrates common properties and CSS examples for borders in your theme design.

Table 13-7	Common Border Properties	
Border Properties	*Common Values*	*CSS Examples*
border-size	px, em	body {border-size: 1px;}
border-style	solid, dotted, dashed	body {border-style: solid}
border-color	Hexadecimal values	body {border-color: #CCCCCC}

Finding additional CSS resources

The time may come when you want to explore customizing your theme further. Here are some recommended resources:

- **WordPress Codex** (`http://codex.wordpress.org`): Official WordPress documentation

- **W3Schools** (`http://w3schools.com`): A free and comprehensive online HTML and CSS reference

- **WebDesign.com** (`http://ewebscapes.com/webdesign`): A premium library of WordPress video tutorials and training

- **Smashing Magazine** (`http://smashingmagazine.com`): Gives numerous tips and tricks for customizing a WordPress theme

Understanding Basic HTML Techniques

HTML can help you customize and organize your theme. To understand how HTML and CSS work together, think of it this way: If a website were a building, HTML is the structure (the studs and foundation) and CSS is the paint.

HTML contains the elements that CSS provides the styles for. All you have to do to apply a CSS style is use the right HTML element. For this example, I break down a very basic block of HTML:

```
<body>
<div id="content">
<header>
<h1>Headline Goes Here</h1>
</header>
<section>
<article>
<p>This is a sample sentence of body text. <blockquote>The journey of a thousand
              miles
starts with the first step.</blockquote> I'm going to continue on this sentence
              and end it
here. </p>
<p>Click <a href="http://lisasabin-wilson.com">here</a> to visit my website.</p>
</article>
</section>
</div>
</body>
```

All HTML elements must have opening and closing tags. Opening tags are contained in less-than (<) and greater-than (>) symbols. Closing tags are the same, except that they are preceded by a forward-slash (/).

For example:

```
<h1>Headline Goes Here</h1>
```

Note that the HTML elements must be properly nested. In line eight of the preceding example, a paragraph tag is opened (`<p>`). Later in that line, a block quote is opened (`<blockquote>`) and is nesting inside the paragraph tag. When editing this line, you could not end the paragraph (`</p>`) before you end the block quote (`</blockquote>`). Nested elements must close before the elements they are nested within close.

Finally, proper *tabbing,* or indenting, is important when writing HTML, mainly for readability so that you can quickly scan through code to find what you're looking for. A good rule to follow is that if you didn't close a tag in the line above, indent one tab over. This practice allows you to see where each element begins and ends. It can also be very helpful when diagnosing problems.

You will use several very basic HTML markup practices over and over in web design and putting together websites. Earlier in this chapter, I discuss how to combine CSS styling with HTML markup to create different display styles (borders, fonts, and so on). The following sections provide you with commonly used HTML markup samples that you will find helpful as a reference for using HTML in your website code.

Inserting images

You will probably want to insert an image into your website, whether it is within the body of a post or page, in the sidebar by using a widget, or within the template code itself. The HTML markup to insert an image looks like this:

```
<img src="/path/to/image-file.jpg" alt="Image File Name" />
```

I break down this code for you in easy snippets to help you understand what's at work here:

- ✔ `<img src=` — This is the HTML markup that tells the browser that the website is looking for an image file.
- ✔ `"/path/to/image-file.jpg"` — This is the actual directory path through which the web browser will find the physical image file. For example, if you uploaded an image to your web server in the `/wp-content/uploads` directory, the physical path for that image file would be `/wp-content/uploads/image-file.jpg`.
- ✔ `alt="Image File Name"` — The `alt` tag is part of the HTML markup and provides a description for the image that search engines will pick up and recognize as keywords. The `alt` tag description will also display

as text on a browser that cannot, for some reason, load the image file; for example, if the server load time is slow, the text description will load first to at least provide visitors with a description of what the image is.

✔ `/>` — this HTML markup tag closes the initial `<img src="` tag, telling the web browser when the call to the image file is complete.

Inserting hyperlinks

You will probably want to insert a link within the body of a website — commonly referred to as a hyperlink, which is a line of text that is anchored to a web address (URL) so that clicking the text takes a visitor to another website or page that appears in the browser window. The HTML markup to insert a hyperlink looks like this:

```
<a href="http://wiley.com">John Wiley & Sons, Inc. </a>
```

To break down that markup, here is a simple explanation:

✔ `<a href=` — This is the HTML markup that tells the browser that the text within this tag should be hyperlinked to the web address provided in the next point.

✔ `"http://wiley.com"` — This is the web address, or URL, that you intend the text to be anchored to. It needs to be surrounded by quotation marks, which define it as the intended anchor, or address.

✔ `>` — This markup closes the previously opened `<a href=` HTML tag.

✔ `John Wiley & Sons, Inc.` — In this example, this is the text that is linked, or anchored, by the web address, or URL. This text displays on your website and is clickable by your visitors.

✔ `</a>` — This HTML markup tag tells the web browser that the hyperlink is closed. Anything that exists between `<a href="..">` and `</a>` will be hyperlinked, or clickable, through to the intended anchor, or web address.

Commonly, designers use URLs, or web addresses, to link words to other websites or pages; however, you can also provide hyperlinks to files such as `.pdf` (Adobe Acrobat) or `.doc` (Microsoft Word) or any other file type.

Inserting lists

Say you need to provide a clean-looking format for lists of information that you publish on your website. With HTML markup, you can easily provide lists that are formatted differently, depending on your needs.

Ordered lists are numbered sequentially. An example is a step-by-step list of things to do, like this:

1. Write my book chapters.

2. Submit my book chapters to my publisher.

3. Panic a little when book is released to the public.

4. Breathe sigh of relief when public reviews are overwhelmingly positive!

Ordered lists are easy to create in a program such as Microsoft Word, or even in the WordPress post editor because you can use the WYSIWYG editor to format the list for you. However, if you want to code an ordered list using HTML, the experience is a little different. My previous step list sample looks like this when using HTML markup:

```
<ol>
<li>Write my book chapters.</li>
<li>Submit my book chapters to my publisher.</li>
<li>Panic a little when book is released to the public.</li>
<li>Breathe sigh of relief when public reviews are overwhelmingly positive!</li>
</ol>
```

The beginning <ol> tells your web browser to display this list as an ordered list, meaning that it will be ordered with numbers starting with the number 1. The entire list ends with the </ol> HTML tag, which tells your web browser that the ordered list is now complete.

Between the <ol> and </ol> are list items designated as such by the HTML markup <li>. Each list item starts with <li> and ends with </li>, which tells the web browser to display the line of text as one list item.

If you don't close an open HTML markup tag — for example if you start an ordered list with <ol> but don't include the closing </ol> at the end — it messes up the display on your website because the web browser considers anything beneath the initial <ol> to be part of the ordered list until it recognizes the closing tag: </ol>.

Unordered lists are very similar to ordered lists, except that instead of using numbers, they use bullet points to display the list, like this:

✔ Write my book chapters.

✔ Submit my book chapters to my publisher.

✔ Panic a little when book is released to the public.

✔ Breathe sigh of relief when public reviews are overwhelmingly positive!

The HTML markup for an unordered list is just like the ordered list, except that instead of using the `<ol>` tag, it uses the `<ul>` tag (UL = unordered list):

```
<ul>
<li>Write my book chapters.</li>
<li>Submit my book chapters to my publisher.</li>
<li>Panic a little when book is released to the public.</li>
<li>Breathe sigh of relief when public reviews are overwhelmingly positive!</li>
</ul>
```

Note that both the ordered and unordered lists use the list item tags, `<li>` and `</li>`, and the only difference is in the first opening and last closing tags:

- ✔ **Ordered lists:** Use `<ol>` and `</ol>`
- ✔ **Unordered lists:** Use `<ul>` and `</ul>`
- ✔ **List items:** Use `<li>` and `</li>`

Customizing Theme Style with Child Themes

A WordPress theme consists of a collection of template files, stylesheets, images, and JavaScript files. The theme controls the layout and design that your visitors see on the site. Almost every WordPress theme can be used as a *parent theme* (or main theme) and allows for the creation of a *child theme,* or a subset of instructions, to override its files. This structure ensures that a child theme can selectively modify the layout, styling, and functionality of the parent theme without touching any of the code of the main, parent theme. The reason you might want to create a child theme based on a parent theme is to keep the template features, functions, and styles of the parent intact so that when you upgrade it in the future, the upgrading doesn't override any of the customizations or changes you made to the design of the child theme. You therefore maintain the integrity of the main theme while modifying the visual look using a child theme.

The quickest way to understand child themes is by example. In this section, you create a simple child theme using a modified style of the parent theme (but leaving the parent theme entirely intact). Currently, the default WordPress theme is Twenty Eleven. Figure 13-6 shows how the Twenty Eleven theme appears on a sample site, without any alterations in the style.

You likely have Twenty Eleven already installed on your WordPress site, and Twenty Eleven is child theme–ready; therefore, it's a great candidate for creating an example child theme. To keep the names simple, I call the new child theme TwentyEleven Child (original, I know).

Figure 13-6:
The Twenty
Eleven
theme.

Creating a child theme

As do regular themes, a child theme needs to reside in a directory inside the
`/wp-content/themes` directory. The first step to creating a child theme is
to add the directory that will hold it. For this example, create a new directory
called `twentyeleven-child` inside the `/wp-content/themes` directory.

To register the `twentyeleven-child` directory as a theme and to make
it a child of the Twenty Eleven theme, create a `style.css` file and add the
appropriate theme headers. To do so, type the following code into your
favorite code or plain-text editor, such as Notepad for the PC or TextMate for
the Mac, and save the file as `style.css`:

```
/*
Theme Name: TwentyEleven Child
Description: My fabulous child theme
Author: Lisa Sabin-Wilson
Version: 1.0
Template: twentyeleven
*/
```

Typically, you'll find the following headers in the stylesheet (`style.css`) of
a WordPress theme:

✔ `Theme Name`: The theme user sees this name on the WordPress Dashboard.

✔ `Description`: This header provides the user with any additional information about the theme. Currently, it appears only on the Manage Themes page (Appearance⟹Themes).

✔ `Author`: This header lists one or more theme authors. Currently, it is shown only in the Manage Themes page (Appearance⟹Themes).

✔ `Version`: The version number is very useful for keeping track of outdated versions of the theme. It is always a good idea to update the version number when modifying a theme.

✔ `Template`: This header changes a theme into a child theme. The value of this header tells WordPress the directory name of the parent theme. Because our child theme uses Twenty Eleven as the parent, our `style. css` needs to have a `Template` header with a value of `twentyeleven` (the directory name of the Twenty Eleven theme).

Now activate the new TwentyEleven Child theme as your active theme. You should see a site layout similar to the one shown in Figure 13-7 (refer to Chapter 11 for more on activating themes).

Figure 13-7 shows that the new theme doesn't look quite right. The problem is that the new child theme replaced the `style.css` file of the parent theme, yet the new child theme's `style.css` file is empty. You could just copy and paste the contents of the parent theme's `style.css` file, but that method would waste some of the potential of child themes.

Loading a parent theme's style

One of the great things about CSS is how rules can override one another. If you list the same rule twice in your CSS, the rule that comes last takes precedence.

For example:

```
a {
color: blue;
}

a {
color: red;
}
```

This example is overly simple, but it shows what I'm talking about nicely. The first rule says that all links ('a' tags) should be blue, whereas the second one says that links should be red. Because CSS says that the last instruction takes precedence, the links will be red.

Figure 13-7:
My Twenty
Eleven Child
theme.

Using this feature of CSS, you can have your child theme inherit all the styling of the parent theme. You can also selectively modify those styles by overriding the rules of the parent theme. But how can you load the parent theme's `style.css` file so that it inherits the parent theme's styling?

Fortunately, CSS has another great feature that helps you do this with ease. Just add one line to the TwentyEleven Child theme's `style.css` file, as in the following:

```
/*
Theme Name: TwentyEleven Child
Description: My fabulous child theme
Author: Lisa Sabin-Wilson
Version: 1.0
Template: twentyten
*/
```

```
@import url('../twentyeleven/style.css');
```

A number of things are going on here, so let me break it down piece by piece:

- ✔ `@import`: This tells the browser to load another stylesheet. Using the `@ import` tag allows you to pull in the parent stylesheet quickly and easily from a particular source (url — explained in the next item).

- ✔ `url('...')`: This file path indicates that the value is a location and not a normal value.

- ✔ `('../twentyeleven/style.css');`: This indicates the location of the parent stylesheet. Notice the `/twentyeleven` directory name. This name needs to be changed to match the `Template` value in the header so that the appropriate stylesheet is loaded.

With the Twenty Eleven theme's stylesheet loaded into the TwentyEleven Child theme, your site now completely adopts the styles included in the parent Twenty Eleven, and you can use the TwentyEleven Child stylesheet to create your own styles while still using the parent theme for all the functions and features included in the template files.

Customizing the parent theme's styling

Your TwentyEleven Child theme is set up to match the Twenty Eleven parent theme. Now you can add new styling to the TwentyEleven Child theme's `style.css` file. A simple example of how customizing works involves adding a style that converts all h1, h2, and h3 headings to uppercase:

```
/*
Theme Name: TwentyEleven Child
Description: My fabulous child theme
Author: Lisa Sabin-Wilson
Version: 1.0
Template: twentyeleven
*/
```

```
@import url('../twentyeleven/style.css');

h1, h2, h3 {
text-transform: uppercase;
}
```

Figure 13-8 shows how the child theme looks with the CSS style additions applied. Getting better, isn't it?

As you can see, with just a few lines in a `style.css` file, you can create a new child theme that adds specific customizations to an existing theme. Not only was it quick and easy to do, but also you didn't have to modify anything in the parent theme to make it work. Therefore, when upgrades to the parent theme are available, you can upgrade the parent to get the additional features without having to make your modifications again.

Figure 13-8:
The updated
child
theme with
uppercase
headings.

More complex customizations work the same way. Simply add the new rules after the import rule that adds the parent stylesheet.

Using images in child theme designs

Many themes use images to add nice touches to the design. Typically, these images are added to a directory named `images` inside the theme. Just as a parent theme may refer to images in its `style.css` file, your child themes have their own images directory. The following sections provide examples of how these images can be used.

Using a child theme image in a child theme stylesheet

Including a child theme image in a child theme stylesheet is common. To do so, you simply add the new image to the child theme's `images` directory and refer to it in the child theme's `style.css` file. To get a feel for the mechanics of this process, follow these steps:

1. **Create an** `images` **directory inside the child theme's directory:** `/wp-content/themes/twentyeleven-child/images`.

2. **Add an image to use into the directory.**

For this example, add an image called `body-bg.png`. I used a simple black-to-gray gradient that I created in Photoshop.

3. **Add the necessary styling to the child theme's** `style.css` **file, as follows:**

```
/*
Theme Name: TwentyEleven Child
Description: My fabulous child theme
Author: Lisa Sabin-Wilson
Version: 1.0
Template: twentyeleven
*/
@import url('../twentyeleven/style.css');
```

```
body {
background: #ffffff url('images/body-bg.png') repeat-x;
}
```

With a quick refresh of the site, you see that the site now has a new background. Figure 13-9 shows the results. You can see how the background has changed from plain white to a nice black-to-gray vertical gradient background image, with the background color changed to match the gray color in the image (indicated by the `#bfbfbf` code).

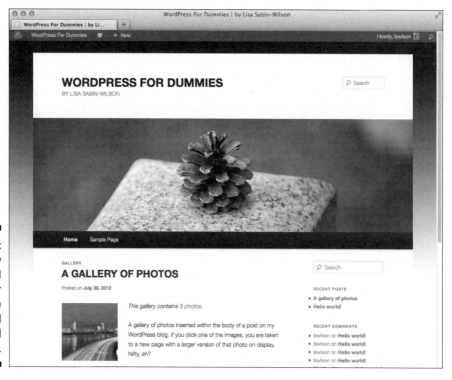

Figure 13-9:
My Twenty Eleven Child theme after editing the background image and color.

Using a parent theme image in a child theme stylesheet

Child theme images are acceptable for most purposes. Sometimes, however, you're better off using images supplied by the parent theme. You could just copy the parent theme image folder, with all its images, to the child theme, but that would prevent the child theme from matching the parent theme if the parent theme image ever changes, such as after an upgrade. Fortunately, you can refer to an image in the parent theme with the @import rule the same way you can reference the parent theme's style.css file.

In the footer of the Twenty Eleven design, a line of text appears stating "Proudly powered by WordPress." In this example, I want to add the logo image in front of the credit text in the footer. Because the logo image already exists inside the parent theme, you can simply add a customization to the child theme's style.css file to make this change, as follows:

```
/*
Theme Name: Twenty Eleven Child
Description: My fabulous child theme
Author: Lisa Sabin-Wilson
Version: 1.0
Template: twentyeleven
*/
```

```
@import url('../twentyeleven/style.css');

footer #site-generator a {
background: url('../twentyeleven/images/wordpress.png') no-repeat
padding: 2px 25px;
}
```

Save the file and refresh your website. Now I'm showing my WordPress pride next to the credit text in the footer. (See Figure 13-10.)

Using a child theme image in a parent theme stylesheet

Looking at the previous examples, you might wonder whether replacing an image used in the parent's stylesheet with one found in the child theme's directory is possible. That would require a change to the parent theme's stylesheet, and the idea behind a child theme is to avoid changes to the parent, so no, that isn't possible. However, you can override the parent theme's rule to refer to the child theme's new image by simply creating an overriding rule in the child theme's stylesheet that points to the new image.

The previous customization helped show my WordPress pride, and I can take that a step further. For example, I think that the WordPress logo in the footer (shown in Figure 13-10) is way too small. I can do better with a larger logo. I will use the Medium PNG: 100 x 100 (grey-m.png) WordPress button that appears on the WordPress.org Logos and Graphics page (http://word press.org/about/logos).

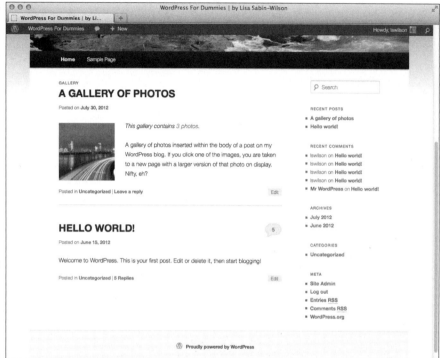

Figure 13-10:
Showing the
WordPress
logo in the
footer.

After you upload the desired logo to your child theme's images directory (by going to `/wp-content/themes/twentyeleven-child/images`) as `grey-m.png`, the following `style.css` file replaces the WordPress logo on the parent theme's footer with the new WordPress button:

```
/*
Theme Name: TwentyEleven Child
Description: My fabulous child theme
Author: Lisa Sabin-Wilson
Version: 1.0
Template: twentyeleven
*/


@import url('../twentyeleven/style.css');


footer #site-generator a {
background: url(images/wp-logo.png) center left no-repeat;
padding: 2px 110px;
}
```

Now your child theme shows your WordPress pride loud and clear with the new, larger logo from the official WordPress.org website. If you ask me, the new look (shown in Figure 13-11) looks quite nice.

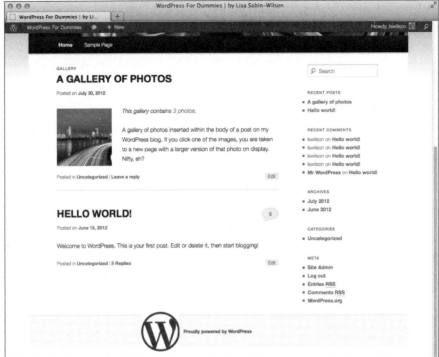

Figure 13-11:
The new,
larger
WordPress
footer icon.

You cannot directly replace parent theme images. Rather, you must provide a new image in the child theme and override the parent's styling to refer to this new image.

Modifying Theme Structure with Child Themes

The previous section showed how to use a child theme to modify the stylesheet of an existing theme. This feature is tremendously powerful. A talented CSS developer can use this technique to create an amazing variety of layouts and designs.

However, this is just the beginning of the power of child themes. Although every child theme overrides the parent theme's `style.css` file, the child theme can override the parent theme's template files, too. However, child themes aren't limited to just overriding template files; when needed, child themes can also supply their own template files.

Template files are PHP files that WordPress runs to render different views of the site (covered in Chapter 12). A site view is the type of content being looked at. Examples of different views are home, category archive, individual post, and page content.

Some examples of common template files are `index.php`, `archive.php`, `single.php`, `page.php`, `attachment.php`, and `search.php`. (You can read more about available template files, including how to use them, in Chapter 12.)

You might wonder what purpose is served by modifying template files of a parent theme. Although modifying a parent theme's stylesheet allows for some very powerful control over the design, it can't add new content, modify the underlying site structure, or change how the theme functions. To get that level of control, you need to modify the template files.

Overriding parent template files

When both the child theme and parent theme supply the same template file, the child theme file is used. The process of replacing the original parent template file is referred to as *overriding*.

Although overriding each of the theme's template files can defeat the purpose of using a child theme — because updating those template files won't enhance the child theme — sometimes you have to override to produce the results you need.

The easiest way to customize a specific template file in a child theme is to copy the template file from the parent theme folder to the child theme folder. After the file is copied, you can customize it as needed, and the changes are reflected in the child theme.

A good example of a template file that can typically be overridden is the `footer.php` file. Customizing the footer allows you to add site-specific branding.

Adding new template files

A child theme can override existing parent template files, but it can also supply template files that don't exist in the parent. Although you may never need your child themes to do this, this option can open possibilities for your designs.

For example, this technique proves most valuable with page templates. The Twenty Eleven theme has a default page template named `page.php`. This page template removes the sidebar and centers the content on the page, as shown in Figure 13-12.

Having the content centered like that isn't a design flaw. The layout was intentionally set up this way to improve readability. However, I like to have a full-width layout option that spans the entire width of the body of the site so that I can embed a video, add a forum, or add other content that works well with full width. To add the full-width layout feature to your child theme, simply add a new page template and the necessary styling to the `style.css` file.

A good way to create a new theme page template is to copy an existing one and modify it as needed. In this case, copying the `page.php` file of the parent Twenty Eleven theme to a new file, called `fullwidth-page.php`, is a good start. After a few customizations, the `fullwidth-page.php` file looks like this:

```php
<?php
/**
 * Template Name: Full width, no sidebar
 */
get_header(); ?>
<div id="primary">
    <div id="content" class="full-width" role="main">
    <?php the_post(); ?>
    <?php get_template_part( 'content', 'page' ); ?>
    <?php comments_template( '', true ); ?>
    </div><!-- #content -->
</div><!-- #primary -->
<?php get_footer(); ?>
```

Figure 13-12:
The default page template in Twenty Eleven.

The key modification is adding `class="full-width"` after the `<div id="content"` markup. This new, full-width class allows you to style the page template without modifying other site styling in the parent theme.

The styling change to make this work is quick and easy. Simply add the following lines after the `@import` rule in the child theme's `style.css` file:

```
#content.full-width {
    margin: 0;
    width: 100%;
}

#content.full-width .entry-header,
#content.full-width .entry-content,
#content.full-width .footer.entry-meta,
#content.full-width #comments-title {
    margin: 0 auto;
    width: 95%;
}
```

Switching to the new full-width page template produces the layout shown in Figure 13-13.

Figure 13-13: The new full-width, no-sidebar page template.

Removing template files

You may be asking why you would want to remove a parent's template file. That's a good question. Unfortunately, the Twenty Eleven theme doesn't provide a good example of why you would want to do this. Therefore, you must use your imagination a bit here, just to understand the mechanics of removing a file from the parent theme, for future reference.

Imagine that you're creating a child theme built off a parent theme called Example Parent. Example Parent is well designed, and a great child theme was quickly built off it. The child theme looks and works exactly the way you want it to, but there's a problem.

The Example Parent theme has a `home.php` template file that provides a highly customized nonblog home page. This template works very well but isn't what you want for the site. You want a standard blog home page. If the `home.php` file didn't exist in Example Parent, everything would work perfectly.

There isn't a way to remove the `home.php` file from Example Parent without modifying the Parent theme (which you never, ever want to do), so you have to use a trick. Instead of removing the file, override the `home.php` file and have it emulate `index.php`.

You may think that simply copying and pasting the Example Parent `index.php` code into the child theme's `home.php` file would be a good approach. Although this would work, there is a better way: You can tell WordPress to run the `index.php` file so that changes to `index.php` are respected. This single line of code inside the child theme's `home.php` is all you need to replace `home.php` with `index.php`:

```php
<?php locate_template( array( 'index.php' ), true ); ?>
```

The `locate_template` function does a bit of magic. If the child theme supplies an `index.php` file, it is used. If not, the parent `index.php` file is used.

This approach produces the same result that removing the parent theme's `home.php` file would have. The `home.php` code is ignored and the changes to `index.php` are respected.

Part VI
The Part of Tens

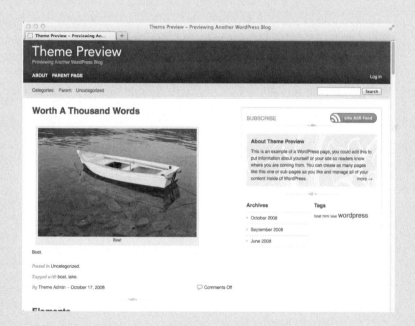

In this part . . .

Welcome to The Part of Tens! In this part, I tell you about ten fabulous WordPress themes and ten useful plugins that you can use to enhance your WordPress blogging.

Chapter 14

Ten Popular WordPress Plugins

In This Chapter

▶ Finding popular WordPress plugins

▶ Using plugins to enhance your blog

*I*n this chapter, I list ten of the most popular plugins available for your WordPress blog. This list isn't exhaustive by any means; hundreds of excellent WordPress plugins can, and do, provide multiple ways to extend the functionality of your blog. And if these ten plugins aren't enough for you, you can find many more at the official WordPress Plugin Directory (`http://wordpress.org/extend/plugins`).

The greatest plugin of all is Akismet, which I describe in Chapter 10. Akismet is the answer to comment and trackback spam; it kills spam dead. It's installed with WordPress. Chapter 10 contains information on how to locate, download, unpack, install, activate, and manage plugins in your WordPress blog.

Jetpack

Developer: Automattic

`http://wordpress.org/extend/plugins/jetpack/`

Jetpack is not just one simple plugin; it's a suite of plugins that connects your self-hosted website running WordPress.org with the hosted WordPress.com service — and brings you many of the features that WordPress.com users enjoy. Jetpack bundles great features such as

▶ **WordPress.com Stats:** This simple statistics program gives you easy-to-read statistics on your site visitors, such as how many visitors you have, where they're coming from, and what content they're viewing on your site.

- ✔ **Jetpack Comments:** This feature is a comment system that integrates with social media login options like Facebook, Twitter, and Google.

- ✔ **Subscriptions:** With this feature, your site visitors can subscribe to your blog posts and/or comments via e-mail.

- ✔ **Sharing:** Your readers can easily share your content across different social networks like Facebook, Twitter, Google+, Pinterest, and more.

- ✔ **VaultPress:** This feature provides a real-time backup and security-scanning service for your site.

- ✔ **Contact Form:** Easily insert an e-mail contact form anywhere on your WordPress site with one click of a button.

- ✔ **Spelling and Grammar:** Improve your grammar, spelling, and punctuation with this integrated proofreading service.

- ✔ **Gravatar Hovercards:** Show a pop-up of your users' Gravatar profiles in comments.

- ✔ **Extra Sidebar Widgets:** Add widgets to your WordPress site like the Easy Image Widget and the RSS Widget.

- ✔ **WP.me Shortlinks:** Create a short URL for easier social sharing with the WP.me service.

- ✔ **Shortcode Embeds:** Easily embed videos and audio files with a WordPress shortcode.

- ✔ **Beautiful Math:** This feature uses the LaTeX markup language for complex mathematical equations within your posts — perfect for the real geeks out there.

Because Jetpack runs and is hosted on the WordPress.com cloud server, updates to this suite of plugins happen automatically — giving you fast and ready access to the latest and greatest bundle of plugins that Automattic has to offer.

In order to use Jetpack, you must have a WordPress.com account, and when you activate it on your Dashboard, it asks you to connect your site to your WordPress.com account — see Chapter 3 for information on signing up for WordPress.com.

Subscribe to Comments

Developer: Mark Jaquith

`http://wordpress.org/extend/plugins/subscribe-to-comments`

The Subscribe to Comments plugin adds a very nice feature to your blog by letting your visitors subscribe to individual posts you've made to your blog. When your readers subscribe to individual posts on your blog, they receive notification via e-mail whenever someone leaves a new comment on the post. This feature goes a long way toward keeping your readers informed and making the discussions lively and active!

The plugin includes a full-featured subscription manager that your commenters can use to unsubscribe to certain posts, block all notifications, or even change their notification e-mail addresses.

Facebook

Developers: Facebook and Automattic

http://wordpress.org/extend/plugins/facebook

This plugin was developed by Facebook for WordPress with a little help from the developers at Automattic. With the importance of a social media presence today, you'll want to make sure that all your content reaches the eyes of your friends and followers on social networks like Facebook. And that pursuit can be time-consuming. The goal of the Facebook plugin is to save you time by easily sharing your new content with your Facebook page and allowing your Facebook friends to discover that content and interact with your website seamlessly. The following great features allow you to

- ✔ Share new content from your WordPress site on your Facebook page automatically. After you connect your site to your Facebook account in the plugin settings, your new content is posted automatically to your Facebook page.

- ✔ Mention friends and favorite pages within the content of your posts and link those mentions directly to their Facebook pages.

- ✔ Include the share, like, and subscribe Facebook buttons on your WordPress site, with easy customization.

- ✔ Display a recommendations box where Facebook makes additional content recommendations for your readers to discover, based on the content they're currently browsing on your site.

- ✔ Include Facebook commenting on your site to allow your Facebook friends to comment in both places at once.

- ✔ Include an Activity Feed Box widget that allows Facebook friends to see what their friends are doing on your site.

- ✔ Determine how well your Facebook presence is doing in promoting your content through Facebook Insights integration.

The Facebook plugin installs easily, and after you connect your Facebook account to your WordPress site through the Facebook plugin settings, you're ready to go!

All in One SEO Pack

Developer: Michael Torbert

http://wordpress.org/extend/plugins/all-in-one-seo-pack/

Almost everyone is concerned about search engine optimization (SEO) in blogs. Good SEO practices help the major search engines (such as Google, Yahoo!, and Bing) easily find and cache your blog content in their search databases so that when people search for keywords, they can find your blog in the search results. All in One SEO Pack helps you fine-tune your blog to make that happen. It automatically creates optimized titles and generates HTML keywords for your individual posts. If you're a beginner, this plugin works for you out of the box with no advanced configuration necessary. Woohoo! If you're an advanced user, you can fine-tune the All in One SEO settings to your liking.

WPtouch iPhone Theme

Developer: Brave New Code

http://wordpress.org/extend/plugins/wptouch

The WPtouch iPhone Theme plugin transforms your WordPress-powered website into an iPhone-compatible browsing experience. It's designed specifically for visitors using an Apple iPhone. As an added bonus, it creates a nice interface for visitors browsing on an Android phone or Blackberry, as well.

This plugin doesn't affect how your WordPress website appears on a desktop or laptop. It affects the view only for people browsing your site on different mobile devices. The switch happens automatically without your having to touch one bit of code, which is always great news!

BackupBuddy

Developer: iThemes Media

http://ithemes.com/purchase/backupbuddy/

Starting at $75 for the personal user and $197 for its entire development suite of plugins, the folks at iThemes have hit a home run with BackupBuddy, which lets you back up your entire WordPress website in minutes.

With this plugin, you can also determine a schedule of automated backups of your site on a daily, weekly, or monthly basis. You can store those backups on your web server, e-mail backups to a designated e-mail address, or store the backups in Amazon's Simple Storage Service, if you have an account there.

BackupBuddy not only backs up your WordPress data (posts, pages, comments, and so on), but it also backs up any theme and customized plugins you've installed (including all the settings for those plugins) and saves and backs up all WordPress settings and any widgets that you're currently using.

BackupBuddy also includes an import and migration script (importbuddy.php) that allows you to easily transfer an existing site to a new domain, or new host, within minutes. You simply download the backup file created by BackupBuddy from your Dashboard (choose BackupBuddy⇨Backups) and install the script on a new domain, follow the steps, and within minutes, your entire site is completely restored on a new domain, or web host, with minimal effort.

This plugin is invaluable for designers and developers who work with clients to design websites with WordPress. Using BackupBuddy, you can download a backup of the site and then use the import/migration script to transfer the completed site to your client's site within minutes — saving all the customizations you did to the theme and the plugins you installed, including the settings and data you've been working so hard on.

WP Super Cache

Developer: Donncha O'Caoimh

http://wordpress.org/extend/plugins/wp-super-cache

WP Super Cache creates static HTML files from your dynamic WordPress content. Why is this useful? On a high-traffic site, having cached versions of your posts and pages can speed up the load time of your website considerably. A *cached* version simply means that the content is converted to static HTML pages (as opposed to dynamically created content pulled from your database through a series of PHP commands) that are then stored on the server. This process eases the efforts the web server must take to display the content in your visitors' browsers.

You can also read a very helpful article written by the plugin developer, Donncha O'Caoimh, on his website here: `http://ocaoimh.ie/wp-super-cache/`.

Twitter Tools

Developer: Alex King

`http://wordpress.org/extend/plugins/twitter-tools`

Social media networking is insanely popular on the web right now. One of the more popular services is Twitter (`www.twitter.com`). Almost everyone who has a blog also has a Twitter account (you can even follow me on Twitter at `http://www.twitter.com/LisaSabinWilson`).

One of the nicer things that came about shortly after Twitter hit the scene was Alex King's plugin for WordPress called Twitter Tools. This plugin lets you tweet an announcement every time you publish a new post on your blog. The announcement appears on your Twitter stream and is read by all of your Twitter followers. People can then click the link and read your article. It's just one more nice way to use social media to promote your blog and content! There's more to this plugin, however; it also has some pretty nifty tools that enable you to

- Publish a post on your blog with your Twitter updates from the day.

- Publish a tweet directly from your blog, so you don't have to use another browser window or application.

- Tag your blog posts with Twitter hash tags — which are like keywords for Twitter that help other people search for and find your content within the Twitter universe.

Google XML Sitemaps

Developer: Arne Brachhold

`http://wordpress.org/extend/plugins/google-sitemap-generator`

This plugin lets you create a Google-compliant site map of your entire blog. Every time you create a new post or page, the site map is updated and submitted to several major search engines, including Google, Yahoo!, and Bing. This plugin helps the search engines find and catalog new content from your site, so your new content appears in the search engines faster than it would if you didn't have a site map.

Sucuri Sitecheck Malware Scanner

Developer: Dre Armeda

`http://wordpress.org/extend/plugins/sucuri-scanner`

With the rise in popularity of the WordPress software came a nefarious group of anonymous hackers trying to take advantage of the vast number of users in the WordPress community by attempting to inject malicious code and malware into themes, plugins, and insecure and outdated files within the WordPress core code.

Protect your website by using the Sucuri Sitecheck Malware Scanner — an easy-to-install-and-use plugin that enables full scan capabilities — for both malware and blacklisting — from Sucuri, right on your WordPress Dashboard. The plugin checks for malware, spam, blacklisting, and other security issues hidden inside code files. It's the best defense you have against malicious hackers and very easy to implement — and for the peace of mind that it provides you, the free price tag is worth every penny!

Chapter 15

Ten Free WordPress Themes

In This Chapter

▶ Finding good WordPress themes

▶ Using popular WordPress themes to style your blog

The list I present here isn't exhaustive by any means. Chapters 11, 12, and 13 give you a few more resources to find a theme that suits your needs.

All the themes in this chapter meet the following criteria:

✔ **They're user friendly,** which means you don't have to tinker with anything to get things to look the way you want them to.

✔ **They're compatible with widgets.** In a word, widgets are wonderful. I cover widgets completely in Chapter 5.

✔ **They're free.** Some very nice premium themes are out there, but why pay if you don't have to?

✔ **They use valid code.** Although you may not notice it, valid code that meets W3C (www.w3c.org) standards won't cause errors in browsers.

Hybrid

Theme designer: Justin Tadlock

```
http://themehybrid.com
```

Hybrid is more of a theme *framework*, or parent theme that can be modified endlessly to create the perfect child theme, than a theme to use straight out of the box, but don't let that intimidate you! It's crazy easy to use, and Hybrid is very user-friendly.

By default, the Hybrid theme is very plain and simple, but it encompasses any and all of the WordPress features and functions that you would want:

- ✔ **It's SEO-ready:** Hybrid comes completely optimized for SEO (search engine optimization).

- ✔ **It's highly customizable:** Hybrid has 15 custom page templates for you to choose from. Each custom page is set up slightly differently, giving you an array of options.

- ✔ **It's widget-ready:** Hybrid has multiple widgetized areas for you to easily drop content into, making your WordPress theme experience easy and efficient.

You can read about the Hybrid theme at the developer's (Justin Tadlock) website at www.themehybrid.com. You can also download and install the theme directly into your WordPress website by using the automatic theme installer built in to your WordPress Dashboard.

Check out options for installing and tweaking WordPress themes in Chapters 11, 12, and 13. Those chapters give you information on CSS, HTML, and theme-tweaking, as well as guide you through working with parent/child themes.

designPile

Theme designer: Smashing Magazine

http://wordpress.site5.net/designpile/

The highlights of this theme are the following:

- ✔ **Three different color schemes:** black and pink, black and green, and black and blue

- ✔ **Sidebar and footer widgets**

- ✔ **Post thumbnails:** supports the WordPress post thumbnails/featured image feature

- ✔ **Space for monetization with ads**

- ✔ **Built-in social networking links and sharing**

The designPile theme, shown in Figure 15-1, is a sharp design and an easy-to-use free WordPress theme for any new user.

Figure 15-1:
Try the
designPile
Theme by
Smashing
Magazine.

Responsive

Theme designer: Emil Uzelac

`http://wordpress.org/extend/themes/responsive`

Responsive design is all the rage right now because of the emergence of mobile and tablet browsing. *Responsive design* ensures that a website looks perfect, no matter which device a reader is using to view it. The Responsive theme by Emil Uzelac features nine page templates including the Blog, Blog Summary, and other static page templates built on a fluid grid system that adapts to the user's browsing environment.

Theme options in this responsive design include webmaster tools, logo management, social icons, and navigation menus as well as multilingual support.

P2

Theme designer: Automattic

`http://wordpress.org/extend/themes/p2`

You can easily see the Twitter-esque inspiration behind P2 by looking at the post text box displayed at the top of the theme. As with Twitter, users can post quick updates, and logged-in visitors can leave feedback on the updates. All this happens from the convenience of the front page of your site — without requiring anyone to click through to a different page on your site, locate the comment form, type, and submit the comment. The P2 theme also features the following:

- Live tag suggestions for your posts and updates
- Threaded comment display
- A show/hide feature for comments
- Real-time notification for posts, updates, and comments
- Keyboard shortcuts

Annotum Base

Theme designer: Crowd Favorite

`http://wordpress.org/extend/themes/annotum-base`

Annotum Base is a scholar's blog theme providing a complete open-access journaling system including peer review, workflow, and advanced editing and formatting for blog posts and pages. The most interesting features in this theme include structured figures, equations, and cross referencing from PubMed and CrossRef (including reference importing).

Other theme options include

- Customized color options
- Custom header image
- Custom background image/colors
- Navigation menus
- Featured images
- Microformats
- Multilingual support

Blackbird

Theme designer: InkThemes

http://wordpress.org/extend/themes/blackbird

Blackbird, shown in Figure 15-2, is a responsive theme (mobile ready) with extensive customization options including the ability to:

- ✔ Use your own logo
- ✔ Include your analytics code
- ✔ Customize featured text using an easy widget
- ✔ Customize background colors and/or images
- ✔ Incorporate post thumbnails using the WordPress featured image feature
- ✔ Customize the header image
- ✔ Use the navigation menu feature in WordPress

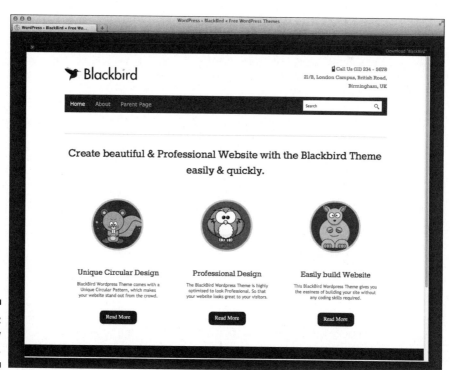

Figure 15-2:
Blackbird by
InkThemes.

iTheme

Theme designer: Nick La

```
http://ndesign-studio.com/demo/wordpress/index.
php?wptheme=iTheme
```

iTheme is a WordPress theme designed with Macintosh lovers in mind. The theme emulates the design elements and features of the Macintosh operating system, with beautiful blue gradients and Mac-like menu headers and icons. This theme has a fully configurable sidebar that allows you to use WordPress widgets, and when they're in your blog, you can drag those widgets around in the sidebar.

Esquire

Theme designer: Automattic

```
http://wordpress.org/extend/themes/esquire
```

Esquire is a free WordPress theme created by Automattic, the company behind the WordPress.com hosted service. It has a distinct visual design with creative typography (fonts), a two-column layout, and visually creative design elements that make it unique (such as the date format and content styling).

Esquire supports all of the expected default WordPress features such as featured images, custom background, custom header, navigation menus, and post formats. The theme design is inspired by the art direction of Esquire Magazine.

WP-Creativix

Theme designer: IWEBIX

```
http://wordpress.org/extend/themes/wp-creativix
```

The WP-Creativix theme by IWEBIX is a very clean, professional-looking free theme for WordPress that you can begin using immediately after you install and activate it. This elegantly designed theme is well suited for a business, portfolio, or photoblogging website.

The WP-Creativix theme provides users with custom page templates (such as no-sidebar templates, portfolio, and blog) and allows you to use default WordPress features such as custom header, custom background, navigation menu, featured images, and threaded comments.

Gridline

Theme designer: Thad Allender

http://graphpaperpress.com/themes/gridline/

Gridline is a minimalist WordPress theme featuring a clean grid layout. The theme has clean, simple, light elements, which lets your design focus mainly on content rather than appearance. The theme uses black, white, and gray tones and a two-column layout, with content on the left and sidebar on the right.

This is a free theme offered by a commercial theme company: Graph Paper Press — and while it is free, to be able to download it, you need to register for a free account on the Graph Paper Press website.

Appendix

Upgrading, Backing Up, and Migrating

*Y*ou may, at some point, need to move your site to a different home on the web, either to a new web host or into a different account on your current hosting account. You may also be reading this book because you're moving your blog from a completely different platform to WordPress. You will also find that during your time as a WordPress user, upgrading the WordPress software is important, as is maintaining backups of your site so that you don't lose precious months or years of content.

In this appendix, you discover the WordPress upgrade notification system and what to do when WordPress notifies you that a new version of the software is available. This appendix also covers the best practices in upgrading the WordPress platform on your site to ensure the best possible outcome (that is, how not to break your website after a WordPress upgrade).

This appendix also covers how to migrate a blog that exists within a different blogging platform (such as Movable Type or Typepad) to WordPress. And finally, this appendix takes you through how to back up your WordPress files, data, and content and move it to a new hosting provider or different domain.

Getting Notified of an Available Upgrade

When you install WordPress and have logged in for the first time, you can see the version number located at the bottom-right corner of the WordPress Dashboard. So, if anyone asks you what version you're using, you now know exactly where to look to find that information.

So, you have WordPress installed and you've been happily publishing content to your website with it for several weeks, maybe even months. Then one day, you log in and see a message at the top of your Dashboard screen that you've never seen before: `WordPress X.X.X is available! Please update now.` You can see such a message displayed in Figure A-1.

Both the message at the top of the screen and the notification bubble on the Dashboard menu are visual indicators that you're now using an outdated version of WordPress and that you can (and need to) upgrade the software.

Upgrade notification

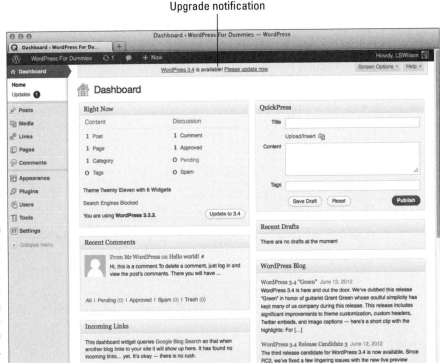

Figure A-1:
Alert notification of the available WordPress upgrade on the Dashboard.

The message at the top of your Dashboard has two links that you can click for more information. The first, in Figure A-1, is a link called WordPress 3.4. Clicking it takes you to the WordPress Codex page titled Version 3.4 that's filled with information about the version upgrade, including

- ✔ Installation/upgrade information
- ✔ Summary of the development cycle for this version
- ✔ List of revised files

The second link, Please Update Now, takes you to the WordPress Updates page on the WordPress Dashboard, shown in Figure A-2.

At the very top of the WordPress Updates page is another, important, message for you (see Figure A-2): `Important: before updating, please back up your database and files. For help with updates, visit the Updating WordPress Codex page`. Both links in that message take you to the WordPress Codex pages that contain helpful information on creating backups and updating WordPress.

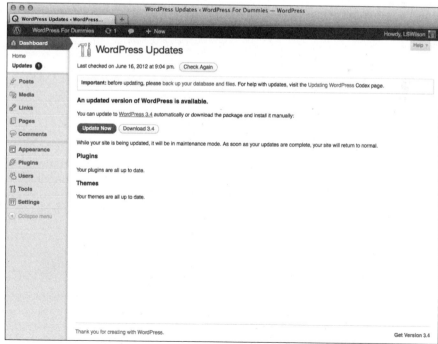

Figure A-2: Get the latest version of WordPress through the WordPress Updates page.

The WordPress Updates page tells you that an updated version of WordPress is available and you have two different ways to update:

- ✔ **Automatically:** By using the built-in WordPress updater
- ✔ **Manually:** By downloading the files and installing them on your server

Backing Up Your Database

One step you should always, always take before upgrading your WordPress software installation is to back up your database. This step isn't required, of course, but it's a smart step to take to safeguard your website and make absolutely sure that — should the upgrade go wrong for some reason — you have a complete copy of all your website data that can be restored if needed.

The best way to back up your database is to use the MySQL administration interface provided by your web-hosting provider.

cPanel is a web-hosting interface provided by many web hosts as an account management tool containing phpMyAdmin as the preferred tool to manage and administer databases. Not all web hosts use cPanel or phpMyAdmin, however; so if yours doesn't, consult the user documentation for the tools that your web host provides. The instructions in this appendix are provided using cPanel and phpMyAdmin.

The following takes you through the steps of creating a database backup using the phpMyAdmin interface:

1. **Log in to the cPanel for your hosting account.**

   Typically, you will browse to `http://yourdomain.com/cpanel` to bring up the login screen for your cPanel. Enter your specific hosting account username and password in the login fields and click OK to log in.

2. **Click the phpMyAdmin icon.**

   The phpMyAdmin interface opens and displays your database.

3. **Click the name of the database that you want to back up.**

   If you have more than one database in your account, the left-side menu in phpMyAdmin displays the names of all of them. Click the one you want to back up, and that database loads in the main interface window on the side of the screen.

4. **Click the Export tab at the top of the screen.**

   The page refreshes and displays the backup utility screen.

5. **Select the Save as File box.**

6. **Select the "zipped" option.**

   This compiles the database backup file in a `.zip` file and prepares it for download.

7. **Click the Go button.**

   A pop-up window appears, allowing you to select a location on your computer to store the database backup file. Click the Save button to download it and save it to your computer.

Upgrading WordPress Automatically

To update WordPress automatically, follow these steps:

1. **Back up your WordPress website; do not skip this step!**

   Backing up your website before updating is an important step, just in case something goes wrong with the upgrade. Give yourself some peace of mind by knowing that you have a full copy of your website that can be restored if needed. My advice is to not skip this step under any circumstances.

2. **Deactivate all plugins.**

   This ensures that any plugin conflicts caused by the upgraded version of WordPress cannot affect the upgrade process. It also ensures that your website doesn't break after the upgrade is completed. You can find more information on working with and managing plugins in Chapter 10; for the purpose of this step, you can deactivate plugins by following these steps:

   a. Click the Plugins link in the Plugins menu on the Dashboard.

      This loads the Plugins page.

   b. Select all plugins by selecting the box to the left of the Plugin column (see Figure A-3).

   c. In the drop-down menu at the top, select Deactivate.

   d. Click the Apply button.

3. **Click the Update Now button on the WordPress Updates page.**

   This reloads the WordPress Updates page with the following messages (as shown in Figure A-4):

   - `Downloading update from http://wordpress.org/ wordpress-3.4-no-content.zip. . .`

- Unpacking the update. . .

- Verifying the unpacked files. . .

- Installing the latest version. . .

- Upgrading database. . .

- WordPress updated successfully

- Welcome to WordPress 3.4. You will be redirected to the About WordPress screen. If not, click here.

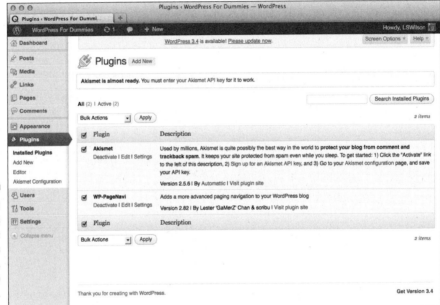

Figure A-3:
The Plugins page with all plugins selected, ready to deactivate.

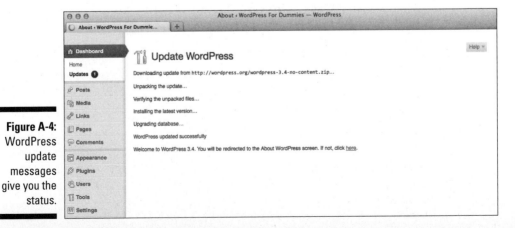

Figure A-4:
WordPress update messages give you the status.

4. **Wait until your screen redirects to the About WordPress page.**

   The Welcome to WordPress page loads in your web browser, and you can see that both the update alert message at the top of the site and the notification message on the Dashboard menu isn't there anymore. The Welcome screen displays a listing of new features in the version you just installed. You're now using the latest version of WordPress.

Upgrading WordPress Manually

The second — and least used — method of upgrading WordPress is the manual method. It's the least-used method mainly because the automatic method, discussed in the previous section, is so easy and quick. In some rare circumstances, you would manually upgrade WordPress because your web-hosting environment can't accommodate the automatic upgrade process, or maybe you just wanted to go through the experience of manually updating the software, for whatever weird reason.

The steps to manually upgrade WordPress are as follows:

1. **Back up your WordPress website and deactivate all plugins.**

   See Steps 1 and 2 in the previous section, "Upgrading WordPress Automatically."

2. **Navigate to the WordPress Update page by clicking the Please Update Now link.**

3. **Click the Download button.**

   This opens a dialog box that allows you to save the `.zip` file of the latest WordPress download package to your local computer, shown in Figure A-5.

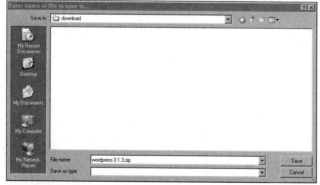

Figure A-5: Downloading the WordPress files to your local computer.

4. **Select a location to store the download package and click Save.**

   The `.zip` file downloads to your selected location on your computer.

5. **Browse to the** `.zip` **file on your computer.**

6. **Unzip the file.**

   Use a program such as WinZip (`www.winzip.com`) to unzip files contained within a `.zip` file.

7. **Connect to your web server via FTP.**

   See Chapter 6 for a refresher on how to use FTP.

8. **Delete all the files and folders in your existing WordPress installation directory** *except* **the following:**

   - `/wp-content folder`
   - `.htaccess`
   - `wp-config.php`

9. **Upload the contents of the** `/wordpress` **folder — not the folder itself — to your web server.**

   Most FTP client software lets you select all the files and drag 'n' drop them to your web server. Other programs have you select the files and click a Transfer button.

10. **Navigate to the following URL on your website:** `http://yourdomain.com/wp-admin`.

    Don't panic: Your database still needs to be upgraded to the latest version; so instead of seeing your website on your domain, you see a message telling you that a database upgrade is required, as shown in Figure A-6.

Figure A-6:
Press the
button to
upgrade
your
WordPress
database.

11. **Click the Upgrade WordPress Database button.**

    This action causes WordPress to initiate the upgrade of the MySQL database associated with your website. When the database upgrade is complete, the page refreshes and displays a message saying so.

12. **Click the Continue button.**

    Your browser loads the WordPress login page. The upgrade is now complete, and you can continue using WordPress with all of its newly upgraded features.

During your time as a WordPress user, you'll upgrade on a regular basis, at least three to four times per year. For some users, this is a frustrating reality of using WordPress; however, because of the very active development environment of the WordPress project, WordPress is the most popular platform available today. Because WordPress is always adding great new features and functions to the platform, upgrading always ensures that you're on top of the game and using the latest tools and features available.

If you're the type of person who is uncomfortable performing administrative tasks such as upgrading and creating database backups, you can hire someone to perform these tasks for you — either a member of your company, if you're a business, or a WordPress consultant skilled in these tasks.

Migrating Your Existing Blog to WordPress

So you have a blog on a different blogging system and want to move your blog to WordPress? This appendix helps you accomplish just that. WordPress makes it relatively easy to pack up your data and archives from one blog platform and move to a new WordPress blog.

WordPress lets you move your blog from platforms such as Blogspot, Typepad, and Movable Type. It also gives you a nifty way to migrate from any blogging platform via RSS feeds, as long as the platform you're importing from has an RSS feed available. Some platforms, such as Myspace, have some limitations on RSS feed availability, so be sure to check with your platform provider. In this appendix, you discover how to prepare your blog for migration and how to move from the specific platforms for which WordPress provides importer plugins.

For each blogging platform, the WordPress.org platform provides you with a quick and easy-to-install plugin that allows you to import and use your content right away. The importers are packaged in a plugin format because most people use an importer just once, and some people don't use the importer tools at all. The plugins are there for you to use if you need them. WordPress.

com, on the other hand, has the importers built right into the software. Note the differences for the version you're using.

Movin' On Up

Bloggers have a variety of reasons to migrate away from one system to WordPress:

- ✔ **Simple curiosity:** The use of WordPress — and the whole community of WordPress users — is generating a *lot* of buzz. People are naturally curious to check out something that all the cool kids are doing.

- ✔ **More control of your blog:** This reason applies particularly to those who have a blog on Blogspot, Typepad, or any other hosted service. Hosted programs limit what you can do, create, and mess with. When it comes to plugins, add-ons, and theme creation, hosting a WordPress blog on your own web server wins hands down. In addition, you have complete control of your data, archives, and backup capability when you host your blog on your own server.

- ✔ **Ease of use:** Many people find the WordPress interface easier to use, more understandable, and a great deal more user-friendly than many of the other blogging platforms available today.

Both the hosted version of WordPress.com and the self-hosted version of WordPress.org allow you to migrate your blog to their platforms; however, WordPress.com accepts several fewer than WordPress.org does. The following is a list of blogging platforms that have built-in importers, or import plugins, for migration to WordPress:

- ✔ Blogger
- ✔ Movable Type and Typepad
- ✔ LiveJournal
- ✔ Tumblr
- ✔ RSS feeds
- ✔ WordPress.com

In the WordPress.org software (self-hosted), the importers are added to the installation as plugins. The importer plugins included in the previous list are the plugins packaged within the WordPress.org software, or they can be found by searching in the Plugins Directory at `http://wordpress.org/extend/plugins/tags/importer`. You can import content from several other platforms by installing other plugins not available from the official WordPress Plugin Directory, but you may have to search a bit on Google to find them.

Preparing for the big move

Depending on the size of your blog (that is, how many posts and comments you have), the migration process can take anywhere from 5 to 30 minutes. As with any major change or update you make, no matter where your blog is hosted, the very first thing you need to do is create a backup of your blog. You should back up the following:

- ✔ **Archives:** Posts, comments, and trackbacks
- ✔ **Template:** Template files and image files
- ✔ **Links:** Any links, banners, badges, and elements you have in your current blog
- ✔ **Images:** Any images you use in your blog

Table A-1 gives you a few tips on creating the export data for your blog in a few major blogging platforms. *Note:* This table assumes that you're logged in to your blog software.

Table A-1	Backing Up Your Blog Data on Major Platforms
Blogging Platform	*Backup Information*
Movable Type	Click the Import/Export button on the menu of your Movable Type Dashboard; then click the Export Entries From link. When the page stops loading, save it on your computer as a `.txt` file.
Typepad	Click the name of the blog you want to export; then click the Import/Export link in the Overview menu. Click the Export link at the bottom of the Import/Export page. When the page stops loading, save it on your computer as a `.txt` file.
Blogger	Back up your template by copying the text of your template to a text editor such as Notepad. Then save it on your computer as a `.txt` file.
LiveJournal	Browse to `http://livejournal.com/export.bml` and enter your information; choose XML as the format. Save this file on your computer.
WordPress	Click the Export link on the Tools menu on the Dashboard; the Export page opens. Choose your options on the Export page and then click the Download Export File button; next, save this file on your computer.
RSS feed	Point your browser to the URL of the RSS feed you want to import. Wait until it loads fully (you may need to set your feed to display all posts). View the source code of the page, copy and paste that source code into a `.txt` file, and save the file on your computer.

This import script allows for a maximum file size of 128MB. If you get an "out of memory" error, try dividing the import file into pieces and uploading them separately. The import script is smart enough to ignore duplicate entries, so if you need to run the script a few times to get it to take everything, you can do so without worrying about duplicating your content.

Converting templates

Every blogging program has a unique way of delivering content and data to your blog. Template tags vary from program to program; no two are the same, and each template file requires conversion if you want to use *your* template with your new WordPress blog. In such a case, two options are available to you:

- ✔ **Convert the template yourself.** To accomplish this task, you need to know WordPress template tags and HTML. If you have a template that you're using on another blogging platform and want to convert it for use with WordPress, you need to swap the original platform tags for WordPress tags. The information provided in Chapters 11–14 gives you the rundown on working with themes as well as basic WordPress template tags; you may find that information useful if you plan to attempt a template conversion yourself.

- ✔ **Hire an experienced WordPress consultant to do the conversion for you.** You can find a list of available WordPress consultants, assembled by the folks at Automattic (the company behind WordPress) at `http://codepoet.com`.

To use your own template, make sure that you save *all* the template files, the images, and the stylesheet from your previous blog setup. You need them to convert the template(s) for use in WordPress.

Hundreds of free templates are available for use with WordPress, so it may be a lot easier to abandon the template you're currently working with and find a free WordPress template that you like. If you've paid to have a custom design done for your blog, contact the designer of your theme and hire him to perform the template conversion for you. Also, you can hire several WordPress consultants to perform the conversion for you — including yours truly.

Moving your blog to WordPress

You've packed all your stuff and you have your new place prepared. Moving day has arrived!

This section takes you through the steps for moving your blog from one blog platform to WordPress. This section assumes that you already have the WordPress software installed and configured on your own domain.

Find the import function that you need by following these steps:

1. **On the Dashboard, click the Import link on the Tools menu.**

   The Import page opens, listing blogging platforms from which you can import content (such as Blogger and Movable Type). Figure A-7 shows the Import page on the WordPress Dashboard.

2. **Click the link for the blogging platform you're working with.**

   Click the Install Now button to install the importer plugin to begin using it.

The following sections provide some import directions for a few of the most popular blogging platforms (other than WordPress, that is). Each platform has its own content export methods, so be sure to check the documentation for the blogging platform that you're using.

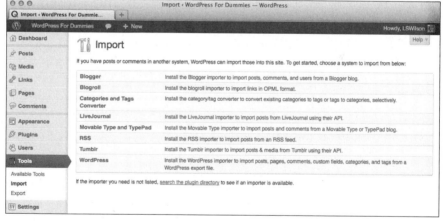

Figure A-7: The Import feature of the (self-hosted) WordPress.org Dashboard.

Importing from Blogspot/Blogger

I call it Blogspot; you call it Blogger — a rose by any other name would smell as sweet. The blogging application owned by Google is referenced either way: Blogspot or Blogger. In the end, we're talking about the same application.

To begin the import process, first complete the steps in the "Moving your blog to WordPress" section, earlier in this appendix. Then follow these steps:

1. **Click the Blogger link on the Import page and install the plugin for importing from Blogger.**

   Click the Activate Plugin & Install Importer link, and the Import Blogger page loads with instructions to import your file, as shown in Figure A-8.

Figure A-8:
The Import
Blogger
page on the
WordPress
Dashboard.

2. **Click the Authorize button to tell WordPress to access your account.**

   A page from Google opens with a message that says your WordPress blog is trying to access your Google account.

3. **Enter the e-mail address and password you use for Google; then click the Sign In button.**

   The Access Request page in your Google Account opens. When you have successfully logged in, you receive a message from Google stating that your blog at WordPress is requesting access to your Blogger account so that it can post entries on your behalf.

4. **Give your permission by clicking the Grant Access button on the Access Request page.**

   If you have many posts and comments in your Blogger blog, the import can take 30 minutes or more.

   After the import script has performed its magic, you're redirected to your WordPress Dashboard, where the name of your Blogger blog is listed.

5. **To finish importing the data from Blogger, click the Import button (below the Magic Button header).**

   The text on the button changes to `Importing . . .` while the import takes place. When the import is complete, the text on the button changes to `Set Authors` (no wonder it's called the Magic Button!).

6. **Click the Set Authors button to assign the authors to the posts.**

   The Blogger username appears on the left side of the page; a drop-down menu on the right side of the page displays the WordPress login name.

7. **Assign authors using the drop-down menu.**

   If you have just one author on each blog, the process is especially easy: Use the drop-down menu on the right to assign the WordPress login to your Blogger username. If you have multiple authors on both blogs, each Blogger username is listed on the left side with a drop-down menu to the right of each username. Select a WordPress login for each Blogger username to make the author assignments.

8. **Click Save Changes.**

   You're done!

Importing from LiveJournal

Both WordPress.com and WordPress.org offer an import script for LiveJournal users, and the process of importing from LiveJournal to WordPress is the same for each platform.

To export your blog content from LiveJournal, log in to your LiveJournal blog and then type this URL in your browser's address bar: `www.livejournal.com/export.bml`.

LiveJournal lets you export the XML files one month at a time, so if you have a blog with several months' worth of posts, be prepared to be at this process for a while. First, you have to export the entries one month at a time and then you have to import them into WordPress — yep, you guessed it — one month at a time.

 To speed the process a little, you can save all the exported XML LiveJournal files in one text document by copying and pasting each month's XML file into one plain-text file (created in a text editor such as Notepad), thereby creating one long XML file with all the posts from your LiveJournal blog. You can then save the file as an XML file to prepare it for import into your WordPress blog.

After you export the XML file from LiveJournal, return to the Import page on your WordPress Dashboard and follow these steps:

1. **Click the LiveJournal link and install the plugin for installing from LiveJournal.**

   Click the Activate Plugin & Install Importer link, and the Import LiveJournal page loads with instructions to import your file, as shown in Figure A-9.

2. **Click the Browse button.**

   A window opens, listing files on your computer.

3. **Double-click the name of the XML file you saved earlier.**

4. **Click the Upload and Import button.**

   When the import script finishes, it reloads the page with a confirmation message that the process is complete. Then WordPress runs the import script and brings over all your posts from your LiveJournal blog.

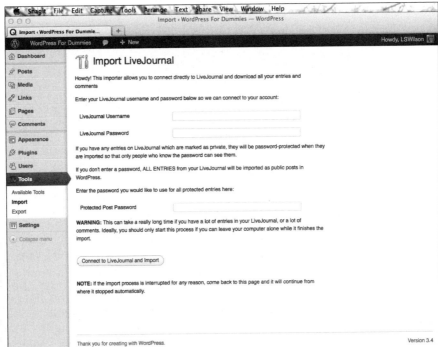

Figure A-9:
The Import LiveJournal page on the WordPress Dashboard.

Importing from Movable Type and Typepad

Movable Type and Typepad were created by the same company, Six Apart. These two blogging platforms run on essentially the same code base, so the import/export procedure is basically the same for both. Refer to Table A-1, earlier in this appendix, for details on how to run the export process in both Movable Type and Typepad. This import script moves all your blog posts, comments, and trackbacks to your WordPress blog.

Go to the Import page on your WordPress Dashboard by following Steps 1 and 2 in the "Moving your blog to WordPress" section, earlier in this appendix. Then follow these steps:

1. **Click the Movable Type and Typepad link and install the plugin for importing from Movable Type and Typepad.**

   Click the Activate Plugin & Install Importer link, and the Import Movable Type or Typepad page loads with instructions to import your file, as shown in Figure A-10.

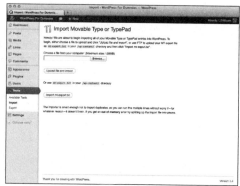

Figure A-10: The Import Movable Type or Typepad page on the WordPress Dashboard.

2. **Click the Browse button.**

   A window opens, listing your files.

3. **Double-click the name of the export file you saved from your Movable Type or Typepad blog.**

4. **Click the Upload File and Import button.**

   Sit back and let the import script do its magic. When it's done, it reloads the page with a confirmation message that the process is complete.

When the import script is done, you can assign users to the posts, matching the Movable Type or Typepad usernames with WordPress usernames. If you have just one author on each blog, this process is easy; you simply assign your WordPress login to the Movable Type or Typepad username using the drop-down menu. If you have multiple authors on both blogs, match the Movable Type or Typepad usernames with the correct WordPress login names and then click Save Changes. You're done!

Importing from WordPress

With this WordPress import script, you can import one WordPress blog into another, and this is true for both the hosted and self-hosted versions of WordPress. WordPress imports all your posts, comments, custom fields, and categories into your blog. Refer to Table A-1, earlier in this appendix, to find out how to use the export feature to obtain your blog data.

When you complete the exporting, follow these steps:

1. **Click the WordPress link on the Import page and install the plugin to import from WordPress.**

   Click the Activate Plugin & Install Importer link, and the Import WordPress page loads with instructions to import your file, as shown in Figure A-11.

2. **Click the Browse button.**

   A window opens, listing the files on your computer.

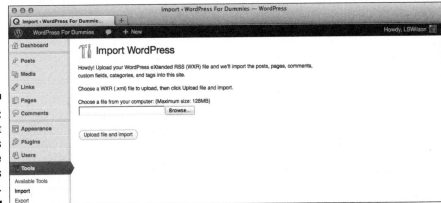

Figure A-11:
The Import WordPress page on the WordPress Dashboard.

3. **Double-click the export file you saved earlier from your WordPress blog.**

4. **Click the Upload File and Import button.**

   The import script gets to work and when it's done, it reloads the page with a confirmation message that the process is complete.

Importing from an RSS feed

If all else fails, or if WordPress doesn't provide an import script that you need for your current blog platform, you can import your blog data via the RSS feed for the blog you want to import. With the RSS import method, you can import only posts; you can't use this method to import comments, trackbacks, categories, or users. WordPress.com currently does not allow you to import blog data via an RSS feed; this function works only with the self-hosted WordPress.org platform.

Refer to Table A-1, earlier in this appendix, for the steps required to create the file you need to import via RSS. Then follow these steps:

1. **On the Import page on the WordPress Dashboard, click the RSS link and install the plugin to import from an RSS feed.**

   Click the Activate & Install link, and the Import RSS page loads with instructions to import your RSS file, as shown in Figure A-12.

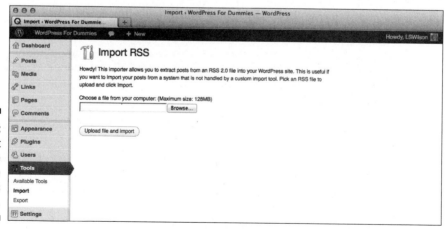

Figure A-12: The Import RSS page on the WordPress Dashboard.

2. **Click the Browse button on the Import RSS page.**

   A window opens, listing the files on your computer.

3. **Double-click the export file you saved earlier from your RSS feed.**

4. **Click the Upload File and Import button.**

   The import script does its magic and then reloads the page with a confirmation message that the process is complete.

Finding other import resources

The WordPress Codex has a long list of other available scripts, plugins, workarounds, and outright hacks for importing from other blog platforms. You can find that information at `http://codex.wordpress.org/Importing_Content`.

Note: The WordPress Codex is run by a group of volunteers. When you refer to the Codex, be aware that not everything listed in it is necessarily up to date or accurate, including import information (or any other information about running your WordPress blog).

Moving Your Website to a Different Host

You may decide at some point that you need to switch from your current hosting provider to a new one. You may have to do this for several different reasons — maybe you're unhappy with your current provider and want to move to a new one, or your current provider is going out of business and you're forced to move. Transferring from one host to another is a reality that some website owners must face, and transferring an existing website, with all its content, files, and data from one host to another, can seem a very daunting task. This section of the appendix should make it easier for you to face.

You have two different ways to go about it:

- ✔ Manually, through backing up your database and downloading essential files
- ✔ Using a plugin to automate as much of the process as possible

Obviously, using a tool to automate the process is the easier and more desirable way to go, but just in case you need to do it manually, in the next section of this appendix, I provide you with the instructions for doing it both ways.

Creating a backup and moving manually

Earlier in this appendix, in "Backing Up Your Database," I provide you with step-by-step instructions on how to make a backup of your database using phpMyAdmin. Follow the steps in that section and you will have a backup of your database with all the recent content you've published to your blog. However, when I say "content," I mean the content that you (or others) have written or typed into your blog via the WordPress Dashboard, including:

✔ Blog posts, pages, and custom post types

✔ Links, categories, and tags

✔ Post and page options, such as excerpts, time and date, custom fields, categories, tags, and passwords

✔ WordPress settings you configured under the Settings menu on the Dashboard

✔ All widgets that you've created and configured

✔ All plugin options that you configured for the plugins you installed

Other elements of your website aren't stored in the database, which you need to download, via FTP, from your web server. The following is a list of those elements, including instructions on where to find them and how to download them to your local computer:

✔ **Media files:** These are the files you uploaded using the WordPress media upload feature, including images, videos, audio files, and documents. Media files are located in the `/wp-content/uploads/` folder; connect to your web server via FTP and download that folder to your local computer.

✔ **Plugin files:** Although all the plugin settings are stored in the database, the actual plugin files that contain the programming code are not. The plugin files are located in the `/wp-content/plugins/` folder; connect to your web server via FTP and download that folder to your local computer.

✔ **Theme files:** Widgets and options you've set for your current theme are stored in the database; however, the theme template files, images, and stylesheets are not. They are stored in the `/wp-content/themes` folder; connect to your web server via FTP and download that folder to your local computer.

Now that you have your database and WordPress files stored safely on your local computer, moving them to a new host just involves reversing the process:

1. **Create a new database on your new hosting account.**

   You can find the steps for creating a database in Chapter 6.

2. **Import your database backup into the new database you just created:**

   a. Log in to the cPanel for your hosting account.

   b. Click the phpMyAdmin icon and click the name of your new database in the left menu.

   c. Click the Import tab at the top.

   d. Click the Browse button and select the database backup from your local computer.

   e. Click the Go button and the old database imports into the new.

3. **Install WordPress on your new hosting account.**

   See Chapter 6 for the steps to install WordPress.

4. **Edit the** `wp-config.php` **file to include your new database name, username, password, and host.**

5. **Upload all that you downloaded from the** `/wp-content/` **folder to your new hosting account.**

6. **In your web browser, browse to your domain.**

   Your website should work and you are able to log on to the WordPress Dashboard using the same username and password as before because that information is stored in the database you imported.

Using a plugin to back up and move to a new host

A plugin that I use on a regular basis to move a WordPress website from one hosting environment to another is aptly named BackupBuddy. This plugin isn't free or available in the WordPress Plugin Directory — you need to pay for it, but it's worth every single penny because it takes the entire backup and migration process and makes mincemeat out of it. This means that it's very easy, and you can be done in minutes instead of hours. Follow these steps to use this plugin to move your site to a new hosting server:

1. **Purchase and download the BackupBuddy plugin from** `http://ewebscapes.com/backupbuddy`**.**

   At this time, the cost for the plugin starts at $75.

2. **Install the plugin on your current WordPress website.**

   By current, I mean the old one, not the new hosting account yet.

3. **Activate the plugin on your WordPress Dashboard.**

   Click the Plugins link in the navigation menu and then click the Activate link under the BackupBuddy plugin name.

4. **Navigate to the Backups page in the BackupBuddy options page.**

   Click the Backups link in the BackupBuddy menu.

5. **Click the Full Backup button.**

   This initiates a full backup of your database, files, and content and wraps it neatly into one `.zip` file for you to store on your local computer.

6. **Download the** `importbuddy.php` **file.**

   Click the `importbuddy.php` link on the Backups page and download it to your local computer, preferably in the same directory as the backup file you downloaded in Step 5.

7. **Connect to your new web server via FTP.**

8. **Upload the** `backup.zip` **file and the** `importbuddy.php` **file.**

   These files should be uploaded in the root, or top-level, directory on your web server. On some web servers, this is the `/public_html` folder; on others it might be the `/httpdocs` folder. If you are unsure what your root directory is, your hosting provider should be able to tell you.

9. **Create a new database on your new hosting account.**

   You can find the steps for creating a database in Chapter 6.

10. **Navigate to the** `importbuddy.php` **file in your web browser.**

    The URL for this would be something like `http://yourdomain.com/importbuddy.php`.

11. **The BackupBuddy page loads in your web browser.**

    Follow the steps to import the backup file and install WordPress, including the database information needed: database username, name, password, and host. This entire process takes about 5–10 minutes or maybe more depending on the size of your website.

12. **Load your website in your web browser.**

    After BackupBuddy does its thing, your website is ready to use just as always.

Index

• E •

• F •

• K •

• L •